Outside Color

Outside Color

Perceptual Science and the Puzzle of Color in Philosophy

M. Chirimuuta

The MIT Press
Cambridge, Massachusetts
London, England

First MIT Press paperback edition, 2017

This book was set in Stone Sans and Stone Serif by Toppan Best-set Premedia Limited.

Library of Congress Cataloging-in-Publication Data

Chirimuuta, M. (Mazviita)
Outside color : perceptual science and the puzzle of color in philosophy / M. Chirimuuta.
    pages   cm
Includes bibliographical references and index.
ISBN 978-0-262-02908-7 (hardcover : alk. paper)—978-0-262-53457-4 (pb.)
1. Color (Philosophy)   I. Title.
B105.C455C45   2015
121'.35—dc23

2014045729

[T]he whole philosophy of perception from Democritus's time downwards has been just one long wrangle over the paradox that what is evidently one reality should be in two places at once, both in outer space and in a person's mind.

—William James (1904, 481)

Contents

Preface   **ix**

1   Color and its Questions   **1**
2   What Everyone Thinks about Color, and Why   **19**
3   Realism, Antirealism, Relationism   **43**
4   Coloring In, and Coloring For   **69**
5   Perceptual Pragmatism   **101**
6   Active Color   **131**
7   True Colors   **159**
8   Outerness without Ontological Commitment   **187**

References   **215**
Index   **241**

Preface

This book is intended as an integrated study of the history, philosophy, and science of color. Each of these disciplines has a chapter devoted more or less exclusively to it: Chapter 2 is historical, chapter 3 is devoted to contemporary philosophy of color, and chapter 4 to contemporary science of color. From chapters 5 to 8 the integration occurs. Sometimes specific sections and subsections contain historical material that holds a mirror to the contemporary issues under discussion. Other sections marshal empirical details pertinent to the philosophical debate at hand. The problem of color ontology is the theme running through the pages, and this unites these different branches of inquiry to a common purpose.

Because this work devotes attention to three rather different disciplines, I have not covered any one of them in all of the depth or detail that would be expected in a study of singular focus. For example, I do not analyze all the philosophical arguments for and against color relationism with the thoroughness that I much admire in Cohen's (2009) *The Red and the Real*. Indeed, I would refer the reader seeking such a focus to that important book. Similarly, my historical treatment is not that of a dedicated historian. In searching out the transitions and traditions in thought that have most shaped the problem of color ontology I have not attempted novel engagements with primary texts and have deferred to the readings of specialist historians. My use of this material has been selective, and may well appear superficial; I hope that the reader will allow some charity here since my goal is not ultimately that of a historical scholar, but of a philosopher taking the long view.

Any review of current science is destined to be out of date by the time it goes to press. While I have attempted to give an up to date, if partial, overview of color psychophysics, psychology, and neurophysiology, it is likely that papers are being published right now that contradict the findings from which I here draw conclusions. Perhaps the best that can be said of compiling a scientific review is that it is like holding one's finger in the air to feel which way the wind is blowing. In chapters 4 and 5 I have aimed to describe some important trends in the direction of research. Needless to say, the wind *may* be about to turn; I have placed my bet that it will not.

In writing this book I owe a sizable debt of gratitude to numerous friends, relatives, and colleagues. The original impetus for my work on color came from Ian Gold, who secured funding from the Australian Research Council to support a three year postdoctoral fellowship for my research on this topic. Ian has also been a wonderful teacher and mentor throughout my transition from the discipline of vision science to the philosophy of science and perception, and I quite literally would not be here without him. Other colleagues from my time in Melbourne also deserve many thanks, not least for making the school of philosophy and bioethics at Monash University a wonderful place to do a postdoc. In particular I'm grateful to John Bigelow, Allen Hazen, Jakob Hohwy, and the late J. J. Smart for their encouragement and comments on early papers and presentations.

The first half of this book was written, roughly, during my time as a McDonnell postdoctoral fellow in the Philosophy-Neuroscience-Psychology (PNP) program at Washington University, St. Louis. I would like to thank the members of the philosophy writing co-op, especially Carl Craver, Dennis Des Chene, David Michael Kaplan, and Mariska Leunissen, and also John Heil, for many helpful thoughts and an honest appraisal of the early drafts.

The second half of the book has taken shape during my time at the University of Pittsburgh. I am much indebted to the faculty and students in the History and Philosophy of Science and Philosophy departments for making Pitt an inspiring place to do philosophy. I am grateful to my chair, Sandra Mitchell, who very kindly gave me the opportunity to hold a graduate seminar on perception and the color project twice within a few short years. I should thank the people who contributed to those seminars—Brian Ballard, Ori Beck, Derek Brown, Laura Davies, Michal de Medonsa, Lucia Foglia, Chuck Goldhaber, Lisa Lederer, Jim Lennox, Rachel Moger-Reischer, Jasmin Özel, Shivam Patel, Evan Pence, Alison Springle, Raja Rosenhagen, Morgan Thompson, Laura Tomlinson, Wayne Wu, and in particular Edouard Machery, my co-teacher during the second seminar—for so many lively discussions and profitable comments. I must also thank Anil Gupta for his many kind, encouraging, and thought-provoking words, and for his organization of a philosophy of perception reading group, participation in which has greatly enriched my understanding of this field.

Work relating to this book has been presented at numerous departmental venues. In roughly chronological order I would like to thank, for their time and interest, the audiences and organizers of research seminars at the school of philosophy and bioethics at Monash University, the philosophy and psychology departments at Glasgow University, biological sciences at St Mary's London, philosophy at Waterloo University, the University of Western Ontario, Washington University in St. Louis, the James Martin seminar at the University of Oxford, the philosophy department and vision institute at the University of Bristol, and the HPS and biosciences departments at the University of Pittsburgh.

I have learned much from audiences at various conferences: The British Society for the Philosophy of Science (2007, 2013), The Joint Session (2012), Progress in Color Studies (2008, 2012), and I am very grateful to Kathleen Akins and Berit Brogaard, organizers of the 2011 Vancouver color conference, John Morrison (2012 Barnard Perception Workshop), Bence Nanay (2013 Antwerp Color and Content Workshop), and Yosuk Boon, organizer of the 2013 Mind-Brain conference at the Korean Institute of Advanced Studies, for invitations to speak at their events.

The final stages of the writing of *Outside Color* were much aided by research leave awarded through the Humanities Center at the University of Pittsburgh. I am much indebted to the directors and committee of the Center for their support, and to the audience members of the Humanities Center colloquium dedicated to the topic of chapter 5, especially my two respondents, Jim Lennox and Jessica Wiskus.

Numerous philosophers have taken the time to read and comment on the work in progress. For their kindness and criticism I must thank Jon Buttaci, Alex Byrne, Carrie Figdor, Anil Gupta, David R. Hilbert, Susanna Schellenberg. I am especially grateful to Derek Brown, for generously agreeing to comment on the manuscript in its entirety, detecting many mistakes and offering many helpful suggestions; and before then for sharing numerous thoughts and insights along the way. I would also like to thank Keith Allen, Jacob Berger, Johnathan Cohen, and Will Davies for challenging and inspiring discussions.

My understanding of color has been constantly shaped and enriched by teachers and colleagues in vision science. In particular, I should thank David Burr, Lars Chittka, Fred Kingdom, Laurence Maloney, Rainer Mausfeld, Concetta Morrone, David Simmons, and Qasim Zaidi. A special mention is deserved by my PhD supervisor, David Tolhurst, who tried to teach me to think as carefully about vision and the brain as he does himself. And tribute is due to the late Tom Troscianko, my first teacher in vision science, who inspired me and many others to enter the field—a unique and generous person, much missed.

As alluded to above, my research has been supported financially by the Australian Research Council (Discovery-Projects Grant, 'The Epistemology of Color Vision'), the James S. McDonnell Foundation, and the University of Pittsburgh Humanities Center. It is a marvelous thing that funds are still available for exploratory, interdisciplinary work across science and philosophy, and I hope that this book lends credit to the idea that the philosophy of visual neuroscience is a fledgling field worth investing in.

I thank Philip Laughlin, senior acquisitions editor in philosophy and cognitive science at MIT Press, for his faith and patience. Thanks also to my comrade Liam Kofi Bright for much assistance at the final editing and proofreading stage.

Not least I must thank my friends and family—especially my husband Mark and my children Tinashe and Tendai—for making my life more colorful. Finally, I would like to mention the debt of gratitude I owe to my mother Rosalind, to whom I have dedicated the book, for everything a mother does and on top of that for being the first person to draw my attention to the fascinating mystery of sight.

1   Color and its Questions

1.1   Preamble

Those outside the profession might be surprised to learn that the philosophy of color exists in its own right. One might assume that all the fundamental investigations into color have been completed by science: Newtonian physics told us that color is wavelength of light, while perceptual psychology has described the seeing faculties of eye, brain, and mind. A peculiar thing about color, in contrast to most other subjects of scientific investigation, is that conceptual analysis of its fundamental nature is conducted in parallel with experimental research. Yet philosophers who concern themselves with color are increasingly preoccupied with the science. Since the 1980s at least, attempts have been made to ground philosophies of color in empirical findings. Color is a rare field in which the practices of data gathering, and of metaphysical speculation, seem to share a common purpose.

But what is the philosophy of color? Philosophical topics are defined by the questions raised under their heading. To ask, "what are colors, do they exist?" is to introduce an ontological concern about the true nature and status of colors among other properties and entities. But why is color more puzzling than shape, say, or texture? Of all the properties that objects appear to have, color hovers uneasily between the subjective world of sensation and the objective world of physical facts. Colors prompt a question of location: "where are colors to be found—out in the world, or only inside the mind?" They set philosophers about the task of metaphysical stocktaking, seeking the proper place for hue, saturation, and brightness, in abstraction from the messiness of the everyday world and the obscurities of mental imagery.

Some concepts are problematic and others not. Some generate deep questions "what is justice, beauty, truth?" others mere trivialities ("what is a brick?"). The interesting thing is that in posing the deep questions, we are already halfway toward presupposing a metaphysical picture. To ask "what is beauty?" is already to tempt one to assume that there is something intellectually tangible, called beauty, that unites all beautiful things. In other words, to abstract beauty away from its manifestation in objects and to give it a conceptual life of its own. As we will see in the course of this book, to ask "what is blue?" has typically meant assuming that there is one kind of chromatic property belonging to all blue things that our visual system detects. So to ask the question is to perform an abstraction of the color away from its context in the material world. At the same time there is radical variability in the colors that things appear to have—they change with the light, with the weather, and with surrounding conditions. This casts doubt on the idea that the sky, say, is simply and truly blue. The ephemeral nature of color leads us to suspect that the eyes are no transparent window onto reality. The relation between perceiver and world becomes problematic.

Philosophers' questions are not so childlike as is sometimes supposed. They are imbued with the legacy of history and branded with contemporary conceit. A philosophical tradition begins to make sense when we understand why some difficulties are intractable and others not. We begin to answer philosophical questions when our motivation for raising them becomes a little transparent to us. The basic idea of this book is that color can better be understood by situating the discussion outside of its usual confines. But getting outside means locating boundaries. The purpose of this and the next two chapters is to examine the significance, origin, and function of some of the assumptions that have channeled thought about color down certain familiar tracks: the worry that colors are illusory, the hope that they are physical, and the resigned acceptance that they are just mental. The aim of the book is to show that these options do not exhaust possibility. The promise is that in taking a glance beyond the usual debate, we begin to see (colorful) things afresh.

1.2   Russell's Brown Table and Eddington's Two Tables

At this early stage some readers might be feeling that there is nothing especially tricky about color. Perhaps that is improbable if the reader has chosen to pick up a book in the philosophy of color, but still the notion, for example, that colors might be illusions can leave a sensible person unmoved. So it is worth saying more at the outset about the kind of ideas and observations that have provoked the debate. There are two important ways of generating the problem of color. The first is the observation of perceptual variation, and the second is the idea of a clash between perceptual appearance and physical reality. There are two well-known passages that exemplify each of these ideas. They both use the example of a table and both date from the early 1900s, even though texts making nearly identical points date back to centuries before. Our celebrated tables provide us with handy illustrations of old ideas.

1.2.1 Russell's Brown Table: Perceptual Variation

The observation of perceptual variation is extremely simple to understand, and it comes in many different forms. It is a case where an object changes in one of its apparent properties (e.g., shape or size) as either viewing conditions alter or the perceiver changes from person to person, or species to species. Instances are not confined to sight, though of course visual cases are the ones of most concern to the theory of color.

In *The Problems of Philosophy,* Russell ([1912] 1980, 2) writes:

Although I believe that the table is "really" of the same colour all over, the parts that reflect the light look much brighter than the other parts, and some parts look white because of reflected light. I know that, if I move, the parts that reflect the light will be different, so that the apparent distribution of colours on the table will change. It follows that if several people are looking at the table at the same moment, no two of them will see exactly the same distribution of colours....

It is evident from what we have found, that there is no colour which pre-eminently appears to be the colour of the table, or even of any one particular part of the table— it appears to be of different colours from different points of view, and there is no reason for regarding some of these as more really its colour than others. And we know that even from a given point of view the colour will seem different by artificial light, or to a colour-blind man, or to a man wearing blue spectacles, while in the dark there will be no colour at all....

Such observations have been used to make various points. Russell himself argues for a sense-data theory of perception, whereby mysterious sensory qualities, rather than ordinary physical items, are the direct objects of perception. What is important to the philosophy of color is the acute description of how, in our experience, impressions of color fluctuate to such an extent that we lose our sense of there being any one canonical color that belongs to the object. This highlights the difference between a property like color and that of shape. Perceived shape is equally variable with viewing angle—a table top rarely projects a rectangle onto the retina. Many would say that we have a "raw impression" as of a trapezoid, and yet we never hesitate to state that the table top actually is rectangular. With color, though, we are troubled by the question, "what is the *real* color of the table?"

As Russell describes, color presents numerous other possibilities for variation. Intrapersonal differences in perceived color come not only on changing angle of view but also by changing the background or lighting conditions, and through time with the aging and yellowing of the eye's lens. Interpersonal variation arises from the physiological differences among members of the population, which cause a great number of discrepancies in the color matches people make. This variation cannot all be put down to color blindness, the existence of a deficient subpopulation. Some trichromats[1] are simply "anomalous." Even though there is much talk of the "standard observer," this is no more than a statistical construct in the scientific literature, an average of individual responses (MacAdam 1997), and in the philosophical debate no consensus has emerged over a principled way to determine which observer is the one seeing colors truly (Hardin 1983; Peacocke 1984; Cohen 2009, 29–33).

Finally, evolution has engineered a remarkably diverse array of color visual systems across species. The number of photoreceptor types ranges from one in some nocturnal animals and deep-sea fish, to 16 in the mantis shrimp. Most mammals have only two cone types, in comparison with which primate trichromacy may look superior. Yet most birds and reptiles have more than three receptor types supporting color vision, and in general, the greater number of receptor classes, the more finely spectral information can be sifted. The horns of the dilemma are these: either we humans must defer to the pigeon or the mantis shrimp and say that the humbler creatures perceive a truth about color that we apprehend only

---

1. That is, individuals with three different cone types in the retina. In contrast, monocromats and dichromats (one or two cone types) are normally classified as color blind or color deficient.

approximately, or we should admit that there is no *one* animal that sees colors truly.[2] The latter horn raises the possibility that there are no animal-independent facts about color. The idea is that color is an animal-relative phenomenon, indeed a perceiver-relative one. Perceptual variation lands us with the problem of color because it stands at odds with intuitions we might have about color being an intrinsic property of objects, one held irrespective of relations with perceivers or circumstances. In other words, it sets a challenge to any simplistic assumption of the objectivity of colors.[3]

The radical conclusion is lent support by the resistance of color to codification. We may have certain beliefs that yellow is a color that belongs to bananas and lemons, and that the true color of a red dress is the one seen in bright sunshine, not the artificial light of the department store.[4] The problem is that this sort of codification of what color belongs to which particular object cannot be brought down to the fine level of shade and hue. If a dress looks redder under the bright glare of sunlight, and more purple in the bluer light of an overcast sky, which is the true color? Both conditions are equally natural, while the likelihood of each just changes with geographical position (dreary London or sunny Melbourne). Definitions of standard conditions have so far been problematic outside of restricted experimental contexts (Wyszecki and Stiles 2000; Hardin 1993, 68ff; Cohen 2009, 34–36), though attempts to put standard conditions to philosophical work continue (Pettit 1999; Allen 2010).

On a deeper level, variation provokes the worry that reality is not as we see it. If we are convinced that our eyes are transparent windows onto a world of preexisting entities bearing mind-independent properties, then it is disconcerting to find that perception makes contradictory claims about that world, when faced with changing conditions. One way to characterize the project of *Outside Color* is as an attack on such misplaced expectations

---

2. Really a trilemma: we could simply stipulate that human vision is our only domain of interest and deny the relevance of the comparative data (Hilbert 1992).

3. Needless to say, there are sophisticated adherents to the doctrine of the objectivity of color who do seek to accommodate the facts of variation. For example, Kalderon (2007) and Allen (2009) advocate *selectionism*—the idea that objects bear a multiplicity of intrinsic color properties, and that each species is responsive to a subset of these.

4. That is, in some circumstances color perception seems to support an appearance-reality distinction that gives weight to the idea that colors are mind-independent properties. In chapter 7 I discuss how this can be so even if there are no canonical colors of things.

of visual perception. That is to say, if we acknowledge that vision involves a complex interaction between objects and seeing animals, then it comes more naturally to be expected that at least some of the properties represented visually are perceiver-relative ones. Vision science is the study of the interaction between stimulus and seer, and much of the material of the book draws on specific findings about the various functions of color vision. Yet no one would deny that perceptual interactions occur as a matter of fact. So within the color debate the expectations of perceiver-independence are articulated as a commonsense or phenomenological intuition about the nature of chromatic experience. The objective of chapters 2 to 4 is to show how this supposed commonsensical view commits itself to an inappropriate model of vision, while chapters 7 and 8 discuss the status of these phenomenological intuitions at length.

Of course, Russell was not the first to make observations of perceptual variability. Burnyeat (1979) describes a rich and ancient debate on this matter. On comparing the historical texts it becomes obvious that there is not just one argument to be made from the observation of variation. As Sextus Empiricus relates, "[f]rom the fact that honey appears bitter to some and sweet to others Democritus concluded that it is neither sweet nor bitter, Heraclitus that it is both" (quoted and translated by Burnyeat 1979, 69). That is, the one observation of the contrasting taste of a substance can prompt the thought that neither the sweetness nor the bitterness are real properties of the honey, or the opposite thought that sweetness and bitterness coexist within the food (see Kalderon 2007). There is a further conclusion advocated by Protagoras, that the taste of the honey be analyzed as relative to subjects. That is to say, honey is sweet for most people, but bitter for a few others. There is no sweetness in absolute terms.

The Protagorean lesson is the one usually drawn in contemporary discussions. Perceptual variation has been cited as the principle grounds for color *relationism*, the thesis that yellow is not an intrinsic property of bananas and lemons but actually a relation that involves the fruit, the seer, and the ambient conditions. This thesis has been argued for most forcefully by Jonathan Cohen in recent years, and is among the points made by Russell ([1912] 1980, 2–3), reflecting on his table:

This colour is not something which is inherent in the table, but something dependent upon the table and the spectator and the way the light falls on the table. When, in ordinary life, we speak of *the* colour of the table, we only mean the sort of colour which it will seem to have to a normal spectator from an ordinary point of view under usual conditions of light. But the other colours which appear under other conditions have just as good a right to be considered real; and therefore, to avoid favouritism, we are compelled to deny that, in itself, the table has any one particular colour.

In short, Russell's example puts to us the problem of reconciling the inconstancy of colors with any expectations we may have of their mind-independent residence in the world. All accounts of color must find a way to accommodate the inconvenient facts about the changeability of color from moment to moment, and from one person or animal to another.

1.2.2 Eddington's Two Tables: The Manifest and Scientific Image

The observation of perceptual variation raises the worry that there is a mismatch between the deliverances of the senses and an underlying reality of which we are only dimly aware. Modern science comes to play a significant role in exacerbating this worry. This is because the physical sciences in particular are often assumed to be offering us an empirically tested and mathematically consistent description of reality, an alternative to the representations of the world generated by our unsound sensory faculties. If there is a discrepancy between the scientific representation and this manifest sensory image, we are advised to place our trust in physics.

Sir Arthur Eddington, the astrophysicist and early expositor of general relativity, also produced works aiming to introduce to a general audience the revolutionary ideas within nonclassical physics. His Gifford lectures begin with an account of the "two tables," a forthright formulation of the clash between science and the world of the senses:

I have settled down to the task of writing these lectures and have drawn up my chairs to my two tables....One of them has been familiar to me from earliest years. It is a commonplace object of that environment which I call the world. How shall I describe it? It has extension; it is comparatively permanent; it is coloured; above all it is substantial. By substantial I do not merely mean that it does not collapse when I lean upon it; I mean that it is constituted of "substance" and by that word I am trying to convey to you some conception of its intrinsic nature....Table No. 2 is my scientific table. It is a more recent acquaintance and I do not feel so familiar with it. It does not belong to the world previously mentioned, that world which spontaneously appears around me when I open my eyes, though how much of it is objective and how much subjective I do not here consider. It is part of a world which in more devious ways has forced itself on my attention. My scientific table is mostly emptiness. Sparsely scattered in that emptiness are numerous electric charges rushing about with great speed; but their combined bulk amounts to less than a billionth of the bulk of the table itself. (Eddington [1928] 2012, xi–xii)

We are now only half a step away from generating the problem of color. Eddington concentrates on the difference in how substantial his everyday table is, compared to his scientific one. He could just as easily have developed the thought that the everyday object is colored, a characteristic not applicable to the scientific table. The point is that color does not make any appearance among the properties of the basic constituents of the world, as put to us by physics. These constituents may be electrons and atomic nuclei, quarks, or strings. Even if we cannot yet bask in the knowledge of a completed fundamental physics, we do know that ever since science began explaining natural processes in terms of the activities of microscopic particles, it has never been necessary to grant them any qualitative chromatic properties.[5] The transparent azure of the copper sulfate solution is explained in terms of the interaction of light with the soluble ions of the crystal, and never in terms of the fundamental blueness of those particles. In short, the reality presented to us through our eyes is colored; the reality given to us by physics and chemistry is not. Another way of explaining the difference is that the senses, in general, present us with a world in which objects have qualitative properties—sounds, tastes, smells, and colors, whereas the only properties ascribed to scientific entities are essentially quantifiable, like speed, mass, length and spin.

Thus Keith Campbell (1969, 132) formalizes the problem of color as a triad of incompatible propositions:

1. In common experience, colors are properties of what is seen.
2. What is seen is, normally, a public, physical, existent, usually a body.
3. In the detailed account scientists are now elaborating of those physical existents, color properties have no place.

---

5. The "color" property of quarks is not relevant here. One concern, however, is that colors could be perceiver-independent properties of physical objects that do not play an explanatory role in the science of physics, and are therefore not to be thought of as "physical properties." For example, they could be properties that supervene on the more familiar properties of physics. Color *primitivism* is, on some formulations, a version of nonreductive physicalism along these lines (Watkins 2010). But importantly, primitivists assert that mind-independent objects *can* bear qualitative properties like hue and pitch (Kalderon 2011a). This is a claim that is usually taken to be ruled out by the modern scientific world view.

Something has to give. The philosophical response is that either "common experience" must capitulate to science, eliminating color from our basic, scientific ontology, or a way must be found to reconcile experience with physical fact. Galileo argued for the first option historically, while others like C. L. Hardin do today. The latter course was plausibly that of Locke, and it is the one pursued by contemporary color realists.

It is not typically suggested that science should back down over any claim to be the truest description of the world. At most, rapprochement may occur as science advances in a way more conducive to explaining features of the conscious world. Sellars is one philosopher who in the course of his career explored these various options. He wrote, notoriously, that "in the dimension of describing and explaining the world, science is the measure of all things, of what is that it is, and of what is not that it is not" (Sellars 1956, 173). He also famously pressed the need for a "synoptic" view to reconcile the scientific and the experiential world. In another celebrated essay Sellars (1963) contrasts the "manifest image," the world of the senses and of humanistic thought, which stands to be displaced by a "scientific image" brought to focus in ever more compelling detail in the research laboratories of the world. Yet, Sellars argues, to lose sight of the manifest image is literally to lose ourselves—our concept of personhood. Should our need to reconcile the two images play a role in directing future scientific theorizing about the nature of sensory experience? This is indeed what Sellars (1981) urges, though few other philosophers of mind and perception have pursued this line of thought.

1.2.3 Which Way into the Problem?
Russell's and Eddington's cases provide us with two distinct ways into the color problem. They can be called ancient and modern, respectively. While there are ample ancient Greek sources for the observation of perceptual variation, the scientific-manifest clash only becomes prominent with the rising influence of microphysical explanation. Interestingly, the figure of Democritus straddles the field. Above he was credited with an argument from perceptual variation. He is more known for his atomism—the doctrine that all material ultimately boils down to collections of indivisible particles, swimming in emptiness. There is a lineage from Democritus to early modern science, via the school of Epicurus. Many moderns perceive

a kindred spirit in the remaining fragments of his writings. In one of the most cited passages in the color debate, Democritus is noted as saying, "[b]y convention colour exists, by convention bitter, by convention sweet, but in reality atoms and void" (Democritus fragment, quoted by Hardin 1993, 59). Perhaps we come across those words often because they so pointedly encapsulate the message that a scientific, atomistic understanding of the universe disqualifies the senses from capturing anything but an illusory, "conventional" reality.

Though Eddington's worry may resound across the centuries, it deserves to be called modern because it certainly comes to prominence during the so-called scientific revolution. Not coincidentally, the problem of color really becomes a problem at this time. The founders of mathematical physics—most prominently Galileo, Descartes, and Newton—set about describing fundamental reality in a purely numerical language. The properties that concerned them were the ones that can be measured, or mathematically defined, and entirely encapsulated within some mathematical system. Physical objects are understood to have mass, length, and motion, while the status of taste, smell, color, and sound becomes unassured. What eludes capture in mathematics is quality—that which is delicious to the palate in the taste of pineapple, or brassy in a trumpet call, or eye-catching in scarlet. The qualitative nature of such properties as taste—the "what it's like" of them—is set aside by the scientific project.

A new understanding of matter as comprising minute, indivisible particles, was advocated by figures such as Gassendi, Boyle, and Locke. They sought to understand all empirical phenomena as the aggregate actions of microscopic atoms or "corpuscles." This picture of material reality as atomistic and mathematically characterized remains basically unchanged to this day.[6] Since the scientific revolution, the building blocks of the natural world have been some sort of quantitatively defined stuff, consisting in whichever particles are posited by the best physics of the day. The extrapolation from physics to metaphysics is a discernible legacy of this tradition.

---

6. Arguably the picture of particulate reality is challenged by post-nineteenth century physics (Ladyman et al. 2007). Yet the standard model in physics still names "subatomic particles," and all properties are resolutely quantitative. So in the loosest sense the picture remains, though the concept of a particle in current physics is very, very far from the billiard ball atoms of the seventeenth century, often retained in the lay imagination.

As Stebbing (1958, 64) remarks, the deniers of the reality of color have simply "made a metaphysic out of a method." In contemporary philosophy of mind, physicalism is a default view. It can roughly be described as the thesis that all properties, including mental ones, will ultimately be explained in terms of the entities and properties of physics. Thus the only hope for the manifest image is that it somehow be shoehorned into physical reality.

Yet there are some crucial assumptions that are taken for granted in the modern way to the color debate, and that happen to be contested by philosophers specializing elsewhere. The first is that science aims to describe the fundamental entities in the world—and does a fair job of doing this. In other words, a scientific realism spawns the physicalistic outlook in the philosophy of mind and perception.[7] It follows, for some, that for colors to count among the real properties of our world, they must be some kind of physical property. A related assumption, quite salient in Eddington's argument, is that science and perception are *in the same business*. That is, it is taken for granted that the proper task of perception is to reveal nature's properties to us, as opposed to interpreting nature in a way most convenient to the perceiving agent. Objectivity is expected of the perceptual world. It is a kind of perceptual realism that mirrors scientific realism. Of course, it is realism that quickly turns to sour skepticism, when it is understood that what we perceive is rather more subjective—much more shaped by the idiosyncratic needs and interests of the perceiver—than was hoped. For once we have learned some rudimentary facts about our perceptual system it is hard to escape the conclusion that we only see what it is that our sensory organs and classifying minds make available to us, and that this is unlikely to be the same reality that is described by physics.

7. Even though physicalism is the predominant view in the philosophy of mind and perception, it has been the subject of serious debate by philosophers wary of the hasty extension of physics into metaphysics, and thence to the philosophy of mind (Crane and Mellor 1990). Furthermore physicalism rests on some version of scientific realism—the belief that the entities posited by our "best" physics are the ones actually inhabiting our universe. This claim is by no means uncontroversial within the philosophy of science. For one thing, most realists within the philosophy of science endorse the weaker claim that scientific theories *aim* at truth to nature. Their rivals urge that scientific theories are instruments for predicting phenomena and manipulating matter. See Chakravartty (2013) for a recent overview, and van Fraassen (1980) for an influential alternative to scientific realism.

Here I have sketched a few of the pitfalls of the modern way. Most of this book is actually an extended discussion of why certain assumptions implicit in the color debate need to be brought into the open and challenged, and why alternative ways of thinking about the problem need to be developed. In order to say something different—and useful—about color, it is necessary to edge outside the confines of the modern debate. And for this, we need to know what those constraints are, pausing to examine the suppositions usually passed over without mention. This is impossible if we uncritically accept that the problem of color is just the task of finding a place for red and green within Democritus's or Eddington's atom-filled void.

1.3   Situating the Debate

"[E]very metaphysical question always encompasses the whole range of metaphysical problems. Each question is itself always the whole" (Heidegger [1929] 1993, 93). Metaphysicians pursuing a piecemeal strategy and attacking problems individually, as is common these days, may dispute the truth of this dictum. But the problem of color is a telling case in point. For one thing, the color question is a single instance of the larger issue concerning the secondary qualities—the ontological status of smells, sounds, tastes, and the tactile qualities. It is assumed, rightly or not, that once we settle on a solution for color, this result will be smoothly translated across to our theories of these other modalities.

Furthermore the secondary qualities confront us with the problem of the manifest. Above I touched upon this. As Wilfrid Sellars saw it, the problem of the manifest not only concerned sensory qualities, but also many notions central to our humanistic understanding of the world, such as personhood, agency, and reason.[8] An antirealist philosopher might fairly easily live her life in accordance with the belief that colors are illusions, but—one hopes—she would find it more challenging to co-exist with

8. Sellars' manifest image is not a pre-theoretical understanding of the world but a world view steeped in philosophical tradition going back to Plato. Many philosophers who discuss the manifest are not as careful as Sellars was to distinguish the manifest image from untutored "common sense." The point is important because pre-theoretical intuition is taken to be immutable in today's philosophical debate. In the next chapter I will describe the connection between a supposed commonsense naïve realism about colors, and the scholastic realism that preceded the so-called scientific revolution.

others while convinced that persons and their responsibilities are equally suspect. Not coincidentally, the question of color has often been treated as analogous to questions in moral philosophy about the status of value judgments in a world of physical facts (McDowell 1985; Smith 1989; Lewis 1989; Johnston 1989).

Ultimately the problem of color leads us to a truly great mystery in the philosophy and science of the mind: consciousness. For it is just one aspect of the problem of finding a place for any qualitative properties—the sensations they belong to and the sentience that apparently gives rise to them—in a world conceived as fundamentally physical. I call the wider issue, that encompasses mind, the manifest, color and other secondary qualities, the *problem of the qualitative*. Philosophers whose goal is a materialistic theory of everything are presented with the seemingly intractable challenge of accounting for the qualitative and mental in terms of the quantitative and physical. A mind-body dualist like Descartes need not be bothered that a thoroughly mechanistic theory of perception can explain sensitivity to external stimuli, and behavioral responses, but not the qualitative awareness that comes with vision and the other senses. In the dualist account consciousness is said to transcend the physical world, so Descartes had the luxury of "kicking upstairs," to borrow the metaphor from Shoemaker (2003), any qualitative aspects of perception into the immaterial realm of the spirit.

Given the relatedness of the issues, it is not surprising that proposed solutions to the problem of color have shared much with proposals in ontology of mind. Reductive color realism has a lot in common with physicalism in the philosophy of mind. Indeed the same "Australian-materialist" philosophers that we associate with mind-brain identity theory and realizer-functionalism were also responsible for analogous views on color. According to mind-brain identity theory, the mind just is the brain or the nervous system (Smart 1959; Armstrong 1968). As such it is a part of the physical world that can be given an objective characterization by science: pain, famously, just is "c-fibres twitching." Likewise, according to reductive color realism, colors just are whatever candidate physical property is identifiable with color, for example, a wavelength of light or spectral surface reflectance, while nonreductive realists take colors to be *sui generis* properties of material objects that supervene on their physical ones (Watkins 2010). In contrast, Hardin (1993) declares himself an eliminativist about color, a view analogous to eliminative materialism in philosophy of mind (Rorty 1970; Churchland 1981).

1.4   Getting Outside: Towards a New Philosophy of Color

In chapter 2 I discuss the historical forces that have shaped the color debate. In chapter 3 we see how these forces continue to constrain contemporary thought. Since the current controversy around color is symptomatic of a more-or-less modern anxiety about the status of sensory awareness in an austere, materialistic universe, it is easiest to understand this debate by beginning with the *antirealist* theories that take the existence of color to be ontologically problematic.[9] The antirealist view of color is often presented as an irresistible consequence of our sophisticated, scientific worldview. Yet it is held unthinkable by many. This is actually for the reason that it goes against "commonsense" or "folk theory" (Stroud 2000). Today's color *realists* are the champions of common sense. While some argue that we can retain the naïve belief that the world just is as we perceive it to be, others seek to reconcile the austere scientific worldview with a straightforward interpretation of visual experience, one that can validate the claim that when I say the sky is blue, it is blue. No one has better summarized the realist ambition than Lewis (1997, 325): "[a]n adequate theory of colour must be both materialistic and commonsensical."

Relationism is the umbrella term for theories that define colors in terms of relations between objects and perceivers (Cohen 2004, 2009). An example of a relational theory is *dispositionalism*, the idea that redness, for instance, is the disposition of an object to appear red to a typical human being in ordinary circumstances. Of greater significance to my discussion are the newer ecological-relational approaches. This approach is grounded in empirical work on cross-species variation in color vision, and the adaptation of perceptual systems to ecological and behavioral niches. Here color is understood in terms of the animal's ecologically appropriate responses to reflectance and other physical stimuli (Thompson 1995). In a related vein

9. Hardin (1993), the most influential advocate of the view, actually calls his position *subjectivist*. I use the term antirealist, to avoid confusion of Hardin's with *relationist* accounts. The relationist such as Cohen (2009) agrees that colors are in some sense subjective (i.e., perceiver-dependent) but does not follow through with the conclusion that colors are not real (not instantiated).

Hatfield (2003, 195) proposes that we classify color as a "psychobiological property"—a relational "attribute of objects that makes surfaces visually discriminable without a difference in brightness or lightness." Ecological relationism has done much to re-animate the discussion, and to bring into focus empirical constraints, especially concerning claims about what kinds of perceptual states can be said to be veridical representations of the environment.

Outside Color can be seen as complementary to the ecological-relationist project. There is a shared methodological tenet that color vision, and therefore color, can best be understood as a means by which organisms make sense of the complexity of the natural environment. The crucial difference from Thompson's work is that this book focuses on the psychophysics and neurophysiology of the *human* visual system. We will see that even before branching out into the comparative literature, a more sophisticated, scientifically informed understanding of perception will help resolve some philosophical puzzles about color.

1.4.1 Destinations

We can now sketch the territory. The next chapter unearths three conventional ways of thinking about color that have had a governing effect on the debate:

1. The detection model of perception, and the idea that color vision can be understood separately from the rest of vision.

2. The assumption that there is one common sense view that colors are intrinsic (perceiver-independent) properties of objects.

3. A rigid demarcation between "inner" and "outer" realms, such that colors must either be located in the brain, or outside in the world of physics.

In the next chapter I argue that much of the familiar conception of color has its origins in the Aristotelian theories of perception that dominated the late Middle Ages. The orthodoxy of Aquinas, among others, was that colors reside in objects just as we see them, and that the resemblance between perception and its object is ensured by *intentional species*, mysterious entities that transmit qualities like color from an object to the eye. This literal realism was rejected with the ontological overhaul that accompanied the rise of modern science. But various features of the old view have set the pattern for the modern alternatives.

In chapter 3 I describe how the three assumptions have shaped contemporary philosophy of color. First, philosophers typically agree that there is a default, commonsense conception of color, one that takes colors to be intrinsic properties belonging to ordinary physical objects. The majority of philosophers take compliance with common sense to be a methodological goal in itself. This has engendered an inhibiting conservatism in the philosophy of color. In most fields of enquiry, such as astronomy or medicine, replacement of a commonsense concept with a scientifically grounded one is taken to be an acceptable outcome. It is problematic that a primary aim of many theories of color is the reconciliation of science with common sense; especially so if, as I argue in chapter 8, the commonsense conception is an unwarranted extrapolation from visual phenomenology.

In philosophical discussion it is typical to analyze color experience as if it were separate and separable from other visual features of an object, like shape and texture. It is a practice that normally goes without question, though it was roundly challenged by the Gestalt school of psychology. Another way of describing this approach is as a coloring-in model: just as in a coloring book, the forms depicted are independent of any coloring scheme, what colors objects appear to have is independent of their shapes, and other spatial properties. Realists and antirealists are then left to argue if these chromatic properties are really out there or if they are mere projections of the mind. Indeed the model has played different but crucial roles in antirealist and realist accounts. It gives antirealists a picture of how the world could be without color. That is, it makes color seem dispensable, something we can eliminate without cost to our perceptual or ontological economy. For realists the coloring-in model informs an understanding of color perception as simply the detection of these sui generis chromatic properties. This blocks a more sophisticated understanding of the function of color vision. Chapter 4 reviews recent work in visual psychology and neuroscience in order to challenge the coloring-in model. The scientific results showing that color vision is not separate or separable from the rest of vision; it serves instead many tasks that are integrated with various visual functions such as perceiving depth and shape. *Coloring-in* is replaced by *coloring-for-perceiving*.

The result of the third assumption, the bifurcation of color into outer and inner components, is that realists and antirealists, respectively, are pushed to focus their attention on either the external or internal causes of color appearances. I present the case that the physicalist account is seriously inadequate, concurring with the observations of Hardin (2003a) on the mismatch between physical and phenomenal color. I also state why the antirealist reduction of color to neural firings is premature. In chapter 5 I diagnose the limitations of both of these approaches as due to their adherence to a particular notion of perceptual success. In the perceptual epistemology that is common ground to realists and antirealists, a perceptual state is veridical if the objects and properties it presents correspond to objects and properties in the perceiver-independent world. Drawing on current vision science, I present a pragmatic alternative whereby perceptual states are understood primarily as action-guiding interactions between a perceiver and its environment. The fact that perceptual states are shaped in idiosyncratic ways by the needs and interests of the perceiver means that some visually presented properties fail to correspond to external counterparts; but this does not automatically render the state falsidical. On this interactionist view, it is natural to say that colors are perceiver-dependent properties, and yet our awareness of them does not mislead us about the world.

The idea is that when we see objects as colored, we are observing subjectively constructed but not merely projected properties. It is necessary to explore the ways in which color is enmeshed in both the physical and the psychological worlds. On my account it is important to consider that:

• Any color visual system is a particular way of sampling the light environment.

• Thus color perception relates perceiver to perceived in a particular way.

• Colors are the distinctive ways that things appear to different color perceivers.

Colors should not be thought of as something belonging either to observers or objects. I propose instead to concentrate on color vision as a process, and to define colors as properties of an interaction between observers and things. What and how we see depends on us—our retinal sensitivities to ambient light, our other neural equipment, and our habitual ways of looking around us. Ultimately, of course, visual experience is shaped by all the things around us. Color vision is a joint product of the perceiver and perceived, so colors are relational in this sense. More specifically, as I argue in chapter 6, an adverbial ontology of color is best able to capture the insights of ecological-relationism: colors are properties of perceptual processes involving particular kinds of spectral stimuli, and spectrally sensitive visual systems.

While there are some precedents for *color adverbialism* in the philosophical literature, the view faces a number of objections grounded in common interpretations of visual experience. So I devote the last two chapters to tackling these concerns. Nevertheless, a conclusive account of color is dependent on some theory of visual consciousness that can explain why objects have the appearances that they do. The question of color will not finally be laid to rest until we have resolved further fundamental issues about the place of mind in nature and the status of our scientific understanding of the mind-world relationship. One may hope, however, that these local innovations in color ontology will themselves form a worthwhile contribution to this grander philosophical project.

2 What Everyone Thinks about Color, and Why

2.1 Overview

Colors were not an ontological problem before Galileo. While ancient arguments from perceptual relativity might have seeded skepticism about the accuracy of some sensory experiences, until the rise of modern mathematical physics the existence or otherwise of external, qualitative properties was not a central concern.[1] Discussions of the philosophy of color normally begin their story in the early modern era, when Galileo, Descartes, Locke, and Newton tell us that colors do not belong to the physical world in the way we apparently see that they do:

And if at any time I speak of Light and rays as coloured or endued with Colours, I would be understood to speak not philosophically and properly, but grossly, and accordingly to such Conceptions as vulgar People in seeing all these Experiments would be apt to frame. For the Rays to speak properly are not coloured. (Newton [1704] 1952, 124–25)

The message of this chapter is that the historical investigation should begin a little earlier, with the Aristotelian theories of perception that dominated the late Middle Ages. The orthodoxy of Aquinas, among others, was that colors reside in objects just as we see them, and that the resemblance between perception and its object is ensured by *intentional species*, theoretical descendents of Aristotle's forms. Subsequent doubts about the existence of color should be seen as a reaction against this view. In particular the Aristotelian-scholastic theory comes with strong ontological commitment

1. Democritus could be cited as the exception that proves the rule, since his picture of atoms and the void is a precursor to modern scientific ontologies. However, the perceptual realism of later atomists, like Epicurus, shows that the ancient version of atomism did not rule out the existence of qualitative color in external objects.

to the existence of colors in external objects: qualitative color is literally
out there in the world. Colors become problematic because this commitment cannot be upheld within the emerging scientific world view.
The problem of secondary qualities, now familiar to us, comes with the
rejection of the scholastic ontology in all spheres of investigation into the
material world. Colors, tastes, and smells can no longer be thought of as
part of a natural order now viewed as inert, mechanical. The interesting
thing is that there is a persistence of the scholastic picture in that ontological commitment to external color is still taken as central to our default,
nonscientific opinions. Indeed the outer-directedness of visual experience
is itself thought by most philosophers to saddle us with ontological commitment to external, mind-independent chromatic properties. By the end
of this chapter it should be clear why this surprising belief is so widely
entertained.[2]

2.1.1 Scholastic Realism

Aristotelian natural philosophy dominated scientific thought in the late
Middle Ages, and the topic of vision was no exception. The scholastic theory of perception, which the moderns rejected, was basically an Aristotelian
realism, with the added refinement of the doctrine of *species*. Put simply,
the idea is that what looks to a human (whose perceptual apparatus is working normally) to be peacock blue, simply is peacock blue.[3] Thus visual presentations of color, as we experience them, are simply manifestations of
properties rightly belonging to the object perceived. The experience perfectly resembles the relevant quality in the object.[4]

---

2. The historical exposition of §§2.1.1 and 2.1.2 is not intended to be ground-
breaking or controversial. Where appropriate I refer to secondary sources on particular points of analysis.

3. See *De anima* (418a, 11–16)—color is the "proper sensible" of sight, and perceptual systems do not err in their reports of these. For discussions of Aristotle and his
medieval followers, see Burnyeat (1992), Everson (1999), Johansen (1997), Gaukroger
(1990), and Lindberg (1976).

4. There is reason to interpret Aristotle's own position as more nuanced than the
naïve realist one that is usually attributed to him. As Jon Buttaci (personal communication) has pointed out, both color realism and antirealism were already established
views and Aristotle can be read as providing a middle path between these extremes.
The potential/actual distinction is crucial to this reconciliation. In particular see
De anima (425b, 26): "the earlier natural philosophers were in error, when they

Aristotle's account in *De anima* assumes a *hylomorphic* physics (where each object is a composite of immaterial form and unformed matter) and explains perception as the reception in the sensory organ of the *form* of the perceived object, without its *matter*. Roger Bacon (c. 1220–1292) combined the Aristotelian theory with the neo-Platonic doctrine of *species*, whereby all objects are said to be constantly shedding off likenesses of themselves into surrounding *media*. *Species* (or *intentional species*) then entered the theory of sensation, to explain how we can come to have truthful perceptions of external objects, especially the distant objects of vision: if objects send out copies of themselves along a line of sight, these can be received by the eye and eventually apprehended by the intellect. Thus the sensory organ may obtain a likeness of the perceived object, without literally becoming that object. This is possible, if the sensory organ does receive something of the object and its properties—*forms* or *species*—without receiving their substance or matter.[5] Combined with Alhazen's (c. 965–c. 1039) formulation of the visual pyramid, which showed how there could be an ordered projection from perceived objects to the eye, the medieval theory of species inspired a robustly realist epistemology of sight.

The theory of species also supported a strong color realism. Indeed, as Aristotle had put it, color is the "proper sensible" of vision, that is, the property to which visual organs are specifically responsive. The perception of a colored object involved the reception of the species of the appropriate color. In order to understand just how color could have been thought to have been present all at once in the object, species and perceiver, it is worth examining the key metaphors that were used to describe species and their

---

supposed that without seeing there was neither white nor black, and without tasting no flavour. Their statement is in one sense true, in another false. For the terms 'perception' and 'perceptible thing' are spoken of in two ways. When they mean the actual perception and the actual perceptible thing, the statement holds good; when they mean potential perception and potential perceptible thing, this is not the case" (R. D. Hicks trans. in Durrant 1993, 52). The idea is that visible objects bear colors (potentially), independently of perceivers, but that color is fully actualized when the visible object is seen. So the realist is right to say that colors (potentially) exist independently of sight, while the antirealist is correct to say that colors (actually) require the presence of perceivers.

5. It is a point of controversy whether or not the sensory organ should be understood as undergoing a purely formal change (Burnyeat 1992), or also a material change (Sorabji 1974; Everson 1999). See Caston (2004) for discussion.

activities. The reception of the species onto the eye is often said to be like the impression of a metal seal on wax. As Aquinas writes:

The disposition of the wax to the image is not the same as that of the iron or gold to the image; hence wax, he [Aristotle] says, takes a sign, i.e. as shape or image, of what is gold or bronze, but not precisely as gold or bronze. For the wax takes a likeness of the gold seal in respect to the image, but not in respect to the seal's intrinsic disposition to be a gold seal. (Aquinas 1945, Lectio 24 on bk. II, §553–54)

Another well-worn comparison is the one made with mirroring. When a colorful object is reflected in a mirror, it imparts its color to the surface temporarily, without permanently altering its constitution. An object's color seems to have the same effect on the eye as when it is reflected in a mirror (Clark 2007, 18–19). In the late Middle Ages colors are very much in the world. There is no mismatch between perceptual phenomenology and scientific ontology. Therefore there is no problem of color. At the same time scholastic realism set color up for a fall. By intimating so strong a notion of the objectivity of vision—that the world *is* as we see it to be—it was inevitable that colors would be found wanting, thus inviting the Galilean criticism that we are entirely wrong in our association of color experiences with physical objects. Indeed the color debate can be understood as a reaction against the scholastic view. In the later sections of this chapter we will return to some specific features of the theory, after first considering how and why it was rejected in the seventeenth century.

2.1.2 The Reaction

Hence I think that these tastes, odours, colours, etc., on the side of the object in which they seem to exist, are nothing else than mere names, but hold their residence solely in the sensitive body; so that if the animal were removed, every such quality would be abolished and annihilated. Nevertheless, as soon as we have imposed names on them, particular and different from those of the other primary and real accidents, we induce ourselves to believe that they also exist just as truly and really as the latter. (Galileo, trans. in Burtt [1932] 2003, 85)

This excerpt from *The Assayer* is familiar to any readers of the current debate over color.[6] Galileo eloquently gestures toward what we would now call an antirealist position, one that asserts that the colors—and other

---

6. This or a similar passage is quoted by Boghossian and Velleman (1989, 81), Thompson (1995, 19), Hilbert (1987, 3), and Giere (2006, 23).

sensory qualities—are never instantiated except in the minds of perceivers. This is an exact reversal of the scholastic scheme, where the red of a strawberry is as real as the matter that it belongs to. Today the quandary that inspires the realist camp is not so much the difficulty of the ideas that colors are only "in the head"; it is that we cannot help but see them "out there" in the world. Wishing to avoid a life sentence of double-think or false consciousness, the contemporary realist seeks a place for colors in the world of physics. This is what Jackson (1998) has called "the location problem."

The explanation of the turnaround from Aristotle and Aquinas on color, to Galileo and Newton, reaches further than just the history of ideas of perception. A fuller understanding comes with an appreciation of how far ontological schemes shifted during the seventeenth century. So what was the new natural philosophy, and why was it at odds with the scholastics' theory of the senses? There is a vast literature on the so-called scientific revolution and the rise of mechanistic accounts of nature.[7] We may restrict our attention here to a few points most tied to the seventeenth century reappraisal of color. The important thing about scholastic natural philosophy was that it proffered explanations of natural phenomena in terms of the numerous qualities, essences and powers of objects whose actions were supposed to give rise to the effect in question, and there was no a priori restriction on how many of these might be at play in the world. As Des Chene (2006, 73–74) has described, the ontological profligacy of the Aristotelian system was disturbing for the mechanists. Among the basic properties of matter—the qualities that were irreducible and had a primary explanatory role—the Aristotelians listed shape, a property acceptable to the mechanists, but also four elemental qualities (hot, cold, wet, dry, and some "occult" qualities, e.g., the attraction to a lodestone), and the proper sensibles of each of the five senses. These are the properties perceived by one sense alone, such as sound for hearing, heat for touch, and, of course, color for vision. Importantly, these are sensory properties, characterized by a qualitative "what it's like" description.

The mechanists, such as Gassendi, Descartes, and Hobbes, sought to explain the same phenomena only in terms of a restricted set of qualities or properties belonging to the basic constituents of matter. The preference was

7. See, for example, Gaukroger (2006), Henry (2002), and Lindberg and Westman (1990) for overviews.

for a catalog of properties that was restricted to those amenable to geometric description or quantification. In effect, to grant irreducible ontological status to qualitative, sensory properties would be to deny the complete intelligibility of nature in mechanistic terms.

For instance, Cartesians conceived of matter as "pure extension," and so inferred that it could possess only the properties of size, shape, position and motion (Hatfield 1990, 114). Boyle, a corpuscularian, took the defining properties of matter to be shape, size and mobility (Alexander 1985, 70). Colors, and the other proper sensibles, formerly basic explanatory properties, were relegated to secondary status.[8] Boyle introduced the terminology of "primary" and "secondary" qualities, though the distinction was assumed by Galileo and Descartes before him, and is now most associated with Locke and his treatment of it in the *Essay Concerning Human Understanding*. This is one of the ways in which Locke draws the distinction:

Qualities thus considered in Bodies are: First such as are utterly inseparable from the body, in what state soever it be; such as in all the alterations and changes it suffers, all the force can be used upon it, it constantly keeps; and such as sense constantly finds in every particle of matter, which has bulk enough to be perceived; and the mind finds inseparable from every particle of matter, though less than to make itself singly be perceived by our senses These I call *original* or *primary qualities* of body; which I think we may observe to produce simple *ideas* in us, viz. solidity, extension, figure, motion, or rest, and number.

Secondly, such *qualities*, which in truth are nothing in the objects themselves, but powers to produce various sensations in us by their *primary qualities*, i.e. by the bulk, figure, texture, and Motion of their insensible parts, as colours, sounds, tastes, *etc.* These I call *secondary Qualities*. (Locke [1690] 1993, bk. II, ch. 8, §§9–10)

The idea that primary qualities are inseparable from bodies dovetails with the idea that these qualities are the ingredients for all physical explanation. As Smith (1990) interprets the primary-secondary distinction, if a property were only occasionally present in matter, not belonging to all bodies at all times, it could not be so useful in a physics that aims to provide exhaustive explanations of natural phenomena—to be a complete

---

8. A point of interpretive controversy is whether colors are themselves to be identified with secondary qualities, or if colors are the ideas in us that are caused by secondary qualities (Alexander 1985, ch. 8). In what follows, I attempt to avoid saying anything controversial about secondary qualities. Where necessary, I specify that the issue in question is the nature of "color," "sensation," and "perceptual experience," as opposed to the nature of the secondary qualities.

description of the world-machine. Thus one definition of the primary qualities is that they are universal. From this era we inherit a world picture, an informal ontology, of matter made up from miniature billiard balls that are colorless and odorless, but whose position and movements can be mapped by an exhaustive mathematical description.

So there is a dramatic fall from grace for the colors, which, as we have seen, had counted among the basic, real properties in the scholastic system. Now a realist theory of sensation satisfied the epistemic requirements of pre-modern natural philosophy. The idea that the senses serve us with a precise picture of reality bolstered the claims of an Aristotelian empiricism. It is worth exploring the ways that a different perceptual philosophy dovetailed with the new scientific epistemology of the seventeenth century. Above, I hinted that the new primary qualities were selected because of their suitability for geometrical or mathematical analysis. There is much more to say about this. The application of abstract mathematics and idealized geometric figures to actual objects and events may seem natural to us, but the relevance of mathematics to empirical science was not at all a given prior to the Galilean revolution. As Hatfield (1990) describes, Galileo had to resort to various rhetorical strategies to convince some of his contemporaries of the value of the mathematical approach. The rise of applied mathematics has come to be known as the "mathemetization of the world picture."[9] Even if, as Hatfield (1990) has argued, there was not a unified metaphysical picture behind the different mechanists' strategies for the application of mathematics to nature, one can detect a strong commitment to what we would now call scientific realism—a belief that scientific theories offer a truthful representation of the natural world. And this has consequences for the status of color, for if scientific theory is taken to be a description of reality, and such theories only grant quantitative properties to matter, qualitative properties—ones marked by a phenomenal what-it's-like-ness—can no longer be thought of as belonging to external objects.

To reiterate, the primacy of the quantitative properties was an exact reversal of the scholastic scheme, and the new approach led Galileo to what would now be called an error theory, the view that our perceptual states cause us to suffer lifelong, systematic delusions because they present us

9. See, for example, Henry (2002), Maull (1978), and Gaukroger (1980).

with colors and other qualitative properties out there in the world. But the path to error theory includes a step that is not often made explicit in the literature on philosophy and color. Error theory is only compelling on the prior assumption that our sensory states present themselves as if resembling states of affairs in the world. Not coincidentally this assumption that perception is mimetic is one of the hallmarks of the pre-modern view, with its metaphors of the wax and seal, and the mirror. Galilean antirealism about color puts itself forward as a challenge to "common sense," what everyone believes about color. Perhaps the scholastic dogma was so widespread that the mimetic theory of perception could easily be mistaken for "what everyone believes...." But we will not understand the color debate properly unless we grasp that what Galileo challenges is not just unschooled intuition, but part of a sophisticated theoretical edifice. We return to this issue in section 2.3 below.

The idea of resemblance often comes into play in the early modern literature. It is worth mentioning the example that everybody knows: that Locke claimed that our ideas of primary qualities resemble their external causes, but ideas of secondary qualities did not, whereas Berkeley denied any resemblance of ideas of one sense to ideas of any other sense, let alone to external objects. Here is the relevant passage from Locke's *Essay* where he uses resemblance as one way to draw the primary-secondary distinction:

> From whence I think it is easy to draw this observation: that the *ideas of primary qualities* of bodies, *are resemblances* of them, and their patterns do really exist in the bodies themselves; but the *ideas produced* in us *by* these *secondary qualities have no resemblance* of them at all. There is nothing like our *ideas* existing in the bodies themselves. (Locke [1690] 1993, bk. II, ch. 8, §15)

Contemporary readers tend to side with Berkeley here and take Locke's resemblance claims to be absurd, even for primary qualities, since he is not making explicit any sense in which this likeness could hold. However, we have seen that the scholastic theory did itself make concrete proposals as to what this resemblance could consist in (i.e., the reception of species in the perceiver's sensory organ). Perhaps we should read Locke more charitably, bearing in mind that at the time that he wrote the scholastic theory was still fresh in people's minds. Although Locke rejects the scholastic account of perceptions for primary qualities as well, he and his readers might not have seen anything intrinsically problematic about the notion of resemblance here.

It is obvious, then, that the modern way of thinking about perception bears the mark of its medieval precursors. In its outright rejection of sensuous colors "out there," the modern theory of perception is an explicit rejection of scholasticism. Indeed the scholastic one was the theory to beat, and for example, Descartes writes in his *Optics* that it is to the credit of his new approach to perception that it need not posit, "all those little images flitting through the air, called *'intentional species'*, which so exercise the imagination of philosophers" (Descartes 1985, 153–54). Yet in other ways the modern approach shows remarkable continuity with the medieval trends. In the next sections we examine specific features of the pre-modern doctrines that have shaped the contemporary color debate.

2.2 Detection and Reification

There is an assumption in the philosophy of color that attracts near universal assent, and probably for this reason is rarely stated. It is the assumption that colors are properties that can be analyzed in isolation from other visual features such as shape and depth. The guiding metaphor is of colors being like paints or dyes that may or may not be part of an otherwise achromatic world. If colors are real, it is the job of the color visual system simply to detect these; if they are not, then it is the mind that paints (i.e., *projects*) these onto its surroundings. I call this a "reification" of color: we have a particular dimension of perceptual experience that is abstracted away from the others, and as a result it becomes a live question whether *this* element of experience constitutes a veridical representation of some particular property of objects.

This picture of the independence of color is strikingly Aristotelian. As we saw, Aristotle wrote that colors are a proper sensible of sight, a visual property that the eye detects separately from the "common sensibles" of motion, form, and the rest.[10] This reification is elaborated in the medieval development of Aristotelian realism. Within the scholastic tradition it was possible to maintain a realism about color vision because of the identity of species as they passed from the external object into the mind. In the new philosophy of the seventeenth century, on the contrary, sensory qualities are said

10. Nevertheless, note that according to Aristotle, we perceive the common sensibles by way of our detection of the proper sensibles.

to *look* as if they were something belonging to material objects while doubt is cast over their external origins. They come to be treated as mental paint pots whose actual origin is within the perceiver—such as the "ideas" or "impressions" of the British empiricists. The modern view is a skeptical attack that specifically targets the medieval assumption of an external source for qualitative color properties.

Furthermore the scholastics reified colors by treating them as separable (at least in principle) from their bodies. One of the central targets of Descartes' attack on the scholastics was their doctrine of "real qualities" (Des Chene 2008). These are sensory qualities, like color and heat, that were taken by the scholastics to be *res*—thing—in that they could exist independently of their normal material substrates. So the qualities are "real" in the sense that they are thing-like, not just in the contemporary sense of "not imaginary." As Menn (1995) argues, the abolition of real qualities was critical to Descartes' scientific project of allowing only geometric properties ("modes of extension") to enter into explanation of natural phenomena. Yet the assumption of the separability of color lingers on in the treatment of this dimension of visual experience in isolation from the rest, as I will argue in chapters 3 and 4.

Reification and detection go hand in hand. If one assumes that the job of sensory systems is to pick up information about ordinary physical properties, then it makes sense to posit that color is whatever property happens to be detected by the color visual system. By the same turn, the reification of color lends us a simple notion of what those chromatic properties might be. Thus we arrive at a compelling model of perception whereby the job of sensory systems is simply to detect physical properties, and hence less attention is paid to alternative functions, such as signaling change or discriminating differences between properties.[11] In the scholastic model, perception is grounded in the sense organs' capturing of intentional species flitting around them. Species have long passed into obscurity, but the detection model lives on in various modern guises. While it is a somewhat amorphous target, the detection model can be thought of as a cluster of all or some of the following commitments:

---

11. The view presented in chapter 4 is that the color visual system serves to discriminate certain sorts of physical properties, and to signal material changes, without detecting any property (or group of properties) that can rightly be identified with color.

1. our sensory organs are analogous to measuring devices;

2. perception aims to represent some of the intrinsic properties of macroscopic physical objects;

3. this representation aims (as far as biology allows) at independence from any idiosyncrasies due to the makeup of the perceiver;

4. and also at independence from modulation by recent experience;

5. failures of independence are departures from veridicality.[12]

It is still common to compare sensory systems with unsophisticated measuring devices like thermometers. Indeed the front line of sensory receptors, such as thermoreceptors and photoreceptors, does seem to invite the analogy with simple physical transducers. The perennial comparison of the eye and photographic camera trades on the idea that the retina passively receives the impressions of light falling on it.[13] The detection model has been key player in the color debate. As I will discuss in chapter 5, antirealists rest their case on there being no one physical quantity that explains all the facets of our color experience. The reductive color realist, however, seeks to isolate certain physical properties—wavelength of light (Armstrong 1969), spectral surface reflectance (Hilbert 1987)—that the color visual system can be said to pick up.

It bears reflection that the detection model fosters extreme views about the validity of the senses, either an entrenched belief in the accuracy of sensory information or the opposite opinion that they get things utterly wrong. On Aristotle's account in *De anima*, the perception of proper sensibles is guaranteed to be incorrigible under normal circumstances. The function of each sensory organ is the detection of its proper sensible. As Gaukroger (1990, 7) argues, Aristotle's case rests on the teleological grounds

---

12. See Akins (1996) for related discussion.

13. Yet even photoreceptors cannot be thought of as photon-catchers, responding to the presence of light in a linear fashion. Their responses are modulated by recent activity and responses of neighboring cells. Likewise thermoreceptors embedded in our skin do not signal absolute changes in temperature. In general, sensory neurons behave after the receptoral stage as if sensitive to contrast between stimulus properties, rather than any absolute physical quantity. For example, the layers of retinal cells following the photoreceptors respond not to light intensity but to spatial differences in light intensity (contrast), such that a black-white border can stimulate an equally strong response over a wide range of lighting conditions from dim candlelight to bright sunshine.

that, "we have the sense organs we do because they naturally display to us the nature of the world we wish to understand." In the medieval version of the account, the grounds become theological: "God has given us the sense organs we have so that we might know His creation" (Gaukroger 1990, 11). In either case, emphasis is placed on the senses as a means to gaining true knowledge of the world. However, skepticism was soon to follow precisely because of a radical shift in opinion about what sort of properties were out there in the world to be detected. In the Aristotelian theory, the eye acts as a simple detector of the colored forms of objects. Likewise, in the scholastic version, the eye and brain register the presence of incoming species. Aristotle took our perceptual systems to be capable of delivering true likenesses of the external world, whereas Galileo suggests that they are systematically misleading. What is different is that Galileo and his contemporaries no longer believed in the objective existence of the sensory qualities that earlier accounts had claimed we detect.

We can also note that in the seventeenth century the comparison of the eye with physical measuring devices becomes explicit. During the scientific revolution the natural operation of sensory systems begins to be compared with performance aided by optical devices designed to enhance perception, tools that are becoming essential to empirical research. The moderns shared with the scholastics an interest in the senses as a means to knowledge of the world. However, the usefulness of natural vision is put under more scrutiny than before because of the possible comparison between the naked and optically aided eye. At the very beginning of his *Optics*, Descartes writes:

[S]ince sight is the noblest and most comprehensive of the senses, inventions which serve to increase its power are undoubtedly among the most useful there can be. And it is difficult to find any such inventions which do more to increase the power of sight than those wonderful telescopes which…have already revealed a greater number of new stars and other new objects above the earth than we had seen there before. (Descartes 1985, 152)

Where naked eye and optical devices conflict in their testimony, the tendency is now to trust invention, not biological endowment (Gaukroger 1990, 13). Telescopes increase our knowledge about the spatial properties of distant things, but they do not improve our perception of color. Microscopes allow us to see structures in minute spatial detail, but provide only ambiguous testimony about their colors. This supports the idea that color is a subjective component of animal vision, which will not, for this reason, be enhanced by machines.[14]

Still, what needs to be scrutinized is the very assumption that unaided biological vision should be compared with the machine-aided sort. The latter is engaged in the specific project of gleaning factual knowledge from experimental situations, while the former does not necessarily have any investment in the gathering of objective facts. So to compare these two is to make the claim that in perceiving we are somehow aiming at an objective description of reality.

In short, if color vision is not there to bring us an objective picture of the world, then there is no error if there does happen to be a mismatch between what we see and the objective picture drawn by measuring instruments. If we step back a moment, we can appreciate how very weird it is to even expect there to be a connection between the manifest visual world, brought to us by our senses, and the rarefied scientific image of a world made up of physical particles, etc. The latter is the product of ever-finer empirical dissection and mathematical deduction, but even then it might only be a tool that enables physicists to predict experimental outcomes. (The debate between realists and instrumentalists in the philosophy of science is far from over!) However, this expectation of a connection between sensible properties and the natures of things was cultivated by generations of Aristotelians, and it still resonates with philosophers thinking about color today.

2.3   The Construction of Common Sense

There is a striking similarity between scholastic color realism and the "commonsense" opinion[15] often discussed in the contemporary debate. Hilbert writes:

14. The famous argument from microscopes appears in Berkeley's *Dialogues*. The observation that blood appears uniformly red to the naked eye, but partly red and partly transparent when viewed under the microscope, is another instance of the perceptual variation described in section 1.2.1. Berkeley's philosophical motives are discussed by Wilson (1999) and Atherton (2003b), among others. The validity of the argument is discussed by Armstrong (1969), Hilbert (1987, ch. 2), and Kalderon (2011b).

15. AKA the "pre-theoretical," "pre-reflective" (Hilbert 1987), or "pre-analytical" (Maund 1981) opinion, "folk theory," or "intuition" (Jackson 1998).

Pre-reflective common sense is robustly realist about colors and does not distinguish color from other fundamental properties of external objects such as shape or weight. Our pre-reflective attitude towards colors takes them to be properties of the things they are seen to qualify, in just the same sense as the shape of an object is a property of it. (Hilbert 1987, 2)

Exactly the same could be said of the medieval theory, in its generous ontology that placed sensory qualities on the same footing as geometric ones. In the contemporary debate, however, the medieval doctrine is practically never mentioned. So is this similarity between pre-theoretical intuition, and scholastic theory important? In this section I argue that it is. Crucially, common sense is accepted as the default view about color, one that cannot be overturned without introducing some disturbing cognitive dissonance. Color realists are, at least in part, motivated by a perceived need to reconcile common sense with science. Any theory of color that rejects one or more tenets of common sense is deemed "revisionary," and this is a major strike against it (Cohen 2009, 65). This is because there seems to be something immutable about common sense. If it is understood simply as intuition, part of our perceptual and cognitive endowment, no matter how scientifically sophisticated we are, we are stuck with it. This is why the problem of color appears to be so intractable. Yet, if pre-theoretical intuition is actually the remnant of scholastic theory, we can hope to shift it. It is far easier to contemplate the rejection of an outdated piece of theory than it is to eradicate a basic feature of our visual phenomenology. The hope is that ontological commitment to colors as perceiver-independent properties can be relegated to the same fate as the scholastics' occult qualities and powers.[16]

An immediate obstacle to this fast way out of ontological commitment is the rejoinder that the scholastic doctrines took the form that they did

---

16. Note that I remain neutral over the issue of whether there *might* be any universal folk theory of color, one that makes weaker claims about the nature of color than those typically formulated under the heading of common sense. For example, it does not seem so implausible that there is a pan-historically and cross-culturally universal commonsense view that holds that colors are properties of ordinary objects or their surfaces, without making any claims about the perceiver-dependent or independent nature of those properties. As far as I am aware, the only experimental investigations into color intuitions have involved Westerners (Cohen and Nichols 2010; Roberts et al. 2014). Thanks to Edouard Machery for raising this issue.

because they were simply the theoretical incarnation of common sense, a statement of what any human would believe about the natural world if not challenged by modern science. In fact the seventeenth-century mechanists deliberately portrayed scholastic theory as the crystallization of the errors of childhood and common sense. For example, Descartes wrote of the juvenile, and also scholastic tendency to confuse mental attributes with physical ones, thus taking sensations to be *real qualities* in objects:

The first judgments we made in our youth, and later also in the common [i.e., scholastic] philosophy have accustomed us to attribute to bodies many things which pertain only to the soul and to attribute to the soul many things which pertain only to the body. They ordinarily blend the two ideas of the body and the soul, and in the combining of these ideas they form real qualities and substantial forms, which I think ought entirely to be rejected. (1641 correspondence, quoted in Garber 1992, 102)[17]

The thought, to be gleaned from Descartes, is that Aristotelian realism was so influential precisely because it appealed to pre-theoretical intuitions about the mind-independence of perceived properties. If this is so, knowing that the pre-modern theory is just like the common sense of today does not help us a bit to loosen the grip of ontological commitment to mind-independent colors. However, I believe there is much more to say than this.

The very idea of an objective world of natural facts—a subject matter of physics, in contrast to the world of human facts and subjective feeling—is itself an innovation of an emergent scientific worldview. Perhaps it is true that all "folk," in all times, have believed in the reality of what they see. But surely their notion of reality has changed over the centuries. Belief in the existence of colors is only problematic if colors are then taken to be objective properties on the same footing as properties in physics—a kind of scientific realism for colors. It is on this point that the correspondence between scholasticism and (putative) common sense is important. It strikes me as implausible to claim that a genuinely pre-theoretical

---

17. See Des Chene (2008, 17) on Descartes' attack on real qualities and substantial forms. He also comments, referring to Book I of the *Principles*, that "Descartes describes the præjudicia or preconceived opinions we acquire early in life when the mind is in thrall to the body. Those opinions turn out quite often to coincide with the opinions of the Schools."

view would make such specific claims for an ontology of properties. It is fair to suspect that this element of folk theory is really a vestige of scholasticism.[18]

Any background assumptions over whether perception is, or ought be, a veridical presentation of the mind-independent world will frame all our thinking about the reality of color. There are networks of attitudes and presuppositions underlying any philosophy of color. Studies in *visuality* are the academic investigation of the visual cultures of various historical periods, and movements, especially in the history of art.[19] Philosophers of color, however, have tended to ignore the possibility of shifting visual cultures. There has instead been a tendency to posit one universal, pre-theoretical understanding of perception.

In the condensed history above, only one strand of medieval thought on vision was mentioned. In fact medieval visual theory was rather diverse, and the dominant view certainly shifted from the early to late Middle Ages. There was a transition from an early Augustinian or neo-Platonic view to the approach developed in the thirteenth century, which combined Aristotle's views with the developments of Alhazen (Lindberg 1976). The earlier theories were *extramissionist*. Sight was thought to happen when illuminating rays were emitted from the eye. The Aristotelian *intromissionist* theories, however, only required that the eyes should receive rays of light emitted by objects. Intromissionism was entirely dominant by the sixteenth century, and there were interesting consequences for the epistemology of sight. Clark (2007, 17) interprets the transition as a move from a conception of vision as partially projected by the mind, and so partly subjective, to one in which vision is the passive reception of objects by the perceiver. On the lat-

18. What if contemporary philosophers only feign interest in the authenticity of folk beliefs, while the actual concern is only with the systematization of axioms that other philosophers have proposed? It could be agreed that the platitudes about color have a history, but denied that this history makes a difference to the philosophical project. (This point is due to Ian Gold.) My response is that these reflections on the origin of beliefs about color should fire our imagination toward alternatives. The problem of color is a clash of contradictory beliefs. Attempts toward straightforward reconciliation, with the realists' assertion that the colors of the "folk" simply are physical properties, has yet to prove fruitful. But if our "prime intuition" is a relic of an otherwise discarded theory, it is time to see if different assumptions will better mesh with our other beliefs. The task of chapter 8 is precisely that of reshaping our intuitions about color sensation.

19. See, for example, Levin (1997) and Clark (2007).

ter view, what we see is more readily interpreted as an objective representation of reality.

Again, there are significant connections between the medieval incorporation of Aristotelian natural philosophy—an important precursor to the more recognizably scientific world views of the seventeenth century—and the rise in importance of the epistemology of perception. The Thomistic motto (originally due to Aristotle) that "there is nothing in the intellect which is not first in the senses," entailed a new regard for natural philosophy, and a new concern with how knowledge of the natural world might be ensured by way of the senses.[20] The theory of species, can be understood as an attempt to theorize vision as the sense that "makes us know." This motivates development of a geometrical theory of sight, and the mimetic aspects of the species account (Biernoff 2002, 63–67). It also reinforces a passive model of vision, where qualitative properties of objects are simply detected by the mind, and with this interpretation of our perceptual experience comes the problematic ontological commitment. In other words, with a less passive model of vision, one that does not insist on the objectivity of what we see but emphasizes instead the relational and perceiver-dependent aspects of our sensory experience, there is no need to equate sensory qualities with perceiver-independent ones. One has reason to doubt that perceptual experience alone saddles us with ontological commitment to perceiver-independent colors.

I would also speculate that along with this desire for empirical knowledge of the world, with its reliance on the senses, comes an altered view of the world itself. The world that is so familiar to us—400 years into the scientific revolution—is of a physical order governed by natural laws, indifferent to the presence of human subjects. In short, this is the idea of objective, human- and mind-independent reality. Crucially, for the philosophy of color, it is from *this* reality that colors are threatened with elimination. As we have seen, Galileo reasons that since there would be no colors in a world bereft of perceivers, there are no colors in the actual world. Not coincidentally, a key innovation of the modern world view has been characterized as the invention of the idea of nonhuman nature. But this "nonhuman" world first comes to prominence with the perceptual realism of the

---

20. See Aquinas, *Summa theologicae* (1a.1.9c). Also see Gaukroger (2006, ch. 2) on the transition from an Augustian to a Aristotelian synthesis.

late Middle Ages. For it only makes sense to posit such a realist understanding of perception if one also takes the *explanandum* of science to be an objective, mind-independent reality, onto which our perception is a window.

I do not suggest that our ancestors were committed idealists who believed that the world was mind-dependent. Rather, I am concurring with Yolton (1984, 6) that there is a connection between the scholastics' emphasis on the concept of objective reality and their perceptual realism. Our image of an objective reality is so entrenched that it can be hard for us to envisage any other way of conceiving things. The issue that is not touched on, though, is why we are so concerned with the facts about the world that are independent of humans. Human beings happen to be a part of the world. So why is it assumed that the best description of reality is as of a world without humans? My point is that this very interest in an uninhabited reality is characteristic of a scientific way of understanding things. Colors are not a problem if your view of reality embraces both inert matter and creatures with minds, heedless of metaphysical divisions between them. The problem of color arises when theoretical emphasis is placed on a physical reality abstracted away from the presence of perceivers, as typified by the Galilean approach, and when doubt is cast over the capability of our senses to picture *this* reality, as happened in the seventeenth century. The importance of this new divide between inner and outer realms is the subject of the next section.

Before moving on it is worth examining a recent account of pretheoretical perceptual realism. Chalmers (2006, 49–50) invokes the metaphor of Eden to convey the idea that primitive color realism is original to human experience, what our kind must believe prior to scientific insight:

When an apple in Eden looked red to us, the apple was gloriously, perfectly and primitively red.... [T]he perfect redness of the apple was simply revealed to us. The qualitative redness in our experience derived entirely from the presentation of perfect redness in the world.

He goes on to write that Eden still plays a powerful role in our perceptual experience of the world. At some level, perception represents our world as an Edenic world, populated by perfect colors and shapes, with objects and properties that are revealed to us directly.

Yet this strong form of perceptual realism in which our eyes are characterized as windows onto an objective reality is, as we have seen, the central tenet of the scholastic account. For the early moderns it was the theory to beat. The mechanists won the ontological battle, but scholastic realism lives on in philosophers' ideas about what perception purports to present. Perhaps it is because that account is *phenomenologically* compelling, but I hope to have given reason to be suspicious of this presumption. To concur with Hume:

The opinions of the ancient philosophers, their fictions of substance and accident, and their reasonings concerning substantial forms and occult qualities, are like spectres in the dark, and are deriv'd from principles, which, however common, are neither universal nor unavoidable in human nature. (Hume [1739] 1985, 275)

2.4   Inner and Outer

Not only did colors take a fall at the beginning of the scientific age—they also broke in two. For one thing that is characteristic of the modern view of color is a splitting off of the subjective experience of color from its physical cause. According to the pre-modern account, there is no dissimilarity between the color we experience and its manifestation in external objects. This is a point most forcefully denied by the seventeenth-century accounts. One of Locke's defining criteria for secondary qualities is that there is no resemblance between the qualities as they are in bodies, and our ideas of them (Locke [1690] 1993, bk. II ch. 8, §15). Descartes writes in the sixth discourse of his *Optics*:

regarding light and colour…we must suppose our soul to be of such a nature that what makes it have the sensation of light is the force of the movements taking place in the regions of the brain where the optic nerve-fibres originate, and what makes it have the sensations of colour is the manner of these movements.

Concluding that, "in all this there need be no resemblance between the ideas which the soul conceives and the movements which cause these ideas" (Descartes 1985, 167).

This is a picture we are now familiar with. Color experience comes to be seen as the inner response to physical objects and forces out there in the world, which are themselves colorless. This looks to be a straightforward way of fitting conscious sensation into a mechanistic world picture. Yet difficulties continue to dog this solution. The first hurdle comes in settling the question of how we should now talk of the colors.[21] Do color words like black, green, and gold refer to our inner sensation, some qualitative experience of hue, or to the external causes of those sensations, even though they bear no resemblance to them? One reason for taking the former route is the strong association holding between color names and our experience of hues. This is the case made by Hardin (1993, xx):

> When somebody tells me that she has a theory about colors, I expect it to be a theory of yellow and green and the like, and if I get a story about spectral luminance or reflectance profiles, or whatever, I want to know how all of that relates to those qualities that I know and love. If a pusher of chromatic theory can't spell out these relationships particularly well, I am disappointed, but if she tells me that colors as she understands them don't include the hues, I feel cheated. Now matter how brilliant her discourse, she has changed the subject.

Yet these words are used to name features of objects in the world, not aspects of our subjectivity. This thought prompts the second route that identifies colors with the physical causes of our chromatic experiences. As Jackson (1998, 93) argues:

Pr. 1 Yellowness is the property of objects putatively presented to subjects when those objects look yellow...

Pr. 2 The property of objects putatively presented to subjects when the objects look yellow is at least a normal cause of their looking yellow...

Pr. 3 The only causes...of objects' looking yellow are complexes of physical qualities.

Conc. Yellowness is a complex of the physical qualities of objects. And likewise for all the colours.

The unresolved debate between realists and antirealists can in fact be seen as a back and forth between the two (as I will argue in the next chapter) rather unsatisfactory options. The lesson to be learned is that colors are not best confined just to the mental or to the physical world.

In chapter 6 I will argue that a better account of color must find a way to encompass both the inner and outer nature of color, suggesting how

---

21. Atherton (2003a, 504) makes a similar point: "Descartes, indeed, may be said to have invented psychophysics. But of course a troubling feature of this new psychophysics is that where before there was a single nature of colour, now there are two, a physical nature and a psychological nature. The anguished cry goes up, but what is colour, really?"

this may be achieved. Here, though, it is worth saying more about the inner-outer divide, and the historical responses to it. Cartesian dualism is the most well-known part of our inheritance from seventeenth-century thought on the mind. It is also the most reviled, since residual dualistic thinking is taken by many to be the obstacle to achieving a naturalistic account of the sentient mind. Yet less attention is paid to the dualism of inner and outer, where the inner realm can be that of the mind *or* brain.

For example, Hobbes, a reductive materialist about the mind and father of mind-brain identity theory, is also a proponent of the inner-outer division. He agrees with Descartes and Locke that there is no external origin for the visual sensation that we experience as light: "light is a fancy in the mind, caused by motion in the brain, which motion again is caused by the motion of the parts of such bodies as we call lucid" (Hobbes manuscript of 1646 quoted in Hatfield 1998, 973). That is, we call bodies lucid because that is how they look to us, not because they are really in themselves lucid. As much as Descartes, Hobbes attributes sensation to the inner workings of the perceiver. The difference is just that those inner workings are conceived as entirely material (Hatfield 1998, 973).

So the distinction established in the seventeenth century that is most relevant to the color debate is not mind-body dualism, but the separation between what is inside the head and what is out in the world. Taylor (2007, 300) describes how one effect of the rise of mechanistic explanation is the decoupling of inner self and outer world, giving us the now familiar concept of the detached or "buffered" subject. As he puts it, "[t]o be a buffered subject, [is] to have closed the porous boundary between inside (thought) and outside (nature, the physical)."

We see the effects of this new version of subjectivity in the philosophy of color. Seventeenth-century theorists like Galileo endeavored to cast colors inward and have them reside just in the mind of the perceiver. In the scholastic view, colors had been taken to pass freely from external objects to viewing subjects, as species. As we have seen, this conceptual merging of the inner and outer is attacked as juvenile confusion entrenched in scholastic miseducation. The problem is that colors do not sit comfortably on either side of the inner-outer divide. The dispositional account that Evan Thompson has called the "received view" can be seen as an attempt to create conceptual space for both the psychological and physical aspects of color, while at the same time upholding the separation between the inner and the outer realms. Yet the view seems to suffer from a chronic structural instability—a continual equivocation over whether colors are truly inside or outside. As noted by Thompson (1995, 11), "[t]his indecision between treating colours as physically grounded, dispositional properties of objects or as subjective 'projections' is one of the central features of the Newtonian heritage."[22]

Locke is the philosopher most commonly associated with *dispositionalism*. This can be characterized as the view that, "the colour of an object is determined by its disposition to produce certain 'perceived colours' in normal or standard viewers" (Harvey 2000, 138), as one philosopher has recently summarized Locke's account. Yet there is a striking lack of consensus among scholars over how to interpret passages in the *Essay* devoted to the primary-secondary distinction. Locke explains that our ideas of colors are due to the effects on us of the "textures" of fundamental particles. It is a further question about what Locke meant to say by "color" or "red." For "red" could be identified with a secondary quality of objects, or with a subjective idea, or with a property that in ordinary talk people erroneously ascribe to external objects (as held by Mackie (1976). At the end of one passage in the *Essay*, Locke writes:

It [*porphyre*] has, indeed, such a configuration of particles, both night and day, as are apt, by the rays of light rebounding from some parts of that hard stone, to produce in us the *idea* of redness, and from others the *idea* of whiteness; but whiteness or redness are not in it at any time, but such a texture that hath the power to produce such a sensation in us. (Locke [1690]1993, bk. II, ch. VIII, §19)

This passage, and the surrounding text, have caused endless controversy among commentators (Rickless 1997). Notably, "redness" and "whiteness" here refer to something said not to be in bodies, motivating an antirealist interpretation. Alexander (1985) takes Locke to be a realist about secondary qualities, understood as properties or powers actually in objects, and a subjectivist about colors: colors are not actually the secondary qualities.

---

22. See Wilson (1999, 473): "Also common to most of these [seventeenth-century] writers is a tendency to vacillate, just as Locke does, over whether terms like 'color' and 'red' denominate physical structures, or the 'powers' that (partly) result from the structures to cause sensations, or (as Locke seems usually to suppose) the sensations themselves."

Bennett (1971), on the other hand, sees Locke as a dispositionalist about the colors themselves.[23]

Descartes can sometimes be read as a dispositionalist, though the interpretation of his theory of perception has also been a vexed matter, complicated by some changes in opinion during the course of his working life. For instance, in the *Principles* (part IV) Descartes writes:

we have every reason to conclude that the properties in external objects to which we apply the terms light, colour, smell, taste, sound, heat and cold—as well as the other tactile qualities and even what are called "substantial forms"—are, so far as we can see, simply various dispositions in those objects which make them able to set up various kinds of motions in our nerves which are required to produce all the various sensations in our soul. (Descartes 1985, 285)

In the same passage of the *Optiks* quoted at the start of this chapter, Newton makes use of the distinction between sensations of color and colors in the physical world, a distinguishing mark of the modern philosophy of color. He also notes the tendency to fall back into the habit of talking of light rays themselves as colored. Indeed this is the way that unsophisticated people will talk about color. Newton offers a complex account whereby "Colours in the Object are nothing but a Disposition to reflect this or that sort of Rays more copiously than the rest; in the Rays they are nothing but their Dispositions to propagate this or that Motion into the Sensorium, and in the Sensorium they are Sensations of those Motions under the Forms of Colours" (Newton [1704] 1952, 124–25). Thus he contrasts

---

23. Perhaps Boyle, who coined the terms primary and secondary qualities, is more explicit about what the dispositional account entails. He writes that though we are forced to conclude that no sensible qualities belong to bodies, we may speak of them as being "dispositively" endowed with colors, due to the arrangement of their corpuscles:

I do not deny but that bodies may be said in a very favourable sense to have those qualities we call *sensible*, though there were no animals in the world. For a body in that case may differ from those bodies that are now quite devoid of quality, in its having such a disposition of its constituent corpuscles that, in case it were duly applied to the sensory of an animal, it would produce such a sensible quality that a body of another texture would not. And thus snow, though, if there were no lucid body nor organ of sight in the world, it would exhibit no colour (for I could not find it had any in places exactly darkened), yet it hath a greater disposition than a coal or soot to reflect store of light outwards, when the sun shines upon them all three...so, if there were no sensitive beings, those bodies that are now the objects of our senses would be but *dispositively*, if I may so speak, endowed with colours, tastes, and the like, and *actually* but only with those more catholic affections of bodies—figure, motion, texture, &c. (Boyle [1666] 1979, 35)

analyses of colors in objects, light rays, and in the "sensorium." Interestingly, his definition of color in objects is reminiscent of Hilbert's identification of color as spectral surface reflectance, which is a dispositional physical property.

As we will see in the next chapter, recent theories have avoided some of the pitfalls and complexities of the early modern accounts, planting color resolutely on one or other side of the inner-outer divide. However, dispositionalism has had something of a revival with Cohen's defense of a role-functionalist account that is akin to the traditional identification of colors with powers of objects to be perceived in certain ways. Some contemporary philosophers have devised new ways to juggle the competing inner and outer claims. The "dual-referent" theories of Maund (1981) and Brown (2006) take it that color words can literally have two different kinds of meanings, referring either to color sensations or to the physical properties that brought them about. While it is an honorable project to attempt to harmonize the conflicting insights of realists and antirealists, the resulting "conceptual fission" is not an ideal outcome for it fails to capture the idea that colors are simultaneously and irreducibly both inner and outer. At best, the dual referent theorist can say that colors are alternately one then the other. But as Mausfeld (2003, 382) writes, "[c]olours fall right on the boundary that we have drawn by bifurcating the world into the physical and the psychological; more than other perceptual attributes, they seem to be Janus-faced."

Before moving on, it is worth asking why it is that theories should continue to pay heed to the dual nature of color. It seems that color does not deserve the name unless it has a qualitative, sensory aspect. Yet, the language of color cannot easily be squeezed into the small space of the intradermal world—as may the language of emotions and desires, depressions, and neuroses. When we are talking about colors, we are inevitably talking about things around us. Even if they are the most ephemeral things, like rainbows, they still reside in the outside world.

3   Realism, Antirealism, Relationism

The purpose of chapters 1 and 2 was to present the problem of color within its relevant historical context. In this chapter I say something about the proposed solutions to the problem that have been put forward in more recent years. I discuss the three main genera of color ontologies— *realism, antirealism,* and *relationism*—and highlight their common ground. We see how the historical factors first noted in the previous chapter have shaped and constrained the contemporary debate. The existing theories are unsatisfactory precisely because they leave unchallenged a conceptual framework that renders color problematic. As Wilson (1999, 456) writes, "one way in which historical understanding can contribute to philosophy is to help us see how traditional and still influential conceptions of philosophical problems may be bound up with assumptions that require fresh evaluation today."

3.1   The Theories

The task in this section is to present the three theory types in broad brush. For more nuanced pictures, and the standard objections to each kind of theory, the reader should consult the references provided in the notes. I have elected not to follow the more elaborate taxonomy of Cohen (2009, 12–14), which takes the fundamental division to be between relational and nonrelational theories. This is because my primary concern is to characterize the theories that have been most influential in recent debates. These do happen to cluster into the three camps, even though the logical space of possibilities is very much more complex. In chapter 5 I will present a novel case for the claim that relationism, conceived as *interactionism* (Giere 2006, 32), is the view most consistent with a naturalistic understanding of perceptual success.

3.1.1 Antirealism

The opening salvo of the color debate originates from the antirealist camp.[1] Thus it is easiest to understand the other types of theories as reactions against the claims of antirealism. Here I discuss, in broad outline, the antirealist's strategy. The antirealist first makes a two tables type observation: that colors do not appear in any physical description of the world. At best, colors enter into biological description of how humans and animals perceive the world. Second, the antirealist notes, is that our experience of color, and our "commonsense" reflection on that experience, take colors to be objective (perceiver-independent) properties of things. In other words, ordinary users of language have a pre-theoretical concept of yellow as an intrinsic property of lemons, a characteristic belonging to lemons regardless of any interaction with humans. This concept conflicts with a fundamental science in which no such properties occur, and insofar as science provides the right description of reality, the deliverance of ordinary experience and common sense must be untrue. The antirealist concludes that color appearances are an illusion. The antirealist stance is often referred to as *error theory* because, following Mackie (1976), the claim is that ordinary discourse commits a pervasive factual error in its attribution of colors to external objects. It is also characterized as *eliminativism* since the claim is that chromatic properties, as presented in visual experience and described in ordinary language, are simply never instantiated and thus should be eliminated from our theoretical ontology.

Here is how Hardin (1993, 111) introduces the claim that colors are illusions:

Since physical objects are not colored, and we have no good reason to believe that there are non-physical bearers of color phenomena, and colored objects would have to be physical or non-physical, we have no good reason to believe that there are colored objects. Colored objects are illusions...

I find much to agree with in the Hardin's rejection of "common-sense" claims for the objectivity of color, and for the willingness to revise

---

1. Representative works are Hardin (1993), Hardin (2004), Boghossian and Velleman (1989), McGilvray (1994), Averill (2005), Chalmers (2006), Maund (2006), Pautz (2013). Opponents of antirealism focus on its inconsistency with common sense. Since the view is a negative one, there are few positive claims to attack. So opponents of the view typically aim to convince us that the antirealist's pessimistic conclusions are premature. See, for example, Cohen (2009, 65).

understanding of color in the light of findings from neurophysiology. However, the claim that nonpathological (and useful) visual functions generate illusions strikes me as counter to naturalistic aims.[2] Perceptual science sets out to understand how the apparently idiosyncratic workings of the visual system manage to inform creatures about the world around them, enough to significantly enhance their quality of life. Labeling normal perceptual states as illusory adds nothing to our understanding of them, and as I argue in chapter 5, that argument rests on the false assumption that the perceiver-dependence of properties presented in a perceptual state is incompatible with that state's being a veridical one.

3.1.2 Realism

How might science be reconciled with common sense? One tactic is to say that the chromatic properties presented in visual experience, and referred to in ordinary language, can be identified with physical properties. Byrne and Hilbert (1997, xxii) provide a definition of *physicalism* as, "the view that colors are physical properties that we sometimes veridically perceive objects to possess." Furthermore "colors are to be identified with properties whose natures (a) are specifiable in ways that do not employ color concepts, and (b) are not constituted by relations to the psychological states of perceivers."

The first influential version of physicalism was D. M. Armstrong's wavelength theory (Armstrong 1968). In his identification of color with wavelength of light, his ambitions were explicitly naturalistic, perhaps inspired by Newton's association of perceived color with the properties of light rays reflected from objects. As it happens, Armstrong's thesis that color experience is the visual representation of wavelength of light then fell out of favor because of its inconsistency with empirical facts about color constancy— the relative stability of perceived color under changing spectral lighting conditions. The wavelengths of light reflected from objects and falling on the eye do not correlate reliably with perceived color. For instance, a banana viewed in daylight will be sending far more shortwave (blue appearing) light rays to the eye than the same fruit viewed indoors under a tungsten lightbulb. This is because the spectrum of the outdoor illuminant is shifted

---

2. But see Hardin (1992).

toward short wavelengths, compared to the tungsten light, that in fact looks more yellowy. However, the color of the banana is not seen to alter drastically when lighting conditions are changed—some difference in shade may be noticed if attention is paid, but it will always still be categorized as yellow.

Reflectance realism is an alternative to the wavelength theory that smoothly handles color constancy phenomena. The property identified with the colors is *spectral surface reflectance* (SSR).[3] This is the proportion of incident light that will be reflected back from a surface, described as a function of the wavelength of the incident light.[4] In a typical SSR graph, proportion of light reflected back from the object is plotted on the y-axis and wavelength on the x-axis. For example, a red object preferentially absorbs light at shorter wavelengths, and reflects light at longer wavelengths, so its SSR plot will step up from left to right. Since SSR is a fixed property of objects, not dependent on incident light spectra, it has been argued that constant color perception is the ability of human vision to detect and represent these properties (Tye 2000, 147).

Physicalists reject the naïve realist claim that there are qualitative chromatic properties 'out there'. For example, they would not suggest that the greenness of the grass, along with its freshly cut smell, are just features of the mind-independent world. Accepting the dichotomy between any possible physical color and color experience, they instead argue that the quantitative physical properties that can be isolated as the causes of qualitative color experiences themselves deserve the name "color." The strategy is set out quite clearly by Jackson (1998, 93) in his argument for the identification of colors with "complexes of physical qualities." The key premise is that whatever it is that deserves the name "yellow" must be the external, physical cause of an object appearing yellow.

Physicalism is vulnerable to a line of attack that, broadly speaking, points out the great dissimilarities between features of color as we expe-

---

3. See Hilbert (1987), Byrne and Hilbert (2003), Matthen (1988), Tye (2000), and Churchland (2007a).

4. Byrne and Hilbert (2003) generalize the theory to all colored objects such as colored light sources and transparencies, by defining *productances* as well as referring to reflectances. For convenience and simplicity, in what follows I will refer only to reflectance. See Byrne and Hilbert (2003, 9).

rience them, such as the structure of color space, and what is known of physical properties, such as SSR.[5] Another objection points out cases of normal perceptual variation—such as intersubjective disagreement over which wavelength of light is perceived as unique green (a green with no tinge of blue or yellow)—and points out that there are no perceptually available facts of the matter as to which subject perceives the 'real' unique green.[6]

Primitivism is an increasingly important faction within the realist camp.[7] This is the contemporary view closest to scholastic realism, in the assertion that colors are sui generis, qualitative properties of objects that cannot be identified with any further microphysical structure. As Campbell (1993, 268) writes, "the qualitative character of the color experience is inherited from the qualitative character of the color." Thus the primitivist can easily bypass the objections to physicalism that focus on the manifest differences between color-as-experienced and color-as-SSR. However, primitivists do face objections from perceptual variation, especially interspecies variation.[8] Another salient issue for primitivism arises over compatibility with a naturalistic ontology, given the claim that the redness of a maple and the fragrance of marigolds just are properties of the extradermal environment. Campbell (1993), for example, talks in general terms about the supervenience of primitive color on ordinary physical properties, whereas Watkins (2005) borrows more of the conceptual apparatus of nonreductive physicalism from recent philosophy of mind.

3.1.3 Relationism

In an influential paper Cohen (2004) employs the term *relationism* as a broad umbrella to encompass all theories that assert that colors cannot be defined independently of their effects on perceivers, but that they are real

5. Hardin (1993), Hardin (2003a), and Pautz (2013).

6. Hardin (2003b) and Cohen (2003). The problem of uniqueness was debated extensively in the pages of *Analysis* by Tye (2006a), Tye (2006b), Tye (2007), Cohen et al. (2006, 2007), Byrne and Hilbert (2007a), and Matthen (2009).

7. See Westphal (1987), Campbell (1993), Yablo (1995), Johnston (1996), Watkins (2002), Allen (2007), Gert (2008), and Kalderon (2011a).

8. See Byrne and Hilbert (2007b) and Kalderon (2007), and Allen (2009, 2010) for responses.

(instantiated) properties nonetheless.[9] Thus the relationist *via media* charts a course between the extremes of antirealism and realism. It rejects the antirealist proposal that color perceptions are illusory or erroneous (Cohen 2010), and in this sense is realist, but in accepting the claim that colors are perceiver-dependent, it amounts to a kind of subjectivism (Hardin 2004). As Cohen (2009, 8) writes:

The heart of color relationism is the claim that colors are relational; in particular, the relationist claims that they are constituted in terms of a relation between (*inter alia*) objects and subjects.

Dispositionalism is the most established of relationist theories. The idea that colors are dispositions or powers of objects to elicit certain sensations in human beings is strongly associated with the secondary quality accounts of the seventeenth century (see section 2.4). Thompson (1995) calls it the received view of that era, and it has had a number of recent adherents.[10] One characteristic of contemporary versions of the view is the recourse to 'standard conditions' and 'standard perceivers'. For instance, Johnston (1992, 230) writes that, "[t]he property of being red = the disposition to look red to standard perceivers as they actually are under standard conditions as they actually are." This raises the challenge of finding appropriate standards.

According to Cohen's characterization, relationism as a general theory is "ecumenical" in that all perceptual variants have equal status as colors, regardless of whether the perceiver or the viewing conditions are standard. Thus relationism need not be bothered by objections to dispositionalism that focus on the absence of scientifically valid criteria for standard perceivers and conditions (Hardin 2004). However, another

---

9. See Thompson (1995, 243) for a similar use of the term. In the interests of brevity, I have omitted discussion of the view known as *relativism*. This is the idea that colors are "centered properties," namely properties that objects possess "only relative to a particular individual and time" (Brogaard 2011, 138). To illustrate, "if this chili instantiates the centered property *being tasty* only relative to an assessor, and the chili is tasty relative to assessor E_1 then it instantiates the uncentered property *being-tasty-relative-to-assessor-E_1* relative to the world as a whole" (Brogaard 2011, 138). *Being-tasty-relative-to-assessor-E_1* is a relational property that corresponds to the centered property. See also Egan (2012) on the comparison between relativism and relationism.

10. See McGinn (1983), Johnston (1992), Levin (2000), and Miscevic (2007). The specific theory that Cohen defends—*role functionalism*—is identical to dispositionalism, on the assumption of a functionalist theory of dispositions (Cohen 2009, 220).

stock objection to dispositionalism is equally pertinent to relationism. This is the argument that colors are simply not presented in visual experiences as relational or dispositional properties (see chapter 8 for extended discussion).

Another important version of relationism is the ecological theory of Thompson et al. (1992) and Thompson (1995). He writes that "being coloured is a relational property because something is coloured only in relation to a perceiver" (Thompson 1995, 243). Thompson's view should be understood as an application of the concepts of Gibsonian ecological psychology in order to bring daylight between ecological-relationism and standard dispositionalism. However, in his definition of being colored a determinate shade as, "equivalent to having a particular spectral reflectance, illuminance, or emittance that looks that colour to a particular perceiver in specific viewing conditions" (Thompson 1995, 245), it is not obvious that the separation from dispositionalism, and even from physicalism, is successful (see section 3.4.3 below).[11]

3.2   Outerness and Ontological Commitment

One core point of agreement among realists, antirealists, and some relationists is in claiming that there is a "commonsense" conception of color, a set of pre-theoretical beliefs about the meanings of color terms that most, maybe all, members of the language community would subscribe to. As I argued in section 2.3, this consensus cannot be understood without reference to the seventeenth-century construction of Aristotelian natural philosophy as an elaboration of childish folk opinions. Contemporary philosophers tend to be more forgiving of common sense. Examples of implicitly held platitudes, attributed to the folk by philosophers, are that green is the physical property of the leaf that causes our color sensation (Jackson 1998), that the

11. Cohen (2009, 226–29) also classifies the sensory-classification account (Matthen 2005) as a kind of relationism. I am unsure of this attribution because Matthen's theory also lends itself to interpretation as a pluralistic kind of physicalism. For example, Matthen (2005, 202) writes, "[w]hat exactly does it mean to say that the colours *really* have these properties? Pluralism is not meant to be a 'relativistic' proposal. The suggestion is not that the colour properties need to be relativized to observers, that truths about colour exist only relative to how particular species experience colour. It is rather that different species might be converging on different properties of distal stimuli...."

green that we perceive is an intrinsic property of the leaf, unrelated to its interactions with perceivers (Boghossian and Velleman 1989), and that our green sensations resemble the intrinsic greenness of the leaf (Mackie 1976). Accordingly, we have access to the true colors of objects, just by looking— what Johnston (1992, 222) calls "perceptual availability."[12] It is also desirable that there be unity in this conception of color. As Maund (1981) summarizes, "[e]ach colour-property is a non-relational, non-disjunctive property of an object. All objects to which the same colour predicate, e.g. 'yellow', applies share the same single, non-disjunctive property."

Philosophers are often explicit about their motivation to uphold common sense or "Moorean facts."[13] Furthermore the primitivist theories are attempts to uphold commonsense realism without reductionistic concessions to a physicalist world picture. What should concern us most here is that many philosophers who hold diametrically opposed positions concerning color ontology still share the same view as to the substance of the commonsense conception. Antirealists resign themselves to the metaphysical costs of subscribing to a theory that is counterintuitive in this respect, expecting to make gains elsewhere, whereas realists take consistency with common sense to be a selling point of their theory.

I characterize the alleged commonsense conception as outer-directedness[14] *with* ontological commitment. On this view the outer-directedness of visual experience is the basis for the folk theory's ontological commitment to perceiver-independent color properties instantiated on the surfaces of ordinary physical objects. The kind of phenomenological and functional observations that exemplify the outerness of color visual experience are:

O1 Color visual experience appears to inform us about things outside ourselves.

O2 Having such experience does actually give us information about external objects. For example, experience of a change in color usually (but not always) indicates a material change in the object perceived

12. In a similar vein Johnston (1992, 223) characterizes "revelation" as the belief that the intrinsic nature of color is fully revealed by standard visual experiences of it.
13. See, for example, Hilbert (1987, 2), Jackson (1998, 87–112), Lewis (1997), Matthen (2005, 201), and Cohen (2009, 65).
14. In order to save syllables, I use "outerness" interchangeably with "outer-directedness."

O3 Unlike pains and itches, color experiences are not felt to be indicative of states of our bodies.

O4 Color vocabulary, unlike the vocabulary of emotions and bodily sensations, helps us refer to objects in the extradermal world.

These observations are consistent both with everyday and scientific practices involving color. They amount to the simple fact that when we think and talk about color, we direct our attention not inward but to things around us. As Wittgenstein (1953, §275) writes:

Look at the blue of the sky and say to yourself "How blue the sky is!"—When you do it spontaneously—without philosophical intentions—the idea never crosses your mind that this impression of colour belongs only to you. And you have no hesitation in exclaiming that to someone else. And if you point at anything as you say the words you point at the sky.

Things become problematic when it assumed that ontological commitment follows inevitably from outerness. Indeed this generates the problem of colors because it is only when certain ontological claims are made for the colors presented in visual experience, or described in ordinary discourse, that there can be a perceived incompatibility between visual experience, common sense, and science. So it is helpful also to articulate the commitment claims, all four of which stand uneasily in a physicalistic conception of reality:

C1 Colors are properties that are instantiated by (the surfaces of) external objects.

C2 When we enjoy color visual experience, the world is presented as if the (surfaces of) objects in it instantiate those very properties.

C3 These properties should be detectable or measurable, like any standard physical property, or they should be identifiable with some other measurable physical properties.[15]

C4 The nature or existence of these properties is indifferent to the presence or existence of perceivers. Colors are perceiver-independent properties.

As described in chapter 1, the modern way into the color debate begins with an Eddington-style observation that common sense posits that the

---

15. C3 can be weakened by allowing that colors supervene on some standard physical properties.

table has a certain brown color, and that this clashes with the physical description of the table as made of hue-less atoms, and empty space. Once the phenomenological outerness of color is appreciated, it may already seem hard to imagine how ontological commitment can be avoided. Yet the connection between outerness and ontological commitment is only tight if there is a subtle reification of color (see section 2.2). If color is conceptualized as some separable property that is painted onto matter, and color vision is understood as the detection of it, then the experience of colors, and our notion of those experiences being informative about objects, will be thought to imply commitment to the instantiation of colors in objects, independently of perceivers. This is because, from within this framework, there is nothing that informative color vision could be, other than the detection of mind-independent color properties. Alternative accounts of the links connecting stimuli perceptual processes and visual experience languish unexamined.

3.2.1   The Relationist Alternative

In subsequent chapters I present one such alternative account. Here, though, it is also worth noting that proponents of relationist theories have tended to dispute the claim that common sense, and perceptual experience by itself, are committed to C4. Numerous authors have rejected the claim that visual experience presents colors as nonrelational properties (see chapter 8). Cohen (2009, 107–108) disputes C4 as a commitment of ordinary language, and Cohen and Nichols (2010) present an experimental philosophy study, which, they argue, shows that the folk concept of color is not that of a nonrelational property.

It is also important to mention the Oxford View of Color, which is the claim that the concept of color employed in ordinary language is that of a perceiver-dependent, dispositional property (Allen 2010). To quote Kneale (1950, 123),

When Locke said that the secondary qualities were powers in things to produce sensations in us, he stated the facts correctly, but he did not realize that his statement was only an analysis of the plain man's use of secondary quality adjectives.... When in ordinary life we say 'The paper isn't really red', we always intend to imply that the paper has some other colour as a dispositional property.

This view has been endorsed notably by Dummett (1979), Evans (1980), and McDowell (1985).

3.3 Detection and the Coloring-In Model

In chapter 2 I described the explicit reification that came with scholastic realism—colors are manifest to the perceiver as detachable *species* that fly through the air from their objects to the seeing eye. Since the doctrine of species was overturned in the seventeenth century, we have not seen such a literal characterization of the separate existence of the sensory qualities. However, there is a sense in which reification remains, in the analysis of color as separate from other visual features of an object, like shape and texture, and unrelated to the activity of perceivers. As Mausfeld (2010, 123) describes the situation within vision science:

Colour is, according to prevailing orthodoxy in perceptual psychology, a kind of autonomous and unitary attribute. It is regarded as unitary or homogeneous by assuming that its core properties do not depend on the type of 'perceptual object' to which it pertains and that 'colour per se' constitutes a natural attribute in the functional architecture of the perceptual system. It is regarded as autonomous by assuming that it can be studied in isolation of other perceptual attributes. These assumptions also provide the pillars for the technical field of colorimetry, and have proved very fruitful for neurophysiological investigations into peripheral colour coding. They also have become, in a technology-driven cultural process of abstraction, part of our common-sense conception of colour. With respect to perception theory, however, both assumptions are grossly inadequate, on both empirical and theoretical grounds.

An analogous methodological practice can be found within philosophy: philosophy of color is debated largely in isolation from the philosophy of perception more generally, and philosophers typically assume an atomistic conception of visual experience whereby color is a perceptual element that, to a first approximation, can be analyzed independently of shape, texture, and so on.[16] Acknowledging that the modern account does not propose as literal a reification as in the scholastic one, I refer to the new picture as the *coloring-in model*. I will now describe how the model has played different—but crucial—roles in antirealist and realist accounts. It gives antirealists a picture of how the world could be without color. For realists it informs an account of color perception as simply the detection of these chromatic

16. For example, Chalmers (2006, 77) "A more complete account of the Edenic content of color experience would require careful attention to all sorts of phenomenological details that I have largely ignored so far, such as the phenomenal representation of the distribution of colors in space, the fineness of grain of color representation, the different levels of detail of color experience in the foreground and background of a visual field, and so on. I cannot attend to all of this here...." (see section 8.4.2).

properties. In the next chapter I will be discussing the scientific evidence that challenges this piece of orthodoxy.

3.3.1 Antirealism and the Coloring-In Model

Antirealism amounts to a forthright rejection of the ontological commitments usually attributed to common sense. The antirealist plays an "unmasking" strategy (Stroud 2000), aiming to show that the true nature of the world is radically different from what is supposed in everyday life, that what we thought to be true-blue is actually an illusion. The picture underlying antirealism is that the perceiver-independent world is achromatic, and that humans systematically misperceive it as being colored. This misperception is usually characterized as a projection of the mind. The idea is expressed beautifully by David Hume ([1777] 1975, 294, app. I), who writes that we have a "productive faculty" that by "gilding or staining all natural objects with the colours, borrowed from internal sentiment, raises in a manner a new creation."

Here Hume is actually using the example of color to describe the projection of value onto the world of facts. Elsewhere Hume does take up a Galilean position toward colors, where these are understood as mere perceptions of the mind, erroneously projected outward (Kail 2007, ch. 7). But what we should notice about the example is the casual reification of color: colors are likened to stains or veneers that can be painted onto a preexisting world of shapes. In order to say that colors are projections it must be assumed that chromatic properties are super-additions to an achromatic world, rather than properties that are bound up with other perceived features such as shape, size, and depth. As described above, this is to assume the separateness of color from other visual features, and to treat color as the specific object of color vision. The metaphor of the coloring-in book is near irresistible.

3.3.2 Realism, Detection, and Color Constancy

When the antirealist employs the coloring-in model the outcome is *projectionism*; when the realist does, the result is *detectionism*.[17] The realist's aim is

---

17. Projectionism and detectionism are complementary approaches, a yin and yang. That is, if it is assumed that sensory experience presents chromatic qualities as some perceiver-independent property that we happen to have detected, then when no external candidates for detection can be found, the natural conclusion is that the chromatic qualities are being projected on to the world. See Kail (2007, chs. 1, 2) on the projective-detective contrast.

to uphold the claim that redness, say, is the property that our visual system detects when we see rubies, ladybirds, and (certain) roses. Primitivists typically do not dwell at length on the perceptual mechanisms underwriting our experience of colors, conceived as simple, perceiver-independent properties. However, the theory is highly suggestive of the idea that we simply detect them.

For the physicalist, each surface has its own SSR, and the task of color vision is the accurate detection and representation of this property. As Tolliver (1994, 415) characterizes physicalism, it is, "committed to the claim that: (i) colors are identical to (or supervenient upon) certain physical features of objects, and (ii) color perception consists in the detection of this physical complex of features and its registration in the nervous system."[18]

The area of vision science that has been most conducive to the physicalism is the *reflectance recovery* approach to color constancy. Lighting conditions vary greatly in their chromaticity, such that wavelength information arriving at the eye is affected as much by light as it is by objects, and yet we are able to converge on fairly stable judgments of the colors of things. In the 1980s there was a proliferation of computer models that formalized color constancy as the problem of estimating the spectrum of ambient illumination and using this information to recover the actual SSR of surrounding objects.[19] This approach assumes a straightforward mapping between physical SSR and perceived color, one that fits the detection framework. Physicalists then interpret constant color experience as reflecting our ability to detect and represent SSR. This is a point made by Tye (2000, 147):

The simplest, most straightforward explanation of colour constancy is that the surfaces of colored objects have features that remain the same as the illumination conditions change—features that are represented in our color experiences and that are responsible for the sameness in their character.[20]

One immediate problem with this simple linking of physicalism to constancy science is that constancy is not perfect. Shifts in illumination do bring about noticeable changes in the perceived colors of things, and troubles then attend in determining which shade of crimson, say, is the

18. See also Byrne and Hilbert (2003, 16) on the evolution of detection mechanisms.
19. For example, Maloney (1986) and Maloney and Wandell (1986); see Maloney (1999) and Hurlbert (1998) for a review.
20. See Byrne and Hilbert (2003, 9).

veridical representation of the tomato's SSR. Of course, deviances from absolute constancy could be explained as due to inefficiencies in the reflectance recovery process. But the point is that this watered down approach to constancy no longer does what the realist like Tye had hoped for: it no longer supports the idea that in virtue of having properly working constancy mechanisms we are thereby gaining perceptual access to the fine grained, physical colors of things.

The reflectance recovery model also takes the color of each surface to be a property had in isolation from the objects around it, since each reflectance belongs to an individual surface, not an ensemble of them. However, it has long been recognized that in order for constancy to obtain, objects need to be embedded in a complex scene, involving various objects of different colors and textures (Smithson 2005, 1339–40). Byrne and Hilbert (2003, 13) account for this fact by asserting that complex scenes are just the best conditions for enabling the visual system to recover SSR. An alternative hypothesis is that the roughly constant colors that we ascribe to individual objects are in fact a function of the whole scene. This was a view expressed years ago by Gestalt psychologists such as Gelb (1938).

The alternative view also leads to a focus on relational rather than absolute color constancy. In the reflectance recovery tradition, constancy is formalized as the problem of maintaining a stable appearance across lighting conditions so that the same SSR will be represented in an identical manner. The alternative is to reformulate constancy as the task of maintaining stable relations between the perceived colors of different objects across lighting conditions, known as "relational color constancy" (Foster 2003). For example, having relational color constancy means that that wine-dark grapes will look bluish compared to cherries, even in a yellow artificial light that would otherwise suppress blue tones. The absolute stability of appearances is of secondary importance, and SSR recovery is not required (Foster 2003, 441). So this approach yields different sorts of computational models from the reflectance recovery ones (Zaidi 1998; Nascimento and Foster 2000). Relational color constancy is often operationalized in experiments where the subject is simply asked to discriminate illuminant changes from SSR changes (Foster and Nascimento 1994; see figure 3.1). Furthermore, as Foster (2003, 441) writes, "[r]elational colour constancy has a plausible physiological substrate." He is referring to the fact that the ratios of cone-receptor

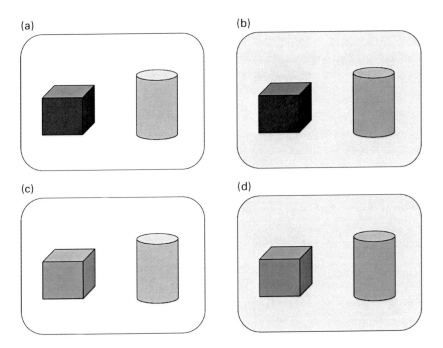

Figure 3.1
Illustration of relational lightness constancy. Lightness constancy is the achromat-ic equivalent of color constancy (see section 4.2.1). In order to measure relational lightness constancy, a subject would be asked to discriminate stimuli in which the intensity of illumination changes from stimuli in which the lightness or gray-level of one of the objects changes. (a) Is the original scene. (b) Illustrates a decrease in illumination level. In (c) the lightness of the cube increases, and in (d) there is both a lightness change and an illumination change. In a relational color constancy ex-periment, the spectral composition of the illuminant, and/or the SSR of one of the objects may change.

excitations in response to pairs of objects seen under different illuminants is invariant under changes in illuminant spectrum. This suggests that infor-mation distinguishing illuminant changes from SSR changes is available to the visual system.

It is important to recognize that theoretical commitments themselves shape scientists' formulation of the problem of constancy, and they chan-nel empirical work in such a way that models and experiments cannot be used simply to decide between these overarching theories. Those who define constancy as reflectance recovery employ operationalizations of constancy that are very different from those who focus on relational constancy. As I have discussed at length elsewhere, the dispute between the contrasting approaches cannot be settled with any crucial experiments but may yield long-term research programs that have different degrees of empirical success (Chirimuuta 2008). One interesting feature of the relational approach to color constancy is that it comes with the implication that constancy works to give us information about the relative similarities and differences between objects, rather than information about intrinsic surface properties. This meshes well with the account of the various functions of color vision to be presented in chapter 4.

3.4   Inside Out and Outside In

Another way of characterizing the debate between color realists and antirealists is as a clash between those who believe that colors belong to the external, physical world and those who think of colors as something generated inside the head that are, if anything, properties of psychological or neurophysiological states. What both sides share is a commitment to a clear separation of these inner and outer realms, and the idea that colors must be found either on one side or the other of the divide—another aspect of the seventeenth century legacy (section 2.4). Yet the interesting thing about color is its "Janus-facedness"—the fact that a plethora of color phenomena demand explanations that draw on physical, neurophysiological, and phenomenal descriptions. As a result both realists and antirealists are forced to offer Procrustean solutions whereby the phenomena that are recalcitrant to their proposed localizations of color are chopped off from the domain of enquiry.

3.4.1   Color in the Brain

One reason for the influence and persuasiveness of Hardin's *Color for Philosophers* was the widely held belief that neuroscience has given us a complete explanation of color appearance. Much of the book is a review of the physiology and psychology of color perception. Most attention is paid to the theory of opponent coding in early visual pathways, and to the psychophysical results of Hurvich, Jameson, and their colleagues. Before going on to discuss Hardin's argument, it is worth saying something about this scientific background—the current state of knowledge and its historical evolution.[21] Afterward I will be taking issue with Hardin's appeal to brain science. My central point is that the evidence presently available on the neurobiology of visual experience is not comprehensive enough to support any strong philosophical conclusions that colors are "in the brain."

A Detour into the Neuroscience of Color

Trichromacy is an essential fact of normal (i.e., not "color deficient") human vision. For a trichromatic subject, a test light of any color can be matched by three primary lights, as long as they appear in the same context as the test. Likewise printers use three primary inks—namely yellow, cyan, and magenta—to fuse and create every hue they wish to reproduce. Trichromacy of color matching has been known of since the seventeenth century, and was later found to be due to the presence of exactly three different cone types in the retina. The cone classes are preferentially sensitive to short (440 nm), medium (530 nm), and long (560 nm) wavelengths of light, and these photoreceptors' differential responses to stimuli of different wavelengths are the first physiological steps toward color vision.

Thomas Young first proposed the three-receptor theory of color vision in 1802. Later in the nineteenth century his ideas were developed by James Clerk Maxwell and Hermann von Helmholtz. All these scientists supposed that the colors we experience are due to the simple summation of responses of the different hypothesized receptors. A dissenting voice came from physiologist Edwald Hering, who in 1878 published a treatise on color that took as its starting point the observation that our experience is of *four*, not three, basic colors. Red, green, blue, and yellow are now known as the *unitary hues* because they can appear as pure colors, not as compounds (Jameson and Hurvich 1955; Valberg 2001).

Binary hues like orange and purple have the phenomenal characteristic of appearing as mixtures of primary hues—red and yellow, or red and blue, respectively. Moreover Hering noted certain antagonistic relationships between the basic colors—for example, that a hue can be reddish or

21. See Mollon (2003) for more detail on the history. See Solomon and Lennie (2007) for a detailed overview of the neuroscience of color, and Palmer (1999, ch. 3) for a more basic introduction.

greenish but not both reddish and greenish; yellowish or bluish but not both yellowish and bluish. In order to explain the binary and unitary appearance of colors, and the relations of exclusion between them, Hering inferred that the responses of color pathways are antagonistic. In other words, that a nerve signaling a red response can only fire when the green response is silent, that a blue response is only possible in the absence of a yellow signal. The modern version of this idea, developed by Hurvich and Jameson, is known as the *opponent coding* theory. Their work brought about a resurgence of Hering's idea in the mid-twentieth century.[22]

A few years later, neurons were discovered in the retina (Monasterio and Gouras 1975) and lateral geniculate nucleus[23] (De Valois 1965) that showed opponent tuning. For example, some cells were excited by the presence of a long wavelength stimulus and inhibited by the presence of a medium wavelength stimulus within their receptive field. These neurons receive input from the photoreceptors and pass signals on to the brain; they seemed to be a physiological substrate for Hering's antagonistic system. Physiological recording of photoreceptors (Rushton 1965) also confirmed the existence and sensitivity profiles of the three different cone types responsible for trichromacy. It was appealing to say that both Helmholtz and Hering had grasped elements of the truth: that Helmholtz had been right about the receptoral stage, and Hering about the post-receptoral stage of color vision.

A Missing Link

What is tantalizing about this research is that it seems to promise a complete account of perceived color—a description of its physiological mechanisms, and an explanation of why the colors that we see have their particular appearances, and why they uphold the relations that they do within subjective color space. To philosophers concerned with showing that physiology can be effective even in explaining features of consciousness, this looks like a gift. Indeed Churchland (2007b) uses details and predictions from Hurvich's account of color appearance to argue for a neurobiological reduction of color qualia. Hardin's concern is not so much the ontology of

---

22. See Jameson and Hurvich (1955, 1956) and Hurvich and Jameson (1955, 1956).
23. Also known as the LGN, this is a "relay" between the eye and neo-cortex, in the mammalian visual system.

mind in general, but the specific problem of color ontology. He proposes a neurobiologically inspired elimination of color. If color talk can, in principle, be substituted by talk of neural processes, Hardin takes it that we have good reason for replacing ordinary chromatic concepts with neurobiological ones:

The tactic that suggests itself is to show how phenomena of the visual field are represented in the visual cortex and then to show how descriptions of the visual field may be replaced by descriptions of neural processes. It will be argued...that we have no good reasons for thinking that such a replacement of the one description by the other would leave anything out, with a consequent loss of information. On the contrary, we have reason to expect that a proper neural description would be richer, more complete, and, in principle, more penetrable by the intellect. Problems that are intractable either at the extradermal physical level or at the phenomenal level promise to yield to analysis in neurological terms. (Hardin 1993, 111)

What Hardin means by "phenomena of the visual field," here, are the qualitative properties of hues. These include the relations of proximity and distance between the different hues, which are mapped out in color spaces (Hardin 1993, 43). Also important are the properties of uniqueness— the tonal purity of red, green, blue, and yellow—as well as the appearance of the binary hues. Hardin (1993, xx) takes these hue properties to be the main explanandum for a theory of color, and he believes that neurophysiology is the discipline most capable of generating satisfactory explanations here. What Hardin means by a "neural description" is illustrated by different examples. Primarily, Hardin (1993, 35) presents the opponent channels of early vision as providing a coding scheme for phenomenal color.

The post-receptoral neurons are taken to be signaling the Hering primaries, four basic hues, plus black and white (the "luminance signal"), into which all other colors may be decomposed. They send signals to the brain that eventually cause one to experience a color with visible components of the hue coded by the channel in question. For example, the firing of (L-M) neurons in conjunction with (L+M)-S neurons, signaling 'redness' and 'yellowness', respectively, would cause you to have an 'orange' experience. The unique hues themselves are thought of as being perceived when one of the opponent channels is giving a zero signal. For example unique red—a red that is neither bluish nor yellowish—is taken to occur when the (L-M) neurons are firing, but no response is made by the (L+M)-S channel.

In Averill's presentation of an antirealist theory it is assumed that there is now a neurobiological account that takes us all the way from the firing of opponently coded neurons in the retina and lateral geniculate to conscious experience of color:

Vision scientists believe that the firing rates of opponent cells are correlated with color experiences. For example, R+G-opponent cells are correlated with red experiences when firing above their base firing rate, and are correlated with green experiences when firing below their base firing rate. (Averill 2005, 224)

Sadly, no references to scientific articles are provided here. In fact most neuroscientists admit that little is understood about the coding of color in the cortex, after the early opponent stages. Remarkably, the relation between the opponent signals and phenomenal color—including the unique hues—is *unknown* (Valberg 2001). The colors that best stimulate the opponent neurons in early vision—known to vision scientists as the cardinal color directions (Derrington et al. 1984)—look nothing like the unique hues. There is certainly no known path from L-M cells to pillar box red. Valberg (2001, 1651) concludes:

It looks like cardinal directions... have little to do with Hering's unique hues, at least at the retina and LGN. This points to the problems encountered when looking for a simple 'neural correlate for your seeing red'.

In his historical overview of color science, John Mollon (2003, 36) describes how on the discovery of opponent coded cells there was an initial enthusiasm in the vision science community, about a potential bridge between perceptual psychology and physiology. These hopes were soon to be disappointed. Mollon concludes that the important features of phenomenal color space are yet to receive a satisfactory neural explanation, since "[t]he properties of our subjective color space still remain to taunt us today. We do not know the status that should be given to the phenomenological observations of Hering and we do not know how to incorporate them into a complete account of color science" (Mollon 2003, 36). So the neural explanation of perceived color relations, and unique hues in particular, remains a subject of ongoing research. It is worth noting that the visual cortex, rather than the early opponent mechanism, has been the focus of this research.[24]

---

24. For example, Hofer et al. (2005), Stoughton and Conway (2008), Brouwer and Heeger (2009), Parkes et al. (2009), Wuerger and Parkes (2011), Horwitz and Haas (2012), and Danilova and Mollon (2012).

It is worrying, then, that philosophers such as Averill (2005) should be basing theories of color on a scientific conjecture—over the link between cardinal color axes and Hering primaries—that has been refuted. Still, Hardin is more cautious in acknowledging the gaps in the account of color in the cortex, and the simplifications assumed by the opponent coding diagram reproduced above. He writes about this proposed neurobiological reduction of color that, "[o]f course, at the present rudimentary state of our knowledge of the visual system, most of this is promise, program, and principle" (Hardin 1993, 111, also see at 35, 54). So Hardin's project is actually a bet on the future likelihood of a complete, purely neurophysiological account of color appearance, even if this has yet to be achieved in practice.

Is this a sensible bet to place? One might be inclined to think that the odds here are good because there are already indications that neurophysiological knowledge has provided indispensable insights into some aspects of color appearance, such as the distinction between binary and unitary shades. If this trend continues, one might anticipate that eventually it should turn out that neurophysiology provides us with a complete picture. One reason to temper this optimism is some work that suggests that certain appearance phenomena will require explanations that look beyond the central nervous system. Philipona and O'Regan (2006) present an ecological explanation of the unique hues and focal colors (i.e., best representatives of the hues red, green, blue, and yellow). Following a statistical analysis of an array of SSRs, they found that surfaces perceived as having unique hues had the characteristic of presenting a simpler reflectance profile to the trichromatic visual system. This finding is consistent with Mollon's observation that there is less interpersonal variation in uniqueness judgments when surface stimuli, which are more ecologically valid, rather than monochromatic lights are used. Thus Mollon (2006, 304) proposes that in our attempts to explain the unique hues we should consider both neurophysiological and ecological factors, and not take these two kinds of accounts to be somehow in competition:

So, what are the unique hues? Are they determined within us, by the organization of our visual system? Or are they ecologically significant, identifying for us particular subsets of spectra in the world? Let us call answers of the former type "constitutional" hypotheses, and answers of the second type, "ecological." The two types of account are not necessarily exclusive, because our visual categories may have evolved to match some feature of the world.

3.4.2 In the Physical World

A major objection to the physicalistic reduction of colors has been the argument from the "axioms of unity." Keith Campbell (1969, 133) introduced these to the debate as a necessary condition on indentification of color with a physical property type. The condition was that, for example, "there must be one physical quality common and peculiar to objects which are turquoise." In a similar vein Hardin (1993, 7) has written:

If an account of the nature of color is to be satisfactory, it must include a set of principles whereby one can understand the resemblances and differences that colors bear to one another.... [F]or instance, what is it about blue things as a group which puts them in a class different from yellow things.

As it turns out, the candidate physical properties do not satisfy such conditions. Hardin (1993, 6–7) points out the complications that arise for the reflectance theory because the spectrum of reflected light reaching the eye from an object can depend not only on its SSR but also on viewing angle, the glossiness of the surface, and its orientation. It follows that from SSR alone one cannot predict perceived color. And what is more, it is unlikely that any two randomly chosen turquoise things will have similar (let alone identical) SSRs, even when their hue is matched in ordinary lighting conditions. This is the phenomenon known as *metamerism*, and it comes about because the human retina contains only three broadly tuned cone classes whose sensitivity profiles substantially overlap. Thus fairly different reflectance profiles will often bring about the same differential cone responses, and hence will be indistinguishable in hue under a certain range of lighting conditions.[25]

The physicalist's response is to acknowledge the idiosyncratic, anthropogenic nature of color classification. Hilbert (1987) is aware of the existence

---

25. The *microphysical realism* of Jackson (1998) faces an analogous problem, the "disjunction objection." Jackson proposes to equate yellow with whatever microphysical property of the object it is that causes it to appear yellow (see McLaughlin 2003). Yet, even for the exact same shade, there is no common physical property shared by canary wings, dandelions, printers inks, or a 575 nm monochromatic light source (Nassau 2001). On Jackson's proposal, the color canary yellow turns out to be a disjunction of all these different possible physical causes of color perceptions. It is a human idiosyncrasy—a result of trichromacy and further visual processing—that all of these are assigned to the same color category. The nub of the issue is that there is no one "natural kind" property that can be singled out as yellow.

of metamers, and does not deny that the human visual system is a very poor resolver of SSR. But he maintains that his own brand of realism is "anthropocentric." While SSR is, in general, a standard physical property, Hilbert concedes that the set of metameric reflectances that humans bundle together as looking scarlet will never play a role in explanatory science. Hilbert points out that scarlet can be an objective property nonetheless, since the set of SSR's that make up this color class can be described in purely physical terms, without reference to human perceptions (Hilbert 1987, 11).

Yet the physicalist must concede that a range of phenomena that are central to color science, such as categorization and matching, have nothing to do with color itself, if we identify color with SSR (Chirimuuta 2014). The physicalist, in other words, has effected her reduction of color to spectral surface reflectance by cutting away from her domain of enquiry what are arguably the central explananda of color theory, such as the question of why two physically very different stimuli should be appear as having the same color, to a trichromatic subject. This is surely a Procrustean solution. At the same time, however, the Hardin-style eliminativist is guilty of an equivalent crime. In her haste to replace chromatic language with neural language she excises a range of topics crucial to the scientific understanding of color perception—the relationships between colors and material properties, and the ways that animals use color vision as a guide to their physical surroundings (see chapters 4 and 5).

3.4.3 In Between?

An ideal ontology of color would not be Procrustean: it would accommodate the fact that color is implicated in a range of phenomena that are not easily confined to a physical, neural, or phenomenal explanation. Furthermore the Procrustean nature of realism and antirealism appears to be symptomatic of the inner-outer divide that has gripped philosophical imagination since the seventeenth century, as was discussed in the previous chapter. Since the relationist, conversely, defines colors both in terms of physical stimuli and perceptual reactions, her view is the most promising way to avoid the Procrustean treatment. However, the dispositionalist versions of relationism that have been dominant so far have not fulfilled this expectation.

We saw in section 2.4 that the dispositionalism that emerged in the seventeenth century is characterized by an equivocation over whether the referent of 'blue', say, is to be thought of as the dispositional property ('power') of items such as sapphires to appear blue to us, as the physical basis of that disposition, or as the blue sensation that we experience. Whatever the case, colors are not held to be somehow in between the mental and the physical, since the point of the theory of secondary qualities was to police the separation of these two domains.

Contemporary versions of dispositionalism have been less equivocal in their location of color within the extra-mental world. A case in point is the "secondary quality" view of Johnston (1992). He defines 'red' as, "the standardly realized disposition to look red to standard perceivers under standard conditions" (Johnston 1992, 230). This seems to place some emphasis on the subjectivity (perceiver-dependence) of color, since colors are defined in terms of their relation to human perceivers, perhaps suggesting that were there no humans, nothing would be colored. However, Johnston (1992, 234) goes on to say that the sort of disposition he has in mind is a "constituted" one, rather than a "bare" disposition:

There are intrinsic features of x which…would cause R [a certain perceptual response] in S [a viewing subject] under C [certain viewing conditions]. These intrinsic features of x are the "constituting basis" of x's disposition to R in S. We may therefore think of a constituted disposition as a higher-order property of having some intrinsic properties which, oddities aside, would cause the manifestation of the disposition in the circumstances of manifestation.

So what Johnston means by 'red' is actually some higher order umbrella term for the basic physical properties that are responsible for the objects having the disposition to be seen as red. A comparison helps illustrate the view. Fragility is the stock example of a dispositional property. It is the disposition of a china teacup, say, to shatter when the conditions are right, as when dropped on a marble floor. In Johnston's account it is the different molecular structures of glass, porcelain, and Pyrex that are the "constituting bases" of fragility; these substances then all share the higher order property of being fragile.

Johnston himself remarks on the similarity between the "secondary quality view" and the microphysical realism of Jackson and Pargetter (1997; see also Jackson 1998; McLaughlin 2003), also known as the "primary quality view." Both the primary and secondary quality theorists take it that there are physical properties of external objects that are the causes of perceivers having color experiences. The point of difference is over the precise schema for deriving less fundamental color properties from these. According to Jackson, the color yellow is the disjunction of all intrinsic properties $P_1 \ldots P_n$ that can cause experiences of yellow in normal observers under standard conditions. For Johnston, however, the color yellow is the higher order property of the same intrinsic properties, defined as the power to cause the manifestation of a disposition to be perceived as yellow (by normal observers under standard conditions). So really both the primary and secondary quality theorists are pointing to the same physical properties to be identified with the colors, but they are cataloguing them in different ways.

Cohen (2009) introduces a different terminology, contrasting the *realizer functionalism* of Jackson and Pargetter (1997), Jackson (1998), and McLaughlin (2003) with his own *role functionalism*. The realizer functionalist exploits the functional relations of color (i.e., its interactions with perceivers) to locate the microphysical bases for these functions and thence to reduce colors to those bases. So the view is analogous to realizer functionalism in the philosophy of mind. Cohen's approach is to define 'red' in the following way: "red for S in C is the functional role of disposing its bearers to look red to S in C…mutatis mutandis for the other colors" (Cohen 2009, 178). Thus his account is like Johnston's secondary quality view, in that both identify colors with the higher order properties of disposing objects to be seen in certain ways, rather than the lower level bases.

Furthermore Johnston (1992, 236) states that, "the difference between Secondary and Primary accounts of color concepts must really be quite subtle," and that it is possible to think that the dispute between them amounts to no more than conflicting taste in "argumentative bookkeeping." Similarly Jackson (1998, 104) writes:

There is…no deep metaphysical dispute between primary quality theorists and dispositionalists. The dispute is over whether the dispositions to look coloured or the physical quality bases of those dispositions should be tagged as the colours; the dispute is ultimately over the distribution of names among putative candidates. And how we answer this labelling question can have no cognitive, epistemic or practical significance.

Consistent with this is the finding that while realizer functionalism is classified as a nonrelational theory, and role functionalism as a relational one, the central difference between the two types of theory is in how they define colors across possible worlds, not in their cataloguing of color in *this* world (Cohen, 2009, 186–87).[26]

In sum, contemporary dispositionalism does not amount to a position that is substantially different from color physicalism. It locates colors "out there" in the physical world, even though it makes use of perceivers' reactions to them for the purposes of definition. Ecological relationism is a view that, at least in its rhetoric, attempts to capture the "Janus-faced" nature of color. For example, Thompson (1995, 244) writes:

For a relational account to be philosophically satisfying and naturalistic it must be ecological. The world outside the perceiver must be considered as an environment, rather than a neutral material universe, and the perceiver must be considered as an active exploring animal, rather than a passive spectator that simply receives sensations from physical impressions.

However, as we saw above, in his own definition of color Thompson (1995, 245) appears to fall back into the mindset common to physicalists and dispositionalists. It appears, then, that if a relationist theory is to offer a genuine alternative to physicalism, eliminativism, or dispositionalism, it will have to be more ontologically revisionary than any of the existing accounts. I make one such proposal in chapter 6. Before then we will examine new accounts of the function of color vision that have emerged from perceptual science.

---

26. For the primary quality theorist/realizer functionalist, color words refer nonrigidly to physical property complexes, since they fill this role only contingently. The result is that if ruby red is discovered to be property X in this world, it is so in all worlds, even if property X appears azure to inhabitants of a neighboring possible world. It is to the advantage of Cohen's role functionalism that ruby red is always the property that makes objects appear that color in whatever world.

4 Coloring In, and Coloring For

4.1 Coloring *In*

The core message of this chapter is that color vision is as a way of seeing *things*—flowers, tables, ladybirds—not, in the first instance, a way of seeing the *colors*. As Akins (2001, 86) writes, "the primary function of color vision is not to see the colors or to see various media as colored."[1] A narrow view of the function of color vision is implied by the coloring-in model. This account supposes that color vision operates in isolation from the perception of form, texture, and the like, and serves simply to color in the shapes presented in the visual field. It pays to clarify at the outset what is meant by saying that color vision is integrated or separate. On the one hand, in the scientific literature, mention of the physiological integration of "color" is shorthand for saying that neurons sensitive to differences in wavelength of light are also sensitive to other stimulus features. Indeed color sensitivity in neurophysiology is normally defined as *wavelength selectivity* of individual neurons. On the other hand, the psychological integration of color describes how perception of the color of a stimulus affects perception of its other visual properties, and vice versa. So none of this should be taken to mean that there is a sui generis color property that can itself be integrated. Precisely the opposite: we will see in this chapter that the chromatic dimension of visual experience cannot be understood in isolation from other stimulus dimensions, and at the neurophysiological level we cannot talk

1. See Akins and Hahn (2014). Akins goes on to state her hypothesis concerning the actual function: "my suspicion is that color vision has evolved to encode a certain kind of general information about the retinal image, not color per se but *spectral contrast* information." The message of this chapter diverges here, as my aim is not to specify any one function but to highlight the variety of functions.

about color per se, only wavelength discrimination. The point is that color vision cannot be isolated as a separate perceptual modality.

4.1.1 The Coloring Book Hypothesis

A common antirealist view is that colors are made up by the brain and then projected onto the world. It is as if the brain colors in the world, adding internally generated color to an achromatic representation of object edges and shapes. Interestingly, there is a scientific equivalent to this view. Neuroscientists Gegenfurtner and Kiper (2003, 199) describe the "coloring book hypothesis" in vision science as the view that "the form of an object is processed first, with color being subsequently filled in."[2] What this means is that the brain processes color separately from form, using purely achromatic information to locate edges and the outlines of objects or their movements through space. Achromatic vision is portrayed as entirely self-sufficient and able to yield a complete representation of what objects are in a scene, and their precise shapes and positions. This leaves no role for color vision in the task of finding out about forms of objects—color looks redundant here, only making an appearance at a later stage to color in the shapes revealed by processing elsewhere. As Mullen et al. (2000, 639) also describe, it is a model where, "the luminance contours and edges of the image...are primarily extracted and used to divide the image up into a number of non-overlapping areas," such that "color has no direct input to the main process of contour or form extraction."

The coloring book model has been influential—if not dominant—in the science up until fairly recently.[3] This is perhaps because the model offers a pleasingly simple view of the workings of the visual system. If the visual system consists of a few separate pathways, each responsible for the processing of different visual properties—form, color, and others like shape and depth—then for the purposes of scientific investigation the

2. Descriptions of visual processing in the brain often use pictorial metaphors: form processing is described as yielding a picture or representation of what objects are where. This usage borrows from computer simulations of vision, where processing stages literally yield a graphical representation of a scene (e.g., the 2½D sketch of Marr 1982).

3. Though Mausfeld (2010, 124) describes how the model—"the entire conceptual framework underlying the idea of a homogeneous and autonomous attribute of 'colour per se'"—faced substantial criticism from the Gestalt school early in the twentieth century.

entire system can be broken down into these subsystems and each of these individual pathways can be studied separately. This makes the task of understanding the visual system much simpler than it otherwise would be. If it is believed that these pathways are separate and not subject to significant interactions between each other, then the vision scientist's task is to devise stimuli that selectively excite one subsystem, like the *isoluminant* (or *equiluminant*) patterns that have been used extensively in color research, and study the neurophysiological or psychophysical responses to those stimuli. Importantly, if it is supposed, for example, that motion is processed independently of color, experimenters need not be concerned that interactions between pathways will affect their results.

It is worth mentioning the specifics of the coloring book model. It posits that color vision is a separate module, isolated from other visual pathways, and that color is processed by a dedicated subset of neurons in the visual cortex. Livingstone and Hubel (1988) describe segregated color pathways running from eye to cortex: the P-stream of retinal ganglion cells and lateral geniculate cells, which project onto the "blobs" in V1. Zeki (1978) reported the discovery of cortical area V4 in the macaque monkey, and because of the sensitivity of its neurons to colored stimuli, he argued that V4 was the color module, the region responsible for color constancy. From his description of patients with cerebral achromatopsia (loss of conscious color vision due to cortical brain damage) Zeki also argued that the human equivalent to V4 is the area necessary for conscious color perception. In other words, he argued that this brain area colors in the visual scene (Zeki, 1993, ch. 26).

Zeki's (1983, 764) writing also reveals a link between the coloring book model and antirealism:

> the nervous system…takes what information there is in the external environment…and transforms that information to construct colours, using its own algorithms to do so. In other words, it constructs something which is a property of the brain, not the world outside. (emphasis original)

One is reminded of Hardin's description of the neurophysiological construction of color, and statement that "chromatic perceptual states" are in fact neural states (Hardin 1993, 111). The point is not that there is a strict entailment between these theoretical suppositions but that the coloring book hypothesis makes this sort of antirealism attractive.

As it turns out, the coloring book hypothesis is not well supported by more recent neurophysiological evidence. For one thing, the hypothesis states that the earliest stages of visual processing compute shapes of objects so that these can be colored in at later stages. But this proposal is countered by findings that much color processing happens at early, pre-cortical stages and that the same neurons that are sensitive to wavelength information also analyze other visual attributes (Gegenfurtner and Kiper 2003, 199). Furthermore the characterization of V4 as the "color center" has been overturned by numerous studies demonstrating the diversity of function in this brain area. As Conway (2009, 286) writes, "Current opinion is that V4 contributes to shape perception, visual attention, and perhaps stereopsis, and not exclusively or especially color."

However, the coloring book hypothesis has been influential in psychophysical research. Livingstone and Hubel conducted a series of perceptual experiments that purported to show that color makes a minimal contribution to visual function, other than coloring in shapes (Livingstone and Hubel 1987; Livingstone and Hubel 1988). Their method was to test visual function with isoluminant stimuli, patterns that have a uniform luminance, and so only provide a signal to neurons sensitive to chromatic contrast. They argue that motion is detected exclusively by the achromatic M-system, that color makes no contribution to the perception of depth and that color information is not essential for linking together parts of an object (i.e., perception of form). One of their findings was that the visual system is insensitive to the contour of an isoluminant edge, a result that has been contested by many. Mollon (1989a, 25) argues that simple Ishihara plates— the ones familiar from opticians' tests for color deficiency—demonstrate the falsity of Livingstone and Hubel's claim. McIlhagga and Mullen (1996) show that Livingstone and Hubel's proposed color channel is almost equally good at resolving edges as is the achromatic luminance channel. This implies that color is as efficient an indicator of shape as luminance contrast. Mullen et al. (2000, 639) contrast the coloring book model with their model in which, "both the color and the luminance system are capable of extracting edges from the visual scene and so dividing the image into distinct regions."

In the next section I will be discussing a number of findings that dispute Livingstone and Hubel's case for the coloring book model. However, one important point is that the choice for or against the coloring book model should not be thought of as a *purely* empirical issue. Prior belief in the model will affect experimental design, especially the choice of stimuli, and this in turn will affect the chances of finding evidence for the model. Psychophysical studies such as Livingstone and Hubel's garnered evidence for the irrelevance of color for many visual functions. This was done by using isoluminant stimuli that elicit responses only from spectrally sensitive neurons.[4] In choosing such stimuli, the researchers are already making the assumption that the color system can be fully characterized in isolation from the rest of vision. But under the unnatural isoluminant conditions, the visual system can behave in atypical ways (Mollon 1989a).[5]

Furthermore isoluminant stimuli are specifically designed to contain no achromatic luminance information. This, of course, means that interactions between color and luminance will not manifest themselves in the experiment. If the alternative assumption is made—that color can only be understood in conjunction with other visual modalities—then different experimental methodologies will be used, ones that have the potential to reveal interactions between color and achromatic processing. In fact the understanding of the interactions between color and other visual subsystems is only at an early stage (Shevell and Kingdom 2008, 152; Solomon and Lennie 2007, 284), and the use of isoluminant stimuli has been cited as a reason for this neglect (Shevell and Kingdom 2008, 156). Different phenomena will be revealed if more naturalistic stimuli are used, ones that combine color and luminance information. As Kingdom (2003, 641) writes,

Important clues to how color vision is involved in form perception may also emerge…from investigations of how color-sensitive and luminance-sensitive mechanisms interact when a subject is presented with stimuli that embody the particular relationship that exists between color and luminance in the natural visual world.

So the interdependence of the perception of color and form, for example, will most likely be discovered to be much more intricate than found to date.[6]

---

4. Though actually isoluminant patterns do not stimulate all spectrally sensitive neurons (Harada et al. 2009).

5. In vision research "natural" stimuli or conditions mean those akin to everyday viewing conditions outside the laboratory. Considerations of ecological validity have encouraged a growing use of natural stimuli in experiments. See the discussion in Chirimuuta and Gold (2009).

6. It is also worth noting the place of the coloring book hypothesis within the influential modular framework. The assumption of modularity in the brain—"the one-area-one-function hypothesis"—has had an important role in vision research. For criticism, see Schiller (1996).

4.1.2 Detection or Discrimination?

Another characteristic of the coloring in model is the focus on *detection* as a primary sensory capacity (see section 3.3). The issue can be understood more clearly if we sketch an alternative to the basic detection model. On this *discrimination* view, a key function of color vision is to flag up differences in surface properties like SSR. For instance, we say that color vision does not track an intrinsic property of lemon rind (seen as yellow), and lime skin (seen as green), but is responsive to the fact that these two surfaces are different in some way (and this is a real physical difference). The color of a particular surface will be a function of its relations to other surfaces and there is no one true color that an object has; colors are not assumed to belong to individual objects—if colors are anything, on this view, they are relations. In agreement with the Gestalt psychologist Gelb (1938), color concerns the structure of our perceptual world in general, not objects in particular.

One reason to take the alternative seriously is consideration of *simultaneous color contrast effects*. Figure 4.1 illustrates the phenomenon. An object, such as the squiggly line, can appear to have quite different colors when seen in different surrounding contexts; yet the physical surface properties of the object remain unchanged. The effect presents no difficulty for the discrimination view because it is assumed that the primary task of the visual system is to represent different objects as contrasting in color. It makes sense that the appearance of an object should change with context, so as to enhance its contrast with surroundings.

As should be clear from the discussion of chapter 3, this example is problematic for the physicalist because she must address the question, "what is the real color of the squiggle?" If color is identified with some physical property of the ink like SSR, which the visual system aims to recover, then we have to ask which is the correct color percept to identify with that SSR (which we know is unchanged from context to context). One option is to stipulate arbitrarily that the one context gives you the veridical color percept, and other context leads you to misperceive the color. But this counters the physicalist's belief that there is a nonarbitrary fact as to what color something is. Alternatively, the physicalist can give up the claim that we have perceptual access to the actual color of the ink, but this would be to

Figure 4.1
Simultaneous contrast effect. The physical surface properties of the squiggle pattern are identical across both backgrounds. Yet the lines appear brighter and whiter when seen on the dark gray background, and darker when viewed against the light gray background.

concede a key tenet of the "commonsense" view that we know what colors things are just by looking.[7]

We cannot ignore color contrast as a side issue. This is because these effects often occur in normal viewing, even though we are unaware of them. Shades of brown and jet black are only ever seen if a high luminance contrast surround is present. Contrast, Shevell and Kingdom (2008, 146) write "not only alters color perception, but also vastly expands the domain of colors we see." These facts undermine any response along the lines of Tye (2000), that the phenomenon of simultaneous color contrast is a mere visual illusion, and therefore not something that a theory of color must struggle to accommodate.

7. Of course, physicalists have made various moves in response to such arguments. See Cohen (2009, ch. 3) for discussion.

Whittle (2003, 135) discusses the significance of such effects and links the relatively scant attention they have received in vision science to the dominance of a detectionist framework where vision is modeled on the operation of a measuring device. It is worth quoting him at length:

> So the phenomena of contrast colours lead us to the ambiguity of colour: that regions of the visual field do not just 'have a colour', but can be seen in different ways. Colours can vary dramatically, depending on how one parses the scene into objects, lighting, and transparent media....[T]hese kinds of ambiguity contradict the notion that perceived colour is just a transduction or transformation of the physical colour. This notion...has dominated psychophysics at least since Fechner. Although many people have argued persuasively against it, it is so temptingly simple, allows just enough space for some neural complexities..., and meshes with so many of our habitual Cartesian assumptions, that it has great staying power. Its dominance is perhaps the deepest reason why contrast colours remain in their uneasy position in colour science: invoked when convenient, but much of the time ignored.[8]

4.2   Coloring *For*

This section develops the alternative to the coloring-in model, looking at evidence for a new view.[9] I focus on the data concerning interactions between color and the other visual modalities that, in the coloring book model, were thought to be isolated subsystems. I describe color *for* depth, color *for* form, color *for* motion, and so on. On this view, the function of color vision should not be characterized as the detection or even the perception of color. The seemingly paradoxical assertion of Akins (2001), that color vision does not help us see color, becomes intuitive. Color helps us see *things* because adding dimensions of chromatic contrast does in fact

---

8. The detection model has also been criticized by vision scientists Alan Gilchrist and Rainer Mausfeld. Mausfeld calls it the "measurement-device misconception of perception" (Mausfeld 2003, 383; see also Mausfeld 1998).On the topic of lightness and brightness perception, Gilchrist (2006, 364) writes that "the doctrine of local determination takes the form of what I have called the 'photometer metaphor' ..: the assumption that the visual system initially encodes the intensity of light at each point in the visual field. Even when not explicitly acknowledged, this metaphor is exposed by a series of symptoms, including the neglect of illumination perception and the obsession with brightness."

9. The view does have a precedent in the Gestalt tradition, however. Take, for example, Koffka, "A general theory of colour must at the same time be a general theory of space and form," quoted by Mausfeld and Andres (2002, 210).

contribute to the perception of geometric properties of objects, especially in complex viewing conditions.

There is no one type of physical stimulus that explains the operation of color vision in all tasks. In most cases the color visual system does not represent an absolute value of any stimulus property, but rather the contrast (i.e., a difference) between stimulus properties. In the *coloring-for* model, color can be thought of as an extra dimension of information that helps the perceiver to solve a number of visual problems, and aids visual processing in a number of ways. Color processing is recognized as an integral part of our visual system. Just as we would not say that our sensitivity to achromatic luminance is an end in itself, but a means to perceiving the boundaries of objects that interact with light, we will see that chromatic sensitivity is another means to perceiving shapes and surfaces of those same objects. It makes little sense to say the visual system is a light detector, or a color detector.

We begin with a list of the functions of color vision, drawn from a review of the psychophysical literature by Shevell and Kingdom (2008). Different vision scientists have found evidence for the contribution of color vision to all of these important visual tasks:

- segmentation of objects
- perception of form or shape
- grouping of objects
- perception of contours
- perception of texture
- object detection
- object identification
- memorization of objects
- perception of depth
- perception of the motion of complex objects
- recognition of shadows

I will now discuss these findings, and other results, grouping them into three rough, and sometimes overlapping, categories:[10]

10. In comparison, Hurlbert (2013, 379) writes that "behavioural studies suggest that color vision serves at least three broad purposes in ensuring survival and reproduction: image segmentation, social-sexual signaling, and object recognition." Due to length constraints I have omitted discussion of social-sexual signaling. For further details, see Hill and McGraw (2006), Bradbury and Vehrencamp (2011), and Stevens (2013).

1. Interactions between color and the processing of other visual attributes
2. Color and cognitive tasks
3. Color and form

4.2.1 Color and the Processing of Other Visual Attributes

The coloring book model posits a separate color module that processes information in parallel with other subsystems dedicated to shape, motion, depth, and the like. The color subsystem is not thought to interact with the other modules nor to assist their functioning in any substantial way. Above we saw that the coloring book hypothesis has been challenged by findings showing how it is possible to recognize shapes and contours of purely chromatic stimuli. This section explores results on the interactions between the processing of chromatic information and other visual attributes. It will emerge that chromatic information has a central role to play in our general visual economy.

Again, we will see the limitations of a simplistic detectionist model of color vision, one that assumes that the primary purpose of color vision is to detect chromatic properties, coloring in a pre-defined visual image. Of course, a detection model could be modified to include interactions between color and other modalities. One could say that colors are detected, and then this information is made available for 3D vision, and so on, or that color processing occurs early on in vision, in conjunction with the processing of form, etc. But then the proposal that the function of color vision is the detection of colors loses one source of motivation.

Depth and Distance

Troscianko et al. (1991) set out to test the claim that color makes no contribution to the perception of depth. They presented observers with red-green equiluminant stimuli that had a "texture gradient" pattern. In the black and white case, texture gradients are indisputably an effective cue for depth, slant, or perspective (see figure 4.2). When viewing such images, it seems we automatically make the assumption that the object depicted has a uniform texture pattern but is receding into the distance in such a way that the units of the texture appear much smaller at the top than at the bottom. So a stimulus that is actually vertical looks as if it is slanted with the top part of the image further away from us.

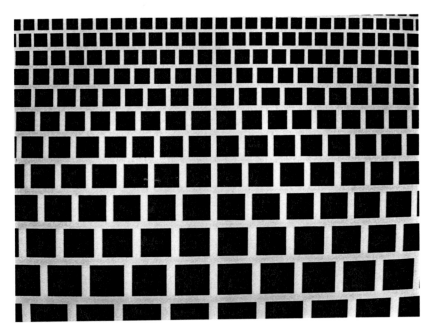

Figure 4.2
Texture gradient stimulus. Troscianko et al. (1991) showed that an equiluminant, chromatic version of this stimulus gives an equally good depth effect, and that this effect is enhanced by the introduction of a saturation gradient—a gradual reduction in color contrast going from the bottom to the top of the image. From T. Troscianko, T., R. Montagnon, J. Le Clerc, E. Malbert, and P.-L. Chanteau (1991). The role of colour as a monocular depth cue. *Vision Research* 31 (11), 1923–30. Reprinted with permission from Elsevier.

Livingstone and Hubel (1987) reported that the equiluminant versions of such stimuli were not perceived as having any depth, a finding disputed by Troscianko and colleagues, who found that they were able to elicit perceptions of distance at equiluminance.[11] This finding counters Livingstone and Hubel's claim that the hypothetical color channel is isolated from the hypothetical depth channel in such a way that color information cannot contribute to the depth tasks. The alternative view is that color is integrated with the mechanisms of depth perception.

11. Troscianko et al. (1991, 1928) discuss the discrepancy. Unlike Livingstone and Hubel's, their experimental design eliminated conflicting context cues, adaptation to the stimulus, and also registered quantitative reports on the angle of slant.

Another finding of Troscianko's group indicates that color has a special role to play in the perception of distance. They showed that the textured depth cue is made more effective by the addition of a color *saturation gradient*. In this case the pattern is strongly colored (saturated) at the bottom of the stimulus, where the texture is large and appears close. The texture pattern slowly washes out to a desaturated gray at the top of the stimulus where the pattern is small and appears to be further away. This greying of the top of the stimulus made it appear even more slanted and distant. What is particularly interesting about the effect of the saturation gradient is that it mimics a depth cue found in the natural world. In an open landscape where one's view stretches for miles around, the colors of very distant objects appear less saturated because of atmospheric scattering. So this loss of color saturation can indicate the distance of hills and mountains over many miles, when other distance cues (e.g., from stereopsis and motion parallax) are absent. In fact it is believed that the saturation gradient is a cue for depth because developmental or evolutionary experience in the natural environment shows that objects with desaturated colors are the most distant ones.[12]

Figure 4.3 shows the saturation gradient of a real landscape. The loss of color saturation from atmospheric scattering is also usually accompanied by a shift to a bluish hue, since shorter wavelengths of light are scattered most. This phenomenon is particularly remarkable at the Australian Blue Mountains pictured here because vaporized eucalyptus oil in the atmosphere increases the scattering. The more blue appearance of distant objects is in itself a cue for depth (Lovell et al. 2005). Note that this function of color vision does not sit happily with a detection model. It is tempting to say that one perceives the distance of the mountains by detecting blueness. But the blueness is not an intrinsic property of the distant trees—it disappears on a nearer view. The blue perception cannot be said to be the detection of spectral surface properties of the trees. There is no blue property of

---

12. This idea is supported by the Troscianko group's finding that a reversed saturation gradient (gray in the foreground and red in the background), the opposite of the natural saturation cue, would cancel the perceived depth of the texture gradient. Below I discuss the "color-as-material" assumption, another instance of the brain interpreting color information in the light of statistical regularities in the natural environment.

Figure 4.3
Blue Mountains panorama. The colors of very distant objects appear less saturated because of atmospheric scattering. They will often appear blue because
short wavelengths of light are scattered most. In the Blue Mountains near Sydney,
vaporized eucalyptus oil from the forest increases scattering. Loss of color saturation
and bluing phenomena are known to cue depth to human observers.

objects out there to be detected. If the blueness belongs to anything, it is a
property of the volume of air between yourself and the horizon (Brown
2014). Yet the blueness is also a function of your distance from the mountain. A better account says that this blueness, and the attendant perception
of depth, is made possible by a relation holding between the perceiver, the
distant mountain, and the atmosphere in between. In general, when perceivers stand in the right relations to things, certain color perceptions occur
that yield useful information about those things. Color is, in the view
developed in chapter 6, not an object of sight but a way of seeing things.

One more result from this study bears on the question of the integration
of color. Troscianko and colleagues found that a saturation gradient alone,
a pattern of shading shifting from red to gray but not combined with any

texture, would not be seen as having depth. The authors argue that this indicates an interaction between texture and color processing:

a texture of some kind is necessary for colour to elicit depth...This suggests that, while colour can code depth, its contribution is contingent upon the presence of texture cues. Such a contingency implies strong links between texture and colour processing in human vision. (Troscianko et al. 1991, 1928)

3D Shape

Above I noted Mullen and McIlhagga's evidence against Livingstone and Hubel's claim for the separateness of color and form processing. The topic will be discussed in further detail below, where I will present the general case that color, in making salient boundaries among objects, has a primary role in helping us recognize and distinguish material surfaces. Here it is worth discussing the role of color in the perception of 3D shape. Zaidi and Li (2006) used abstract flow patterns that elicit a sensation of depth. They found that isoluminant images made at least as effective a depth cue as the gray-scale ones. Their results provide evidence for the existence of neurons that are orientation tuned and sensitive to both chromatic and luminance contrast. In other words, this sort of 3D form perception could best be understood as the result of neurons able to "multitask"; there was no evidence for separate banks of neurons only sensitive to color or to shape.

There is also evidence that shape—specifically, the perceptual interpretation of the 3D structure of a stimulus—affects color. Hurlbert's group used a stimulus equivalent to the Mach card. It is simply a stiff paper folded in half and stood up vertically, like a greetings card. The stimulus is viewed with the opening of the card face on to the subject. For this experiment, one-half of the inside of the card is painted a deep magenta, the other left white. On normal viewing, there is a strong inter-reflection between the two halves of the card, so that the white half is seen in a pinkish light. Bloj and co-workers introduced the manipulation of presenting the card through a device that reversed the stereoscopic information in the stimulus, so that it appeared convex, like a rooftop, rather than concave like an open book. In the convex condition the unpainted half of the card looked to be a fairly saturated magenta, no longer pinkish-white. The explanation given is that under normal viewing, where the card is seen as concave, the visual system is able to interpret the pinkish hue as due to inter-reflection between the two surfaces. This assumption is not made in the convex viewing condition, since such reflection would not occur outside of the laboratory, so the pink-ness of the unpainted card is taken to be an actual surface color. As Bloj et al. (1999, 877) write, "The effect demonstrates that the human visual system incorporates knowledge of mutual illumination—the physics of light reflection between surfaces—at an early stage in colour perception."

That is to say, the perception of color is not isolated from the interpreta-tion of the layout of objects in a scene. I would resist any presumption that the pale pink seen in the concave condition is veridical, and the saturated magenta illusory (as would be urged under the physicalist hypothesis that color is spectral surface reflectance). The colors that we see in any circum-stances are actually part of an overall best interpretation of the scene, derived not only from the spectral cues coming from individual objects but also sensitive to the relations among them.[13]

Motion

Findings concerning the physiological interaction between color and motion processing are more controversial. Evidence has been reported for low-level chromatic motion detectors, namely responsiveness to the motion cues of isoluminant stimuli (Cropper and Derrington 1996, review in Cropper 2006). Croner and Albright (1997) report that color segmenta-tion aids the detection of motion in a pattern of random dots, but their findings were challenged by Li and Kingdom (2001; see also Michna and Mullen 2008 on the perception of global motion in colored random dot patterns). Overall, however, Livingstone and Hubel's claim for the isolation of color and motion channels is not supported by the recent psychophysi-cal or neurophysiological evidence.

In the well-known effect of the Benham disc, perceptible colors are gen-erated from the rotation of a patterned achromatic disc. The most likely explanation of this phenomenon is that different wavelength sensitive cells in the retina vary also in temporal sensitivity (Campenhausen and

13. I suggest that this conclusion is further supported by the finding of Yang and Shevell (2002) that color constancy is reduced when scenes are viewed in the absence of stereoscopic information about the distances of objects. However, their results are also subject to the physicalist interpretation that stereoscopic information is a cue to the illuminant spectrum, such that, without it, the visual system is less able to discount the illuminant and achieve color constancy (see section 3.3.2).

Schramme 1995). The point of interest for us is that the stimuli for color need not be anything like a typically colored surface. Motion (more specifically, a certain temporal pattern ordering) can itself be a cue for color. No *object* need have the colors that we see. Of course, the reflectance realist can reply that Benham disc hues are peculiar and illusory, and therefore not a counterexample to the claim that colors are SSR properties of objects. This claim would seem to be supported by the intuition that the disc is not actually colored because, when it stops spinning, we see that it is "really" black and white. But my point is that motion-generated colors are just as convincing, phenomenologically, as any others, so their exclusion from the class of "real colors" is question begging. In fact this case is no different from the example of the rainbow. There is no spectral bridge in the sky. Its appearance vanishes if we take slightly the wrong point of view. Yet, if any manifestation is an iconic example of color, it is the rainbow.

Lightness Constancy

Lightness (or *albedo*) is a stable property of a material object, the proportion of light that it will reflect averaged across all wavelengths of incident light. It is the achromatic equivalent of spectral surface reflectance, and perceptually it is the apparent darkness or brightness of a surface, often characterized as shades of gray. There is overlap between lightness and color research: color can be thought of as a special case of lightness perception, since lightness relates to how much light of all wavelengths is reflected from an object, whereas surface color is affected by the proportional reflection of light of certain wavelengths. Indeed it may be that perception of lightness is the primary task. Campenhausen (1986) argues that spectral sensitivity may have evolved to ensure *lightness constancy* (i.e., the stable perception of the brightness of objects) in all lighting conditions.

The point is that a monochromat cannot use information about the light reflected from individual objects to estimate their lightness. This is because changes in the perceived brightness of an object will be ambiguous between changes in material reflectiveness, or changes in background illumination. For example, to a monochromat whose one receptor type is maximally sensitive to mid-wavelengths, a red apple will look darker than a green granny smith in the broad spectrum light of the midday sun. But at sunset when the spectrum of light shifts to longer wavelengths the red apple will be reflecting more light than the other, which will make it the

Figure 4.3 [Plate 1]
Blue Mountains panorama. The colors of very distant objects appear less saturated because of atmospheric scattering. They will often appear blue because short
wavelengths of light are scattered least. In the Blue Mountains near Sydney, vaporized eucalyptus oil from the forest increases scattering. Loss of color saturation and
bluing phenomena are known to cue depth to human observers.

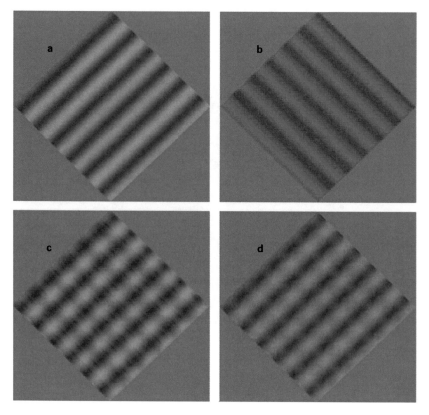

Figure 4.4 [Plate 2]

Color-shading effect. A sinusoidal luminance grating (a) and red-green equiluminant grating (b) are not found to elicit an impression of depth or corrugation. However, when these two images are superimposed (c), there is a strong depth effect. This effect is abolished if a colored grating is then superimposed onto the luminance grating (d). Image reprinted with permission from Shevell, S. and F. Kingdom (2008). Color in complex scenes. *Annual Review of Psychology 59*, 143–66. Copyright © 2008 by Annual Reviews.

Figure 7.1 [Plate 3]
Tree Fungus. Photographs of tree fungus among the undergrowth of a north Australian rainforest.

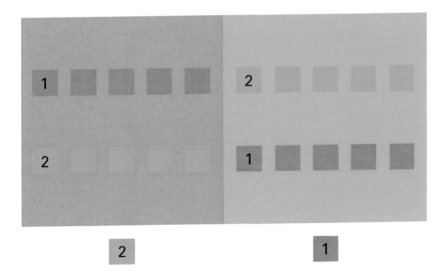

Figure 7.2 [Plate 4]
Color contrast effect. Squares in the top row all appear as roughly the same gray color. However, squares on the top left have the same physical spectral values as the other squares labeled 1, which appear mushroom pink in other contexts, and squares on the top right have the same physical spectral values as the other squares labeled 2, which appear sage green in other contexts. Image adapted from website of Akiyoshi Kitaoka, reproduced with permission.

Figure 7.3 [Plate 5]

Color contrast effect and color constancy. The top tiles of Rubik's cube, which appear blue on the left-hand side and yellow on the right-hand side, actually have the same reflectance, which appears gray if seen against a white background. The equivalence can be demonstrated by viewing these tiles through a paper cutout that masks the surrounding area. Image created by Beau Lotto, reproduced with permission.

brighter of the two fruits. A monochromat viewing the fruit under these two different conditions risks misidentifying the one for the other because of this failure of lightness constancy.[14] The ambiguity can be resolved by summing the activity of different photoreceptor types. Campenhausen (1986, 675) writes that,

During the course of evolution the need for lightness constancy may have been the original cause for the development of the cone system in vertebrates and the corresponding receptors in invertebrates. Color vision would then be a secondary achievement developed after the appropriate photoreceptors had become available.

If a perceiver with only one receptor type (and therefore no capacity for color vision) will experience continuous fluctuations in the lightness or darkness of objects, then visual information cannot be relied upon for identification and recognition of objects. The proposal that the need for lightness constancy actually drove the evolution of different photoreceptors remains speculative, but the deficiency in lightness constancy experienced by totally color blind, achromatopsic patients has been documented. Oliver Sacks describes the experience of the "color blind painter" whose higher level visual system had been damaged by a cortical lesion. He writes that,

Though he now lived wholly in a world of lightnesses and darknesses, he was very struck by how these changed in different illuminations; red objects, for instance, which normally appeared black to him, became lighter in the long rays of the evening sun, and this allowed him to infer their redness. This phenomenon was very marked if the quality of illumination suddenly changed, as, for example, when a fluorescent light was suddenly turned on, which would cause an immediate change in the brightnesses of objects around the room. Mr I. commented that he now found himself in an inconstant world, a world whose lights and darks fluctuated with the wavelength of illumination, in striking contrast to the relative stability, the constancy, of the colour world he had previously known. (Sacks 1995, 18)

What is tantalizing about Campenhausen's suggestion is that it completely breaks with the idea that color vision is there to enable us to see

---

14. Trichromats are in fact subject to a failure of lightness constancy in very dim light, known as the Purkinje effect. Because rod photoreceptors, used for night vision, are relatively more sensitive to shorter wavelengths of light than the average cone response, the apparent brightness of objects changes as cone-mediated day vision is substituted by rod-based scotopic vision. For example, Purkinje observed that red petals, which in daylight are brightest, at early dawn appear dimmer than blue petals or surrounding leaves (Wade and Brožek 2001). Note that rod vision is effectively monochromatic.

colors. Again, the position we arrive at is one in which *color vision doesn't help us see the colors of things; it helps us see things.* The idea that color vision is required for a stable representation of the visual world would explain why it is pervasive in the animal kingdom. It is worth emphasizing how ancient and widespread color vision is. Most seeing animals have some sort of color capacity, and genetic evidence points to its very early evolution in most lineages. It seems that if you are going to bother to have vision, you might as well have color vision. That is to say, it is not an "optional extra" but something invaluable for efficient spatial vision. As Jacobs (2004) discusses, it may be that color vision is "inevitable."

The fact that color vision aids lightness constancy might be taken as evidence by realists that the visual system is representing surface reflectance as a stable property of objects. But this need not be so. Just as color constancy is possible without the detection of SSR (see section 3.3.2), the contribution of color vision to lightness constancy is made possible just by sensitivity to differences in wavelength of ambient light. In a light environment full of fluctuating and ambiguous signals, the adaptation of the early visual system to changing lighting conditions makes possible invariant perception of objects (Zaidi 1998). Sensitivity to changes in illumination color actually enables a representation of material objects as themselves unchanging. Color perception is crucially involved with our arriving at a stable view of the material world. Yet, in order to have this function, it need not represent any intrinsic property of objects.

The message of this section has been that the perception of color is integrated with that of other visual features, like depth and lightness. Now one straightforward, realist interpretation of this would be that color exists as a physical property of external objects, and its presence affects our perception of other properties, because of some crossed neural pathways. Nothing in the empirical literature rules this out directly because the experiments do not work at that level of abstraction. However, I would say that the literature does suggest a different interpretation. Most important, there is no one physical stimulus type that is implicated in all of these cases. The fact that other visual features influence perceived color suggests that color experience is a result of interactions across the brain, with complex physical triggers. The colors we see are the appearances of ensembles of things, not sui generis chromatic qualities. We must break with the assumption that each object has a particular color that is sometimes modulated by contextual effects. Color, we learn, is a fundamentally spatial attribute, a significant part of our interpretation of how objects are arranged in space. To quote Koffka (1936, 134), "colour, localization, shape and size must be regarded as different aspects of one and the same process of organization."

4.2.2 Color and Cognition

Here I dwell on the contributions made by color vision to more high-level cognitive tasks such as identification and memorization of objects. The sort of functions I have in mind are not exclusive to humans or higher mammals. The idea that "color vision is cognitive" has been advocated by Lars Chittka, an expert on bee vision (Skorupski and Chittka 2011). His interest is in the way that these insects use color to track the location of flowers, and learn which flower types are the richest sources of food. The real distinction here is between approaches that define color vision as a simple response to physical triggers and those that take it to be the processing of stimuli in such a way as to allow specialized interpretations of objects in a scene.

In a much cited article John Mollon describes how color vision in primates aids identification of objects like edible fruit, and the understanding of their material properties. This is possible because changes in color often correlate with changes in chemical composition. An obvious example is ripeness. Mollon ([1989] 1997, 384) states that, "[i]n the case of fructivorous primates, one of the most important functions of trichromatic colour vision must be to judge the state of ripeness of fruit from the external appearance." Although it is hard to gather concrete behavioral evidence that animals use visual cues, rather than olfactory or tactile information to choose ripe fruit (Dominy, 2004), we know that at least for humans color is an extremely significant quality in determining food preference. (The ubiquity of artificial coloring in mass prepared foods is testament to this).

What is more pertinent to the discussion of color and cognition is the evidence that animals' responses to color are flexible and can be adjusted according to the needs of different tasks. This comes across most clearly in the numerous associative learning experiments performed on bees. It is believed that the primary function of color vision in bees is in foraging for flowers laden with nectar. Honeybees are generally attracted to flowers that appear blue or violet to us, or that have UV reflecting petals. But it has long been reported that these insects can readily learn to associate specific hues with nectar rewards, and selectively fly only to certain colored stimuli.[15] Other work shows that bumblebees are sensitive to combinations of ambient light color and flower color, learning to associate a reward from yellow flowers under green light, and from blue flowers under blue light (Lotto and Chittka 2005).

Skorupski and Chittka (2011) contrast true color vision with "wavelength-specific behaviors," reflexive actions that are initiated by the presence of light at certain wavelengths, such as the attraction of male fireflies to light at 545 to 575 nm. They are also keen to distinguish color vision from simple wavelength discrimination, the ability to perceive chromatic contrast in the absence of any achromatic luminance contrast. Instead, they propose, "a cognitive view of colour vision, where colour is used in learning about and classifying regularities in an organism's environment" (Skorupski and Chittka 2011, 252)

What these authors avoid is the reduction of color vision to one particular stereotyped reaction to a particular sort of stimulus property. They take instead a functional approach that examines the role played by color vision in an animal's learning about objects and interaction with them. Color vision is more than an inflexible response to an external stimulus, and likewise, more than just an internal sensation. Again, we find that no one physical property accounts for all of an animal's responses. For example, in Lotto and Chittka's (2005) experiment, bumblebees using color to search for nectar sometimes behaved as if responding to an invariant SSR property of artificial flowers, and sometimes took their cue from wavelength of ambient light.

So color is, among other things, *for* cognition. Experiments on humans also bear this out. Gegenfurtner and Rieger (2000) conducted a study designed to test the contribution of color both to early sensory coding and later cognitive stages such as memorization. They found that compared to black and white images, color images were more easily recognized in a task where observers were asked to distinguish novel from previously viewed pictures.[16] Liebe et al. (2009) found that monkeys and humans benefited

---

15. Frisch (1914) and see Kelber et al. (2003) for recent review. The stimuli typically used are artificial flowers: small pieces of colored paper or plastic that surround a portion of sugar solution.

16. See also Nijboer et al. (2008) who report that the strength of this effect depends on a relatively long time interval between stimuli. And see Ling and Hurlbert (2008) on the relationship between visual memory and color constancy.

equally from color information in a task involving recognition of naturalistic images. Less formally, a study performed on medical students in the 1970s, around the time that color broadcasting became standard, found an improvement in learning and long-term memorization of up to 15 percent when educational programs were shown in color as opposed to black and white (Bergstrom et al. 1974)!

Note that the functions described in this section require some degree of color constancy, for it would be impossible to use color for the identification, recognition, and memorization of objects, without some fairly stable color percept to be associated with an individual object. This constancy need not be absolute in the sense that there is no apparent difference in hue as the lighting changes. Rather, there needs to be some sort of label that stays relatively fixed from one viewing occasion to the next. The gross perceptual categorizations named by our basic color terms do this remarkably well. To know that lemons are yellow is enough of a guide for finding lemons in different situations, even when subtle changes in lighting, shade, and the peel of the fruit cause noticeable changes in perceived hue.

Reports also show that color constancy in humans and animals is not perfect, but that the limited color constancy is a feature of most visual systems examined, including the bee's. One reason why this is so is that color constancy need not involve complex processing in the brain. Some degree of constancy comes about simply from the physiology of photoreceptors, which tend to adapt to chromaticity of ambient stimuli.[17]

4.2.3 Form, Segmentation, and Saliency
Form

The most contentious claim made by Livingstone and Hubel (1987) is that color makes no contribution to the perception of form. They hold that visual pathways for color and form are separate enough to be effectively autonomous: grasping the shape or contours of an object is in no way enhanced by adding chromatic contrast, while patterns that exclusively stimulate the color pathway yield only ghostly, inadequate presentations

---

17. Ives (1912), Smithson and Zaidi (2004), and Smithson (2005). Conversely, Lotto and Chittka (2005) argue that the type of color constancy demonstrated by the bumblebee indicates that more processing is involved than just receptor adaptation.

of form. As we have seen, Mollon ([1989] 1997) takes Livingstone and Hubel's claims to be immediately countered by the existence of Ishihara patterns designed to test for color blindness. People with normal color vision perceive a number that goes unnoticed by those with color deficiency. By definition, such shapes would stimulate only Livingstone and Hubel's color pathway, and not the form pathway, which is sensitive only to luminance (black and white) information. So the existence of color-defined forms tells us either that the putative color pathway is also a form pathway, such that color sensitive neurons are also sensitive to spatial structure, or that there is significant interaction between these two pathways, such that they cannot be truly separate from each other. Such hypotheses have come under empirical scrutiny. For instance, Clifford et al. (2003) presented psychophysical evidence that color sensitive neurons in primary visual cortex are also selective for stimulus orientation (see Flanagan et al. 1990).

If one considers the information available in natural surroundings, it makes perfect sense that color should contribute to form perception. In the world outside the vision laboratory, pure luminance signals often tell an ambiguous story about where objects lie, because of the prevalence of shadows. Mollon (1989a) argues that a clue to the primary function of color vision comes from looking at tasks that color blind viewers find difficult. The problem of detecting objects in cluttered surroundings, with multiple shadows, is exactly analogous to the Ishihara test. Because of the randomness of the lightness of the different dots, the camouflaged number cannot be picked out by an achromatic signal alone. It only stands out against the background because of its difference in color. This corresponds to the everyday task of picking flowers or fruit in dappled, leafy surroundings. Mollon (1989a, 382) concludes that, "[a] primary advantage of colour vision is that it allows us to detect targets against dappled or variegated backgrounds, where lightness is varying randomly."

Segmentation

Color vision helps us perceive form and therefore to segment a visual scene into its component objects. *Segmentation* is the problem of finding the boundaries between different objects in a scene. It is, writes Mollon (1989a, 382), "an important preliminary to the actual recognition of objects." On introspection, it may seem a trivial task because it is something we do so effortlessly. But the difficulties encountered by programmers attempting to have computer systems accomplish the same thing demonstrates the actual challenge involved. The problem is complicated because of the presence of shadows and the way that objects overlap and occlude each other in cluttered scenes. In fact it is in cases where objects are numerous, and when there is "luminance noise" due to a multiplicity of shadows, that color vision seems to be most useful for segmentation. Thus Morgan et al. (1992, 294) write that,

there are sound computational reasons for preferring colour to luminance as a method of segmenting scenes. Non-specular [i.e. matt] objects lit by dappled light will often be more spatially uniform in the shape of their reflectance spectrum than in their luminance.

In other words, in dappled conditions the SSR measured across different parts of an object will be relatively uniform, compared to the wild variations in absolute light levels. Therefore any segmentation of a scene into regions having roughly the same SSR will map onto most changes in material objects, whereas a scene segmentation based not on spectral information, but on total light reflected, will display an array of shadows and highlights as well as objects. As these authors continue, "[o]n functional grounds, we might…expect colour to be a powerful determination of early segmentation, and our results suggest that this is the case." From the analysis of information available to the eye, we have a theoretical reason to think color important for scene segmentation, and this prediction is borne out by empirical study.

Saliency

Color makes things stand out—a cluster of pink flowers will be obvious against a busy background of leaves, a lady in a pink hat will stand out from the crowd. This is the idea of visual saliency. Psychophysicists study saliency by means of visual search experiments, where the task is to locate an odd object (the *target*) in a field of different objects (the *distracters*). Tresiman and Gelade (1980) developed the *feature integration theory* to explain the results of a series of experiments measuring how time taken to locate the target varied as a function of the number of distracters. For some types of targets and distracters, the search time would remain constant, no matter how many distracters were added to the field. The target is said simply to "pop out." Color is a prime example of a popping out feature. The saliency of color differences is thought to underlie many of the important visual functions of color. As we have seen, a basic challenge faced by the visual system is that of segmenting the scene into a meaningful array of separate objects. Color is an important cue for segmentation, and this has been linked to its attentional saliency (Wichmann et al. 2002, 511).

The question of how a scene is to be segmented, and what objects are made salient, depends on the perceptual system of the animal. That, in turn, depends on its ecological niche and lifestyle—what sort of food it eats, what its conspecifics look like, what regions it inhabits. Given that no system would be able to discriminate every spectral stimulus—nor would it be useful to, given the information explosion entailed—color visual systems appear to be tuned to particular objects of interest (Osorio and Vorobyev 2005; but see Chittka and Briscoe 2001). This leads to the important point that there is no absolute best color vision system. Even for a task like scene segmentation, any "best" segmentation will be relative to the animal. For a hypothetical fruit-eating animal, an ideal segmentation of an image of fruit-laden tree, for example, gives leaves a uniform shade while the different fruits show strong chromatic contrast against the leaves, and take on a range of discriminable hues (to enhance the visual recognition of different varieties of fruit). Conversely, for a hypothetical leaf-eating creature, it would be beneficial to have a color visual system that can discriminate leaves of different plants, and can tell young leaves apart from old. Again, it is not helpful to think of color vision as a detecting instrument. There is no one property that color vision picks up. Color vision makes possible different ways of enhancing the salience of perceived objects. How this is done depends on the actual color visual system of the animal, and its specific perceptual needs. Color vision could not serve this purpose by detecting any one physical property.

It has often been argued that the problem of spotting ripe fruit in a dappled context of green foliage was a driver of the evolution of primate trichromacy.[18] Most mammals are dichromats, possessing short wavelength and longer wavelength sensitive cones in their central retina. Primate

18. For example, Regan et al. (2001), Sumner and Mollon (2000a, b), and Osorio and Vorobyev (1996, 2005).

trichromacy, where both medium and long wavelength sensitive cones are present, is an evolutionarily recent mutation and scientists have sought a functional explanation for it. It is still an issue of some controversy in the literature, since primate trichromacy cannot be said to be *optimized* for foraging for fruit or edible leaves, and has not been proved behaviorally useful (Hiramatsu et al. 2008; see Jacobs 2009 for review).

Still, none of my claims depend on the truth of the frugivory hypothesis. The important point is that color vision is linked to our perception of the shapes of objects, recognition of objects against cluttered backgrounds, and scene segmentation, and there are sound computational reasons why color should be useful for such tasks. These lie in the nature of the physical signal that comes from spectral contrast, as opposed to achromatic, luminance contrast. To summarize, in many lighting situations in which the luminance signal is varying randomly, the spectral signal will remain correlated with object boundaries. This is the reason for widespread usefulness of color in segmenting scenes and perceiving edges and boundaries. We should not be overly impressed with our ability to interpret black and white film and photographic images, or read too much into the fact that "color blind" people only appear minimally impaired. For one thing, most "color blind" individuals in the population do have dichromatic color vision. That would be enough to support most segmentation tasks. Furthermore sitting back and watching a movie is not the same task as hunting in a forest or even negotiating a busy city street. In real life situations where objects need to be spotted and recognized virtually instantaneously, we would likely feel the lack of the fast disambiguation of objects afforded by color vision, as evidenced by Sacks's case study of achromatopsia.

4.3   Color as Material

An interesting demonstration of the role of color in the perception of objects and scene layout is found in the work of Kingdom et al. (2004), who show that color vision helps disambiguate shadows from objects in a scene. We effortlessly recognize which edges and borders are due to shadows and not due to changes in material objects. But it needs to be appreciated that the disambiguation of shadows from objects is a significant problem that the visual system must confront. If shadows were not disambiguated, it would not be clear to us that the tree's shadow cast on the ground is not some dark object lying on the earth, or some alteration in the material of the ground. What Kingdom's group found psychophysically was that achromatic luminance edges that are not aligned with chromatic edges are more likely to be perceived as shadow borders, and luminance edges that are aligned with chromatic edges are less likely to be perceived as shadow borders. This is not just a recondite psychophysical finding. A piece of anecdotal evidence of the importance of color vision for shadow recognition comes from Sacks's case study of cerebral achromatopsia. Sacks (1995, 7) relates how the patient had trouble distinguishing shadows from changes in material structure: "[a] major problem occurred when he drove, in that he tended to misinterpret shadows as cracks or ruts in the road and would brake or swerve suddenly to avoid these."

Kingdom's results also demonstrate the interdependency of form and color vision, for example, that "[a]lthough shadows are primarily luminance-defined features, their perception appears to be significantly impacted by colour" (Kingdom et al. 2004, 913). According to the coloring book hypothesis, luminance-defined features should only be processed by the achromatic form channel, and their interpretation should not be influenced by color information. This work shows that the opposite is true.

Kingdom's interpretation of these findings is that the visual system operates on the assumption that color informs us about material differences between objects. He calls this the "color-is-material assumption" (Kingdom 2008).[19] It is a heuristic employed by the visual system to the effect that color is likely to be informative about material properties in the scene. The role of color in our perception of scenes is shaped by prior assumptions about typical correlations in the natural environment, namely that chromatic borders are associated with material changes, whereas achromatic borders are not. As Kingdom et al. (2004, 913) write, their findings are "consistent with the idea that the human visual system has inbuilt

19. In this book I refer to it as the "color-as-material" assumption to avoid any suggestion that we are always compelled to interpret color as being a material property, and never see colored lights, shadows, and the like. The heuristic can, of course, be overridden by conflicting visual evidence.

assumptions about the origin of colour-luminance relationships found in natural scenes."[20]

The "color-shading effect" is another example of the color-as-material assumption at work (see figure 4.4). An achromatic luminance grating pattern gives no impression of rippling or depth. But, if the pattern is superimposed with a pattern of red and green stripes, an impression of corrugation can be observed. According to Kingdom (2003), the colored pattern is assumed to be due to a material surface, and the black and white superimposed grating is then assumed to be a shading pattern, due to changes in depth of the material surface (i.e., the peaks of the surface are light, the valleys shadowed). If a red-green pattern is superimposed on the black-white one, the effect of depth is abolished.

These analyses do not attribute any unlikely reasoning processes to visual neurons. Rather, Kingdom's idea should be interpreted in terms of the Bayesian approach to brain function. Many low-level visual operations can be modeled in terms of Bayesian inferences to what was the most likely external cause of the neurons' firing pattern. Such inferences are affected by a *prior* term that captures the statistics of the relevant external stimuli, one that says that external cause is most probable, independent of incoming neural information (Rao et al. 2002; Kersten et al. 2004). Kingdom is saying that the visual system acts as if under the influence of prior knowledge that a color change is likely to be accompanied by a material change, and that a luminance change unaccompanied by a color change is probably not a material change. This prior can be overridden if there is a strong probability of an alternative scenario.

When discussing color phenomenology, I believe that we should look to such "inbuilt assumptions" in order to understand the outer-directedness of color experience. Color vision informs us about material surfaces, how they are arranged in space, how they are different from each other. A difference in color is interpreted as a difference in material. But, in order for this to happen, there need be no attribution of an intrinsic chromatic property

---

20. The phrase "color-luminance relationships found in natural scenes" should not be understood as assuming the realist thesis that colors are instantiated in scenes, independently of perceivers. Instead, the phrase can be glossed as, "relationships between spectral and luminance information typical of natural scenes." Kingdom (2011, 10–11) explicitly rejects the realist interpretation of the color-is-material assumption and endorses the relationist interpretation of Chirimuuta (2011).

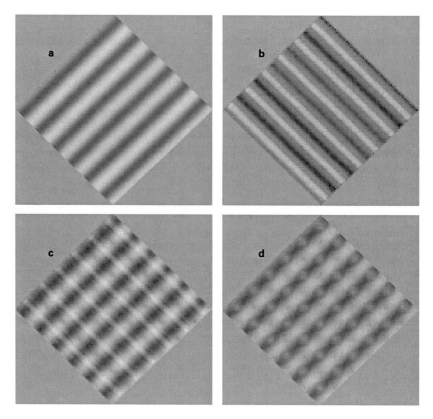

Figure 4.4
Color-shading effect. A sinusoidal luminance grating (a) and red-green equiluminant
grating (b) are not found to elicit an impression of depth or corrugation. But when
these two images are superimposed (c), there is a strong depth effect. This effect is
abolished if a colored grating is then superimposed onto the luminance grating (d).
Image reprinted with permission from S. Shevell and F. Kingdom (2008). Color in
complex scenes. *Annual Review of Psychology* 59, 143–66. Copyright © 2008 by Annual Reviews.

to any of these surfaces. Outer-directedness need not entail ontological commitment. Red and yellow contrast with each other. Because of this we can know just by looking that skins of strawberries and lemons are made of different kinds of matter. All this can be known even if there is no special red or yellow property that strawberries and lemons possess. As I will argue in chapter 8, the alleged phenomenological fact, that colors are presented in visual experience as properties intrinsic to physical surfaces, is an intellectual step beyond the manifest color experience.

Why should color vision work like this? The answer is in the nature of light information around us, as introduced above in the discussion of form and saliency. Numerous scientists have noted the association between the perception of color and material change.[21] Indeed it is a "sensible" assumption for the visual system to make for the very reason that edges defined by color can consistently indicate material changes, whereas achromatic edges are not so well correlated with material changes. This is because of the prevalence of shadows in natural viewing. Since the spectral composition of light reflecting off any surface is more constant within object boundaries than across them, wavelength information can be used to differentiate objects. The color associated with each surface, ultimately derived from wavelength discrimination, will be roughly stable even when there are shadows.

What is more, the visual system is endowed with various color constancy mechanisms that stabilize perceived color under conditions of changing illumination. As Osorio and Vorobyev (2005, 1745) write:

Chromaticity is probably relatively stable (constant) in natural illumination, so that it gives information about surface reflectance, pigmentation and other material properties....Colour vision is therefore likely to be important for object detection or classification.

Thus color may turn out to be the best indicator of change and continuity in material surfaces. If any two surfaces differ in material constitution, it is likely that they will differ in SSR. This difference in SSR will probably be perceived as a difference in color, so this chromatic contrast reliably indicates a boundary between objects. I use the words "likely" and "probably" here because there are significant exceptions, namely instances

---

21. See, for example, Rubin and Richards (1982), Switkes et al. (1988), Maximov (2000), Gegenfurtner and Kiper (2003), and Osorio and Vorobyev (2005).

of metamerism where two surfaces have very different SSRs but are perceived to be identical in color. These create problems for the simple reduction of color to SSR, and the claim that color vision represents SSR (see section 3.4.2). Even though the use of color vision for finding out about objects is made possible by our having some degree of color constancy, this can be achieved without the recovery or representation of SSR (see section 3.3.2; Hurlbert 2013).

4.3.1 Conclusions

The central message of this chapter is aptly captured by perceptual psychologist Steven Shevell (2012, A337):

[t]he influences of chromatic and non-chromatic features are reciprocal. Shape affects color perception, but also color affects perceived shape. The direction of motion of a chromatic object can alter its perceived color, but also the similarity of colors among objects can influence their perceived direction of motion. Studying color in isolation, even if possible, would neglect basic properties of neural pathways as well as the full role of chromatic coding in visual perception.

Yet, at the end of this long review of psychophysical and neuroscientific findings, it is worth considering how all this relates to the philosophical problem. It might be objected by someone committed to realism that all I have shown is that color vision makes a causal contribution to the processing of other perceived properties, which is to say, there is no ground for claiming that the function of color vision is not the detection of colors but rather the enhanced perception of things and scenes. For example, the hypothesis that primate trichromacy evolved in order to aid the discrimination of fruits and leaves, or the observation that the visual systems of many animals are tuned to the color signals of conspecifics, might lead one to think that *the* function of color vision (what color vision evolved to do) is the detection of particular surface properties of objects, and these properties may be identified with the colors.[22]

In response to this concern, it is worth considering the sheer range of observed functions of color vision described above. Unless one has an antecedent commitment to realism, and the detection framework, there is no reason to privilege the frugivory hypothesis over the hypothesis that color vision evolved in order to facilitate lightness constancy, or in order to

---

22. I thank Edouard Machery and Alison Springle for raising this point.

enhance scene segmentation. Indeed the fact that primate trichromacy is a very recent mutation speaks against the idea that this could be a general account of the evolution of color vision. As to the signaling hypothesis, nothing can be known from the fossil record about the colors potentially signaled by the Cambrian creatures whose eyes first employed color vision. Thus the claim appears impossible to substantiate. However, what we do know about the ecologically specific color adaptations of today's marine creatures, such as fish, is that they typically serve to enhance contrast between the watery background and the animals swimming either above or below them (Lythgoe 1972). At the same time color signaling is an obvious characteristic of marine ecosystems such as coral reefs, where intensely colorful life forms abound. If I were forced to speculate on the "original" adaptational factor that led to color vision, I would bet on contrast enhancement in the ancient oceans rather than signaling. What is more, in my theorizing about color I give priority to the information that we have about the functions of color vision in contemporary species, and I prefer to put aside speculations about their evolutionary origin and priority. What is uncontroversial is that these functions are various, and there is no theory-independent reason to assert that SSR detection is the primary function and that the others are secondary.

So what further bearing do findings reviewed in this chapter have on the philosophical debate? For one thing, it drops us a big hint that accounts of color experience that have been assumed by philosophers are informed by the narrow, coloring in account of the function of chromatic vision. In chapters 7 and 8 we will see that replacement of the coloring in picture with the coloring for account allows us to defuse standard objections to relationism and the new relationist theory, color adverbialism. In the next chapter I discuss how realists and antirealists have all assumed a correspondence account of perceptual success. This is closely related to the coloring in model: a color perceptual state is veridical if it correctly represents a chromatic property intrinsic to an object's surface, and if not it is falsidical. The idea of color vision that has emerged in this chapter is of a multifaceted sort of visual enhancement. It does not make sense to evaluate the success of color perceptual states in terms of correspondence to specific color properties, but instead in terms of the other visual functions, and the behaviors, that are made possible by the state.

5 Perceptual Pragmatism

5.1 Naturalized Color Ontology—The Very Idea

In this chapter I ask whether or not it is feasible to attempt to derive a color ontology from perceptual science—to find a metaphysics within the psychophysics, so to speak. As we will see shortly, sometimes clear conceptual claims do emerge from the scientific community, ones that seem to make transparent the ontological commitments of the empirical endeavor. Yet there is a striking lack of consensus among scientific theorists. So the danger in taking any one such claim to be *the* naturalistic color ontology is that with a little more digging, one easily uncovers alternative claims that bolster rival ontologies. To illustrate this point, in the next subsection I discuss some quotations from vision scientists that can be taken as expressions of the three important theory types: realism, antirealism, and relationism. On pain of inconsistency, an ontology of color cannot simply be read off from scientists' definitions and theoretical commitments.

This result might suggest that there can be no ground for an argument that relationism is the kind of philosophical theory that harmonizes best with perceptual science. So in section 5.2 I set out on a different track. I begin with a naturalized *epistemology* of perception, asking how the truth and informativeness of perceptual states is understood by contemporary perceptual science. I argue that the commonplace idea that perceptual activity aims at *correspondence* between external stimulus and inner states should be replaced by the pragmatic ideal of *usefulness*. This follows from some truisms of perceptual science, the primary point being that perceptual systems do not deliver any uniquely true description of world; instead, each description is partial and interest relative. Thus, while one cannot read off a consistent ontology of color from scientists' theoretical statements, an epistemology of perception can be derived from the scientific "orthodoxy," and this is significant for the problem of color. In section 5.3 I spell out the ontological lesson that was implicit here, arguing that color relationism offers important resources for getting clear on the scientific understanding of perceptual success, and that it suggests an interesting avenue toward rethinking what we mean by realism.

5.1.1 A Spectrum of Views

In a *Journal of Philosophy* article Hardin (2003a, 191) writes that "it is a curious sociological fact that many philosophers, but very few visual scientists, are color realists." To be a color realist is to hold that colors are perceiver-independent properties that are instantiated on the surfaces of things, whether or not anybody is there to look. What the realist denies is that color is in any way a by-product of neural activity. In agreement with Hardin's antirealism, vision scientists have variously claimed that color is identifiable with states of the brain, or that it is created or constructed by the brain:

At this point in time our ideas concerning the nature of color are still largely speculative. For now, the most convincing account, in conflict with few if any facts, is that color is identical to a particular brain state. (Kuehni 1997, 26)

We know from psychophysical and neurophysiological investigations that color is created somewhere in the brain, although the exact location of this process is still unknown, and we even have no idea what entities the sensations called color are....In short, colours appear only at a first naïve glance to be located in objects. (Backhaus and Menzel 1992, 28)[1]

However, in making his sociological claim, Hardin is ignoring the numerous scientists working in the field of computational color constancy who do express views akin to realism. Of course, color realism appears in a number of different varieties. On the one hand, primitivists believe that colors inhere to the surfaces of things in exactly the manner that we experience them. That is to say, the world beyond our perception is a full Technicolor one: the saturated reds, whites, and pinks of geraniums *are there* in the petals just as they *appear* to me. There is no split at all between appearance and reality. As far as I know, no vision scientist has expressed such a

---

1. Quoted by Byrne and Hilbert (2003). See Sekuler and Blake (1985, 181), Goldstein (1989, 140), and Zeki (1983, 764).

commitment. On the other hand, physicalism or reflectance realism posits that color experiences are simply visual representations of objective, physical properties such as SSR. Thus, even though a physical property like SSR could not be pink in the way we commonly experience that hue, experiences of pink could be the "signs" of physical properties that elicit them. The SSR *is* pink, while the visual sensation we associate with pink should be thought of as a *representation of pink*.

Similarly Maloney (2003, 285–86) reviews his color constancy research and introduces the notion of "intrinsic color." He defines this as the "objective correlate of the perceived color of a surface" that, he adds, could be measured by some computation of the surface's reflectance. Like the color physicalists, Maloney interprets the phenomenon of constancy as our perception of a stable color property existing independently of us (Hilbert 1987, 65; Tye 2000, 147–48; see also section 3.3.2).

In order to study how humans achieve color constancy, it is fairly intuitive to frame the problem in a realist way: to say that color constancy is about the recovery of a hypothetical objective property. This leads researchers to posit primary-like qualities—"intrinsic colors"—and then develop models of how these might be recovered. Yet, as I have discussed elsewhere (Chirimuuta 2008), this is not the *only* theoretical approach to constancy. So color physicalism is not a compulsory commitment of color constancy research, even though it does harmonize with some color constancy models.[2]

I now want to emphasize that the idea that color is (at least in part) created or constructed by the brain *is* compatible with color relationism. The core relationist thesis is that colors are "constituted in terms of a relation between (*inter alia*) objects and subjects" (Cohen 2009, 8), and one way to cash out this perceiver-dependence is in the idea that the brain has a role in "constructing" color by partly governing how chromatic properties are perceptually manifest.

Thus, as Giere (2006, 32) observes, one of the textbook passages that is frequently quoted as an example of antirealism is as much an expression of relationism: "There may be *light* of different wavelengths independent of an observer, but there is no *color* independent of an observer" (Palmer 1999, 97; emphasis in original). Palmer's primary point here is that we cannot

---

2. But see Hurlbert (2013), a vision scientist who has recently argued that color constancy research is *not* compatible with reflectance realism.

identify color with a perceiver-independent physical property. As Fairchild (1998, xv) also writes, "without the human observer there is no color." This is, of course, in keeping the relationist thesis that color must be understood in terms of the relationship between perceivers (human or nonhuman) and objects. An antirealist theory like Hardin's only follows *if* one assumes that perceiver-dependence is incompatible with the reality of color.

Here is another statement of relationism from the vision science literature, one that could not also be interpreted along antirealist lines:

> The adoption of the psychophysical position not only admits but asserts that an evaluation of color has an inherently medial nature; implying at once an appraiser, the human observer, and an object of appraisal, radiant energy. This course seems to be amply justified on purely philosophical grounds, but, if less academic justification is desired, the purely practical considerations are fully sufficient. (Jones 1943, 542)

This quotation comes from a fascinating document published in the *Journal of the Optical Society of America*. The author, Loyd Jones, was chair of a committee appointed with the task of putting definitions and concepts of color into good working order. Jones reports on a series of debates between color scientists (psychologists, psychophysicists, and colorimetrists) that preceded the committee's eventual report.[3] The committee, formed in 1933, was given the task of replacing an earlier definition of color as a *sensation*, or as Jones (1943, 536) puts it as a "purely subjective concept."

The new proposal was to define color as a "psychophysical concept." In effect this is a relational approach where, as stated in the quotation above, color must be defined in terms of relations to perceiving subjects and to a physical quantity (radiant energy). It is "a characteristic of light dependent on human vision" (Jones 1943, 541). Interestingly, the first reason Jones gives us for this shift is a felt need for consistency with the standard psychophysical (i.e., relational) definition of *light*.[4] The second reason stated for adopting the psychophysical definition is the need for a conception of

---

3. This was published as *The Science of Color* (Jones 1953).

4. "*Light as a Psychophysical Concept....* It is evident that light, as thus conceived, is neither a physical nor a psychical quantity. It is rather a psychophysical notion, involving c.g.s. units, on the other hand, and a psychical dimension, which we may designate as ψ, on the other. Light can neither be identified with brilliance nor with radiant energy. It has the properties of both, taken together" (Troland 1929, quoted by Jones 1943, 540). Perhaps today's prejudice would be to define light purely in physical terms.

color suitable for the practices of colorimetry.[5] As Jones (1943, 539) writes, "the measurement of color, as it is practiced at the present time, is admittedly not a purely psychological measurement, nor, on the other hand, are such measurements purely physical." Rather, they are somehow both—relating the psychological to the physical.

We have seen that vision science presents no unified account of its ontological commitments. Perhaps it is the case that the different practical demands of many subdisciplines of the science each push for a conception of color that best suits the tasks in hand. Thus the professed conceptions of color are various. In this vein Wilson (2006, 456–57) describes how the contrasting exigencies of color *design* (e.g., painting and graphic design), and color *reproduction* (e.g., manufacture and use of dyes) have fostered quite different conceptual norms. In the former domain, appearance of the color in the circumstances in which the final product will be viewed is of primary consideration. Therefore attention must be paid to the influence that illumination and context have on human visual responses, and color is treated in a more relationist way. If, however, the practice concerns consistent reproduction of a particular color, such as in clothing manufacture, then the best way to achieve this is by stipulating a normal observer and standard viewing conditions, and then proceeding to ignore the perceiver-dependence of color appearance. This fosters a more realist theoretical stance.

If this picture is broadly correct, and if our only methodology is this rather direct reading off of theoretical commitments from the scientific literature, then the result will at best be a set of naturalized ontolog*ies* of color. However, it is my thesis here that there is a path from vision science to a more unequivocal and revisionary metaphysical view. This path will not be direct. In the next section I outline an *epistemology* of perception that is implicit in visual science, and in section 5.3 I unpack the ontological lesson.

5.2   Perception as Interaction

We have seen that because of the lack of consensus between different research traditions there is a serious problem with any attempt to read off

5. According to the definition of Fairchild (1998, xvi), the business of colorimetry is to provide "the fundamental color-measurement techniques that are used to specify stimuli in terms of their sensory potential for an average human observer."

a naturalistic color ontology from scientists' conceptual claims. So how might perceptual science offer revisions to color ontology? My proposal is that we should first take an excursion to the naturalistic epistemology of perception. By this I mean we should examine the ways in which scientists have addressed questions such as the following:[6]

• What does it take for a perceptual state to be *right*?

• How does perception inform us and other animals about the environment?

• Under what circumstances can perceptual states be said to be illusory?

In order to recover the answers to these questions that are implicit in perceptual science, I will begin by setting out four "truisms" of the discipline. These are commonplace assumptions that I believe are almost universally accepted by researchers. I will then argue that by considering these points, one is able to outline a minimal epistemology of perception that is assumed in scientific research. This is the view I call *perceptual pragmatism*, and it should be taken as a philosophical articulation of the minimal perceptual epistemology that is in the background of the empirical research. Perceptual pragmatism can be characterized through the contrast with a perhaps more intuitive, and philosophically dominant epistemology of perception. Whereas the dominant view takes perception to be a kind of detection of objects and properties in the world that aims at a matching between inner and outer states, perceptual pragmatism treats perception as a kind of interaction with the world that is more active and interest relative than the rather passive process of detection. On the pragmatist view, the ideal perceptual state is simply one that is useful to the perceiver, not one that can make a claim of correspondence to perceiver-independent states of affairs. So, following the delineation of the four truisms, I will flesh out the perceptual pragmatist approach by discussing the detection–interaction,

6. Note that this notion of "epistemology" does not give an account of knowledge with a capital K. My account really is delimited by these three questions. However, other philosophers have asked under what circumstances the perceptual states of reason-giving agents like adult human beings provide warrant for their beliefs, and how one can refer to perceptual states in order to justify one's beliefs before other reason-giving agents. This examination of the rational role of experience is simply not my project here. See Gupta (2006) and McDowell (2011) for recent discussions.

correspondence–utility, and passive–active contrasts. Here are the four truisms or starting assumptions:

1. Perception is an action-guiding interaction between perceiver and environment.

2. Perceptual systems do not deliver a uniquely true description of the world.

3. Each description is partial.

4. Each description is interest relative.

The first point, that the process of perception is an action-guiding interaction between an animal and the extra-dermal environment, seems hardly contestable. What bears emphasis, though, is that I have deliberately focused on "interaction" as an (almost) neutral starting point. To say that perception is an interaction is to say simply that when an animal perceives, something goes on in the environment and something happens in the animal, and that these two goings-on are related to one another in an important way. One *could* go further and say that this interaction is supported by a particular type of causal mechanism. But that would be to load up with theoretical commitments that were not there at the outset. In section 5.2.2 I talk about one very entrenched way of characterizing the interaction: the detection model.

The significance of this first point is that it highlights the fact that perception is not an inner process like (ideally) the circulation of blood. As such, in order to understand perception researchers have to direct attention both to the inner mechanisms of the sensory system and the environment that they are responsive to. This is common ground between researchers of very different theoretical persuasions—Gibsonians and Marrians, ecologists, and computationalists.[7] Furthermore it is uncontroversial that perception is there for guiding activity—finding food, avoiding predators, and so on. The implications of this are discussed in section 5.2.1.

The second item might sound more contentious. But let me be clear that by "description" I do not mean anything so concrete as a "representation." The point is just that if one considers perception beyond the narrow human example, one finds an incredible variety of different kinds of sensory systems

---

7. See notes 13 and 15; Mausfeld (2010) is one dissenting voice here.

that make possible an array of states that humans literally cannot imagine.[8] Thomas Nagel, famously, could not imagine what it would be like to be a bat and fly around at night guided by echolocation. For myself, I cannot imagine what it would be like to be a homing pigeon endowed with pentachromacy, magnetoreception, and possible sensitivity to the direction of polarization of light. In some sense the perceptual systems of the bat and the pigeon must be "describing" the world differently. Nobody would argue that any of these creatures has *the* correct way of apprehending the world. This is because each description is partial, as stated in point 3.[9] For instance, what the honeybees gain in the ability to detect patterns of ultraviolet light, they lose (in comparison with humans) in their inability to see patterns of long wavelength light; dogs may hear at higher frequency than we can, but we can see with greater spatial acuity. It is beyond doubt that no animal who has ever walked the Earth has ever been responsive to all possible perceptual stimuli (i.e., *all* the frequencies of sound waves that some animals can hear, all the wavelengths of light that some animals can see, all the possible chemicals that some animals smell and taste, plus all of the exotic sensory modalities like sensitivity to magnetic fields; see Wolfe et al. 2006, 3), simply because it takes biological resources to build a sensory system, and these resources are finite.

Since animals are limited in what they may sense, it pays to choose wisely. The fourth point follows from the third. In saying that a description is "interest relative" what I mean is that the practical needs that a perceptual system must meet will have a bearing on what is perceived and the manner in which it will be perceived. For example, a species that uses vocalizations as a means of communication will have an auditory system sensitive to those sounds; there is no point having a sense of taste if it can never discriminate nutritious from poisonous foodstuffs. This point again should be uncontroversial, though I have been careful to phrase it in a way that will not immediately raise accusations of adaptationism. In his book *Seeing, Doing, and Knowing* Mohan Matthen provides an important discussion of the tight connection between perception and the practicalities of life, but he goes as far as to say that each system has evolved to serve a particular function (Matthen 2005, 206). It is not hard to find

8. See Prete (2004) to get a sense of the alienness of invertebrates' sensory worlds. A classic study on this theme is von Uexküll ([1935] 1957).

9. "[S]ensory systems are actually filtering systems that let in only the information that is potentially biologically meaningful" (Prete 2004, 3).

counterexamples to this claim—such as creatures that spend their lives buried in mud but have perfectly good color visual systems (Chittka and Briscoe 2001). So my assertion is just that at a certain level of generality it makes sense to say that perceptual systems serve a function and that this implies that the "descriptions" they yield are interest relative.[10] I will now say more about the perceptual pragmatist account by comparing it with the nonpragmatist foil.

5.2.1 Correspondence and Utility

At the heart of the view I call perceptual pragmatism is the rejection of the correspondence theory of perceptual accuracy. In answer to the question "what does it take for a perceptual state to be right?" the perceptual pragmatist replies "it must work—it must be a *useful* guide to the surrounding environment." This is in contrast to a view more dominant in the philosophy of perception that says a perceptual state is right if it is veridical—if its contents correctly correspond to states of affairs in the surrounding environment.[11] If the rejection of correspondence as the standard of evaluation for perceptual states is the more radical move, why should one be tempted

---

10. See Goldstein (1999, 258–59): "perception evolved for the purpose of survival, and the variations in perceptual mechanisms we can observe across species reflect the specific survival needs of each animal. One of the best ways to draw a connection between perceptual mechanisms and survival is to consider the eye—a structure found throughout the animal kingdom, but in different forms that are designed to meet each animal's specific needs."

11. But note that the correspondence theory is no longer uniquely dominant in the philosophical debate over truth (Glanzberg 2013). Also the commitments of pragmatist philosophy have been contested from the very beginning of the movement. In introducing the term "perceptual pragmatism," I do not mean to claim the whole tradition but only to allude to a source of inspiration. One theme of American pragmatist philosophy—at least in the more "relativist" lineage from William James (James [1907] 1981, lecture VI) to Richard Rorty (e.g., Rorty 1979)—has been the rejection of the correspondence theory of truth (see Misak 2013 for discussion and criticism of this lineage). In James's late philosophy of mind, and in the work of his student Edwin Holt, the implications of this for the understanding of perception were brought out. As Heft (2001, 80) writes, "Only if the relation of knower and known is accepted as one of 'inside and outside' does it make sense to treat error and illusion as correspondence problems. It is precisely this sort of distinction that James's radical empiricism, and Holt's elaboration of it, does not accept. Consciousness is not a mental state as such; it is a *relation*, an 'awareness of' an object of experience. The notion of correspondence does not fit with this type of framework. Two distinct domains are not being mapped accurately or imperfectly onto one another; rather, awareness is relational." As Heft (2001) discusses, the James–Holt tradition was a major inspiration for the ecological psychology movement (Gibson 1966, [1979] 1986).

by it? The primary reason is that it gets to a core commitment of perceptual science.

Consider the question "what are perceptual states for?" A natural response is "to tell us what is where." This chimes easily with the correspondence way of thinking, but it is not the most fundamental of responses. The answer that predominates in perceptual science is "to help you to live by guiding your activity in the world,"[12] and "telling you what is where" is but one way to achieve this. From the naturalistic perspective, having something that works is the key constraint on perceptual systems, not accuracy for the sake of accuracy. Something like the contrast between correspondence and utility based analyses is discussed by Palmer (1999, 6–7) who writes that "perception is *not* a clear window onto reality, but an actively constructed, meaningful model of the environment that allows perceivers to predict what will happen in the future so that they can take appropriate action and thereby increase their chances of survival."

Consider the much abused example of the frog's "bug detector"—the reflexive tongue lash in response to peripheral visual stimulation. Following Barlow (1953), it is commonly held that this visual-motor loop serves the frog by finding and capturing food. The implication is that it would be inappropriate to impose some abstract standard of correctness on the frog's visual states, such as the precision with which they relate the fly's shape and contour, or even the ability to deliver internal states that reliably correlate with the presence of specific external objects. In order to interpret and analyze *what* the animal selects to find out about its environment, and *how* that information is conveyed, one must be cognizant of the needs, interests of the animal, and its behavioral repertoire (e.g., whether it is nocturnal or diurnal). This is because perceptual "descriptions" are inherently selective and interest relative. In ignoring this, one risks a distorted image of one's topic of enquiry and will likely forgo valuable insights.[13]

---

12. For example, "Human senses have evolved to help us act in ways that encourage our survival" (Wolfe et al. 2006, 3).

13. In the concluding chapter of the textbook *Visual Perception* the authors reject the Gibsonian ecological framework in favor of the Marrian computational one. Even so, they assert that the insights of ecological psychology are a crucial component for understanding visual representation and processing. They write that "[i]t is in understanding how simple animals such as flies perceive their surroundings that a

However, that is not to say that accuracy in reporting the distinct shapes of flies is always irrelevant. If the frog lives in a location where almost identical looking edible and poisonous flies coexist, then the animal will need a system sensitive to their subtle differences. In other circumstances, having a more acute visual system could even be detrimental to the frog, namely because of the additional cost it would take to build a larger, more discriminating eye.[14] The question "what does it take for a perceptual state to be right?" can only be addressed by first considering the system's function or use. Correspondence and accuracy are secondary considerations. In other words, the application of accuracy conditions to actual biological systems is not a meaningful exercise without prior specification of the function of the system.[15]

5.2.2   Detection and Interaction

It might well be objected that the correspondence view that I have just sketched as a foil for perceptual pragmatism is a straw man: for no one

---

combination of the two approaches [ecological and computational] has achieved most success, specifying the ecological problems vision must solve for the animal, devising appropriate algorithms, and unravelling their implementation by the nervous system" (Bruce et al. 1996, 379).

14. "Visual information is only useful if the animal can improve its behavior on the basis of it. For every species there is thus a limit to how much spatial information it can use. There is, of course, also a cost involved in making and maintaining eyes, and it is this final balance which determines how much vision each species can afford" (Land and Nilsson 2002, 10).

15. It might be objected that the computational tradition in vision research, exemplified by the work of David Marr and discussed in detail by Burge (2010), is very much committed to the correspondence-detection model. As Marr (1982, 6) notes, this tradition is an extension of representational theories of mind that were dominant from the seventeenth to nineteenth centuries, so it is hardly surprising that it shares something of the correspondence thinking that characterizes this approach to the philosophy of mind and epistemology. Yet even so, Marr (1982, 32) makes it very clear that any analysis of the representations that on this view constitute perceptual states must make reference to the particular tasks for which those representations are suited: "Vision...is used in such a bewildering variety of ways that the visual systems of different animals must differ significantly from one another. Can the type of formulation that I have been advocating, in terms of representations and processes, possibly prove adequate for them all? I think so. The general point here is that because vision is used by different animals for such a wide variety of purposes, it is inconceivable that all seeing animals use the same representations; each can confidently be expected to use one or more representations that are nicely tailored to the owner's own purposes." It follows that no one of these representations is *the* correct description of the environment. Each representation can be assessed according to how well it enables the perceiver to do particular tasks.

would claim that perceptual systems should be evaluated by standards entirely abstracted from any ecological and behavioral context. To make the contrast between the two outlooks clearer, I will now say more about an initially appealing way of understanding perception in terms of inner-outer correspondence: the detection model. In seeing the limitations of this model, the virtues of perceptual pragmatism will come into sharper focus.

In response to the question "how does perception inform us and other animals about the environment?" the perceptual pragmatist will reply "in virtue of some kind of perceiver-environment interaction." This leaves the nature of the interaction open, for the time being, though I will say more about it in section 5.2.3 below. In contrast, someone committed to the correspondence view will typically give a more pointed reply: "because perceptual systems are able to detect surrounding objects and their properties." This process of detection need not be restricted to simple sensory transduction, such as the photoreceptors' detection of incoming photons; it may involve a complex reverse optics calculation or Bayesian inference from proximal sensory stimulation to the most probable distal object (Burge 2010). Yet the basic idea is that the perceiver is concerned to know what is where, and that some elaborate process of detection is employed in order to achieve this.[16]

I will follow Kathleen Akins in rejecting this model for the reason that it becomes stretched or empty when one examines real perceptual systems.[17] The correspondence-detection model begins with the idea that perceptual systems report on the external world "without exaggeration or omission" (Akins 1996, 344). The governing metaphor is that sensory and perceptual

---

16. Pautz (2013) characterizes an influential version of the detection theory, which he calls "tracking intensionalism": "The rough idea is that you sensorily represent an objective sensible quality (on this view, a physical property), and are thereby aware of it, just in case you undergo an internal state (a 'representation') that 'registers' or 'tracks' the instantiation of that property by external items." Dretske (1995) and Tye (2000) are influential proponents of this view, with Millikan (1989) cited as a more sophisticated variant. Akins (1996) targets philosophers as divergent in their opinions as Churchland and Churchland (1981), Dennett (1987), and Fodor (1990) for their shared detectionist commitment.

17. Akins's (1996) article fames the discussion in terms of *sensory* systems and states. So one might object that the sensation-perception distinction means that this work is irrelevant here. I doubt this because the topic of the paper is the aboutness or intentionality of sensory states, and any robust sensation-perception distinction must treat perceptual, rather than sensory states as intentional (about the external environment).

systems are like a technician's measuring devices—for instance, that our systems for thermoreception are like the body's own thermometers. But actual perceptual systems do not conform to the expectation that they veridically report on external events without bias or distortion. Instead, they are typically "narcissistic," which is to say that their ineradicable self-interestedness gets in the way of their ever achieving a neutral (i.e., perceiver-unrelated) view of the world (Akins 1996, 345). For example, the responses of thermoreceptors on the skin do not correlate with fixed dermal temperatures, but they do signal events of rapid heating or cooling that could lead to tissue damage.

Now an adherent to the correspondence-detection model could simply say that what states of the system correspond to are not temperatures, per se, but something more related to the perceiver's interests, like "thermal perils."[18] But what must then be conceded is that the ideal of perceptual veridicality as the achievement of correspondence with something in an external, perceiver-independent reality has been quietly dropped. A more considered response is to say that while "thermal perils" is a notion inextricably tied to a perceiver's interests, there is still a set of objectively measurable temperatures (and temperature changes) that constitutes thermal perils (for particular animals). That set of objectively measurable temperatures can be defined in purely physical terms, without reference to biology and psychology, even though it would not be of interest to a thermal physicist. So one can still claim that thermoreceptors detect that set of temperatures, without conceding that what is detected is a perceiver-dependent property.[19]

Gerrymandered sets of physical properties, with no claim to physical significance, are held up as the objective correspondents of our perceptual

---

18. This is one way to read the "anthropocentric realism" of Hilbert (1987).

19. This is the entrenched position of contemporary color physicalists. It is clear that the human color visual system cannot be treated as analogous to the spectrophotometer, a measuring instrument that detects SSR. This is because the sets of reflectances that humans classify as having the same colors appear in no physical description of the world. Still, the color physicalist says, all of those reflectances that we see as cherry red are properties that belong to their objects independently of our seeing them. Thus, when we see cherry red, we can still be said to be detecting a perceiver-independent property of the world (Smart [1975] 1997; Byrne and Hilbert 2003). See section 3.4.2 and Chirimuuta (2014) for criticism of this approach to color; Pautz (2013) presents objections to this doctrine applied to other sensory modalities, including smell and taste.

states, and it has to be admitted that this eviscerates the original detection-ist model whereby perceptual systems inform us about the environment just by picking up on external goings-on. For many *salient* features of our perceptual experiences—such as the boundaries between hue categories--cannot be thought to map onto perceiver-independent reality, but are strange beasts like "thermal perils" and "cherry reds." Do they cause us to suffer illusions because they get in the way of any apprehension of a perceiver-neutral world, or are they veridical just because there are, out there, some optical stimuli that cause them, even though such stimuli have no place in a physicist's catalog of the world? In section 5.3 I argue that the conceptual framework that leads into this dilemma is misguided. First I will say more about the perceptual pragmatist alternative.

5.2.3 Passive and Active

A distinguishing feature of the correspondence-detection model is its con-strual of perception as a passive, receptive process whereby external stimuli bounce onto sensory receptors and eventually leave their trace on an inner register. Until now I have been quite noncommittal about what kind of interaction could be put forward as an alternative to detection. Yet it should be noted that the word "interaction" is not itself free of connotation. "To interact" is typically to engage in a back-and-forth with someone or some-thing. The implication is that there are two active participants, and further-more that activity on one side affects the other, and vice versa. So to declare that perception is an interaction is already to gesture toward a more active account.[20]

Enactivism is an influential movement in recent philosophy of perception that takes perception to be a capacity that is on a continuum with an

---

20. The passive–active contrast under discussion here is not to be confused with the distinction between mental states not under any voluntary control, and those that are (i.e., vision being passive in the sense that we cannot will ourselves to see a rain shower made of golden pennies). The notion of perceptual activity outlined in this section includes any subpersonal, involuntary processing that shapes perceptual states in ways not predictable from the external stimulus. Examples under this head-ing are phenomena of perceptual categorization, classification, and "interpretation," as well as overt attentional modulation and bodily movement involved in perceptual exploration. For instance, when Martin (2009, 3498) writes that "color is not a prop-erty of the objects *per se* but is a result of the brain's ability to interpret the spectral reflectance of an object, relative to the reflectance of other objects in the visual field," I take him to be emphasizing the active nature of color perception.

animal's ability to act in the world.[21] For example, Noë (2004, 17) rather controversially characterizes all perceptual awareness as requiring the use of "sensory-motor knowledge." Since my task here is to articulate a minimal, naturalistic perceptual epistemology, it would not suit my purposes to take on any such contested claims. Instead, I will say simply that perceptual states inform us about the environment because they are the result of interactions (the specific mechanisms of which are the topic of empirical investigation) that allow the perceiver to seek out the information needed to guide current activities. The key idea—one that is, I believe, the current scientific orthodoxy—is that the perceiver must actively seek out stimuli, and that this activity necessarily shapes the resulting "descriptions." The activity of the perceiver is most striking in a modality like touch, where the exploratory gestures of the hand are obviously integral to resulting perceptual states. But this is no less the case in the seemingly passive modality of vision.

For instance, the phenomenologist Hans Jonas believed that vision and touch are utterly dissimilar, writing that, "[t]ouch has to go out and seek the objects in bodily motion and through bodily contact…whereas in sight selection by focusing proceeds non-committally within the field which the total vision presents" (Jonas 1954, 512). On his conception, vision is the distanced, contactless sense, a pure reception of information rather than an active engagement with the world. This way of understanding vision is empirically false. As it happens, we would be unable to read or view photographs if our body and eyes were static because of the fatiguing of our photoreceptors by constant stimulation. And because of the heterogeneity of the surface of the retina, movement of the eyes (saccades) with precise gaze control is essential for normal vision (e.g., see Findlay and Gilchrist 2003; Burr and Morrone 2004). Recent scientific work gives credence to the idea of Merleau-Ponty (1969) that the gaze is something like a grasp. That is, we use the foveating gaze, the targeting of an object on the highest acuity region of the retina, to gain a visual handle on the thing (e.g., Schütz et al. 2009 on saccades and object recognition). But subjective experience has been found to be an unreliable guide to eye movement because of the effect of saccadic suppression, the momentary impairment of vision for the duration of the saccade. So it is no wonder that the surface phenomenology of vision suggests to us that our eyes are relatively passive and immobile,

21. Seminal works include Thompson et al. (1992), Hurley (1998), and Noë (2004).

even though, just as much as the sense of touch, sight relies on our active probing of the environment. As Land and Nilsson (2002, 178) summarize, "our eyes search the surroundings for information rather than simply absorbing it." Naturally, how we search depends on what we need to do (Yarbus 1967).[22]

The passive-active distinction brings us to one last question, which will underscore the difference between perceptual pragmatism and its rival: "under what circumstances can perceptual states be said to be illusory?" If one assumes the passivity of perception, as presented in the detection-correspondence model, anything that the subject brings to the resulting perceptual state—any classification, omission, or exaggeration of the external signal—risks being construed as a distortion, in other words, as a perceptual error or illusion. For if the perceptual process is ideally just a passive reception of external stimulation, any element in a perceptual description that fails to correspond to an external stimulus because it arises not from the stimulus but from the perceiver's way of interacting with the stimulus (or a way of interpreting the stimulus, to employ a more metaphorical notion of activity) is of dubious epistemological standing. I will give an example to illustrate the point

In his criticism of Cohen's (2009) color relationism, Tye (2012) brings up the example illustrated in figure 5.1, the Adelson checkerboard. Citing the authority of Wikipedia, Tye calls this an illusion: the two squares A and B have an identical physical characteristic (lightness), yet we perceive them as being different shades of gray. Tye's analysis is entirely grounded in the correspondence-detection view because it assumes from the outset that the task of the visual system is to behave like a photometer, passively noting the proportion of light reflected from each element of the image and bringing no interpretation to bear on the resulting "description." What happens if we drop the correspondence-detection picture? On the assumption that perception is active and interpretative, then there need be nothing illusory about the way in which we perceive this image, except in the trivial sense that all pictorial representations can be called "illusions" (i.e., for the fact that we interpret graphical images in ways that mimic our apprehension of concrete scenes). This is because our parsing of the image can be holistic, in

---

22. The comparison of vision and touch is discussed at greater length in Chirimuuta (2011a); see also Chirimuuta and Paterson (2014).

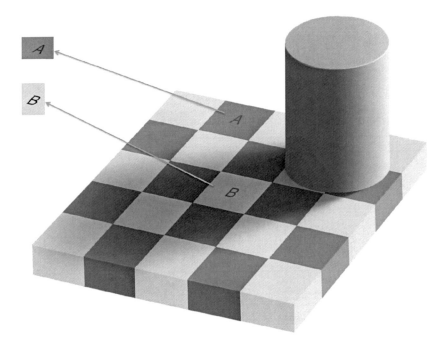

Figure 5.1
Adelson checker shadow "illusion." Squares A and B have the same physical light-ness, as can be determined from the cutouts on the left. However, in the context of the whole image, square B is interpreted as falling under shadow, and so is perceived as being made from a material that is different (a brighter shade of gray) from square A. Source: Image adapted from Wikimedia commons.

contrast to the localized process of detection, and our perception of the gray levels will be informed by a global interpretation. To take square A to be illuminated strongly, and square B to be lying in shadow is a perfectly viable (and useful) interpretation of the image as a whole, and this affects our impression of the gray levels of the tiles.[23]

23. Tye (2012) presents the Adelson image as a counterexample to color relationism. According to the theory of Cohen (2009), the different shades of gray that we per-ceive the squares to have, in and out of context, would all count as genuine colors. But according to Tye, only the colors perceived out of context are the genuine ones because in that case our perception of the squares can be thought to indicate the physical identity of surfaces of A and B. In his response to Tye, Cohen (2012) does not take the line of defense that I have outlined here and asserts that the relationist can still call this image an illusion, albeit one that requires a different interpretation from that of Tye.

We can now see how this rethinking of illusion bears on the ontological problem of color. In general terms, the relationist thesis is that color cannot be understood without considering what subjects themselves bring to perceptual states. That much is common ground with the antirealist. Yet the relationist parts company with the antirealist and argues that we should not treat those states as illusory or misinformative, since the colors are real enough, even though they are "subjective" or perceiver-dependent. Perceptual pragmatism gives the relationist the resources to make this case, by considering the utility of perceptual states involving color. States will not count as illusory just because they are "subjective," as long as they are useful interpretations of the surrounding environment. In effect what the relationist must do is *redefine perceptual realism*.

5.3   Color Relationism Is Realism Enough

Realism debates are the province of ontology. To ask whether a substance or property is real is typically to ask whether its existence is mind-independent. Thus debates over the existence of time, Platonic objects, material objects and God, all share a structural similarity (Dummett 1993). The same can be said of the color debate, as traditionally conceived. The task of this section is to show how the contrasting epistemologies of perception that were described in the previous section are connected to perceptual ontology. What will now become clear is that the traditional way of framing the debate over color realism is bound to the detection-correspondence model of perception. The pragmatic, interaction-utility outlook allows for a reformulation of what counts as realism, and so fosters a distinctive ontological position.

According to the framework typically evoked in ontological discussions, the real world is the one consisting of objects and properties outside the mind. The unreal world is like a dream—full of stuff and qualities that are merely "in the head." "Real" is often used synonymously with "objective," meaning "out there in the world whether or not any human is around." "Intersubjectivity" is often taken to be a good enough proxy for objectivity. If enough people agree that something is there, at least it is not a figment of one person's imagination gone awry. Dreams and hallucinations lack intersubjectivity; the sky and Mount Kilamanjaro do not, and their existence is an uncontroversial objective fact. The blueness of the sky and the beauty of the mountain, like the virtues of chivalry and vices of liberated women, are the interesting cases. They lack a full majority of subjects' endorsement, and science, often used as the ultimate arbiter of objective existence, has nothing clear-cut to say on such matters.

Now to focus on the purely perceptual, and not the aesthetic or moral qualities of objects, the ontological question is standardly one of correspondence: *which, if any, properties of objects in mind-independent reality can be said to correspond to the properties my perceptual experience presents those objects as having?* It is natural, then, to think of perceptual systems as having the role of detectors of mind-independent objects and properties. The path of influence seems also to run in the other direction. If it is assumed that perceptual systems are detecting devices then it is natural to discuss the ontological status of perceived qualities in terms of their correspondence to external, mind-independent properties. I am not in a position to claim that the reality-as-mind-independence view in ontology is more fundamental than the detection-correspondence model in the epistemology of perception, or vice versa. The important point is that they are mutually reinforcing and come as a philosophical package. If one accepts one of these views, then the other becomes practically irresistible (even if there is a position in logical space by where one can hold the detection model without the ontological framework, and vice versa).

Without the detectionist epistemology of perception and its ideal of correspondence, the ontological positions of realism and antirealism both lose their motivation.[24] Without correspondence in place as a governing metaphor, why would it seem imperative to match inner perceptual states to outer physical properties, and why would failures of correspondence count as evidence of the unreality of color? This is the force of the perceptual pragmatist's claim to revise color ontology. No refutation of either realism or antirealism

---

24. It bears emphasis that the targets here are the versions of realism and antirealism that have dominated the color debate, and were discussed in chapter 3. These various physicalist, primitivist, and eliminativist theories adhere to a correspondence picture and are incompatible with perceptual pragmatism. However, if by realism one means just the thesis that colors are instantiated, and if by antirealism one means just the thesis that colors are not mind independent, then both realists and antirealists can be perceptual pragmatists. Thanks to Derek Brown for raising this issue.

is on offer; rather, the idea is to remove the framework according to which one is tempted to hold one or other of those positions.

On the other hand, it follows naturally from perceptual pragmatism that the subjective/objective, mind-dependent/mind-independent and appearance/reality distinctions should *not* be treated as equivalent.[25] If it is accepted that all perceptual states are the result of selective and interest-relative interactions between a perceiver and an environment, then it is unwise to think of them as representing an objective, mind-independent reality, and equally unwise to treat all of them as mere appearances, unconstrained by reality. On the perceptual pragmatist view, a different notion of realism is to be invoked. Reality is there as that which the mind bumps against, rather than that which the mind fortuitously records from a transcendent state of serene detachment. Therefore to say that perceptual states and perceived qualities earn their keep by utility and not by correspondence to mind-independent reality is to be a fundamentally different kind of realist. As Rorty (1999, xxiii) puts it, "there is no way in which tools can take one out of touch with reality. No matter whether the tool is a hammer or…a belief or a statement, tool-using is part of the interaction of the organism with its environment."[26]

In sum, the question for color ontology is not whether internal color experiences can be said to map on to color in the external world. Instead color perception should be examined in terms of what seeing with color allows one to do—such as to recognize and recall familiar items, and the numerous other functions discussed in chapter 4. Taking up the tool analogy, there are always various ways to get the same practical result (just as there are numerous kinds of color vision), and yet they can all

25. In other words, the point of relationism is to open up conceptual space between the real, the objective, and the perceiver-independent. The polysemy of the very terms "subjectivity" and "objectivity" is a common theme authors writing on color relationism. See, for example, Hatfield (2003) and Cohen (2010).

26. Needless to say, my concern is not to defend Rortean pragmatism, in general, but to point out the advantages of this outlook in the context of color theory. The tool analogy quickly becomes stretched. For instance, whereas tools such as can openers have one specific function that they are designed to perform, and an item such as a blunt can opener is said to be broken if it fails to perform it, on my account the functions of perceptual systems are flexible (dependent on the tasks a perceiver happens to engage with) and success is much more graded. A human dichromat is not a "broken" color perceiver!

be said to get us in touch with reality. There is no concession to "anything-goes" relativism because the environment constrains which tools will work, and what kinds of perceptual systems will be informative.[27] This approach to color will now be illustrated with a discussion of perceptual categorization.

5.3.1 The Warping of Perceptual Space

Color perception is categorical in the sense that any colored object is readily assigned to a particular hue class, one that contrasts saliently with other classes. Any color space, though it may comprise the millions of hues that a normal perceiver can discriminate, is seen to contain a small number of distinct regions, like countries on a globe. These are clusters of hues that look similar to each other but very different from the other hue clusters. At the category boundaries, one perceives a fairly sharp transition from one class to another, even though the physical stimulus is varying smoothly.

An obvious example is the rainbow spectrum of visible light. Here the stimulus is a continuum of wavelengths between about 400 to 700 nm. A continuous physical quantity like this does not, in itself, contain any distinct regions. However, to the human eye the spectrum appears as a series of marked colored bands. There are only a tiny number of these (Newton's seven), so the bands cannot even be taken to be a discrete approximation to the continuum of wavelengths. Importantly, we can still resolve differences in shades of color within the bands, perhaps millions of distinct

27. Interestingly, the reworking of realism along pragmatist lines has recently gained some prominence in the philosophy of science. For example, Chang (2012, 217) introduces the notion of *active realism* as a way to rethink the realism/antirealism debate over scientific theories, writing that "'[s]cientific realism' should mean a scientific stance that commits us to expose ourselves to reality, rather than some metaphysical hubris about how we can obtain or have obtained objective truth." Thus he urges, "I think *realistic* people (including most empiricists and pragmatists) should re-claim the label of 'realism'! Being realistic means concerning ourselves with what we can plausibly do and know, with conditions of actual inquiry rather than pipe dreams of ultimate truth and certainty. In this vein a great slogan for active realism can be taken from Charles Sanders Peirce: 'Do not block the way of inquiry.'" Another example of a pragmatic realist theory is *scientific perspectivism*. In an influential presentation of the view Giere (2006) draws on an analogy between color vision and scientific theorizing. According to Giere, both of these ways of finding out about the world are selective, interactive, and deeply shaped by the needs and interests of the subject.

shades. The bands of color categories should be thought of as a "system" that imposes order on those millions of shades.

Given the phenomenological obviousness of color categories, it is perhaps surprising that there is an ongoing scientific controversy over how best to conceptualize them and connect them with our knowledge of the visual system (Witzel and Gegenfurtner 2013). On the one hand, the *Whorfian* view on color categorization is that the phenomenon is language mediated, and therefore cognitive in origin (Davidoff 2001), whereas the *universalists* take color categories to reflect features of our basic perceptual physiology (Berlin and Kay 1969). Here I intend to sit happily on the fence between Whorfians and universalists, holding a pluralist position like the one advocated by Dedrick (2006). If universalism is starkly associated with the view that "physiology determines named colour categories," and Whorfianism with the thesis that "physiology plays no interesting role in the development of named colour categories," then both positions seem implausible. The substantive debate is over the extent to which physiology or language dominates color category formation. I will be noncommittal about this, only asserting that physiology must have some role, as do language and cognition.

My central point is that the principles of categorization are shared broadly across perceptual systems. For instance, simple nonlinearities in sensory responses can serve as categorization mechanisms. If a sensory neuron has a strongly accelerating response function, it can be thought of as classifying stimuli into two categories, namely low or high intensity. Moreover the exact specification of the mechanism can also serve to make salient certain physical differences while eliding others. A sigmoidal response function will exaggerate the difference between a stimulus just below the acceleration threshold, and one just above it, while treating two stimuli both above or below the threshold as relatively similar or indistinguishable, and those in the middle, accelerating range, are more distinguishable (see figure 5.2).

Similarly the early stages of human color perception can also be understood as giving rise to "low-level categorizations." The first signal for color vision is the differential response of the three retinal cone types. Our photoreceptors cannot finely resolve the wavelengths of incoming light to perform a detailed spectral analysis. Instead, countless different stimulus spectra produce the same signal, while opponent coding at the

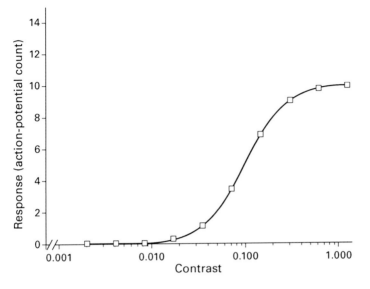

Figure 5.2
Naka–Rushton model. The Naka–Rushton model represents the nonlinear (sigmoidal) contrast response function of a neuron in primary visual cortex (V1). Mean neuronal response (*y* axis) is plotted against contrast of stimulus (*x* axis). See Chirimuuta and Tolhurst (2005) for details.

post-receptoral level exaggerates the difference between the physically quite similar stimuli that maximally excite the M and L cones.[28]

A high-level color category, on the other hand, is one that is marked by an individual's language and is associated with a conscious experience of

28. Note that I have been careful to avoid the claim that these opponent mechanisms explain our conscious experience of color categories. This was the universalist line advocated by (Hardin 1988), but it faces criticisms not only from Whorfians but also from visual neuroscience (Valberg 2001; Mollon 2003; also see section 3.4.1). My claim is that some form of categorization takes place at the low level, and that it constrains but does not determine the high-level categorizations of which we are consciously aware. Nor do I want to invoke rigid demarcation between perception and cognition, and deny that perception is culturally influenced and informed by cognition. I have focused here on categorization mechanisms in the sensory periphery where it is safe to assume that neurons are encapsulated from cognitive processing. For example, the retinal neurons receive no top-down connections from the brain. But that is not to say that perception, in general, is like this.

perceptual similarity among co-classified objects.[29] High-level classification schemes are also a feature of nonvisual modalities. The canonical examples of categorical perception are from research on perception of phonemes, a clear case of categorizations that are language relative. However, unlike the classifications of smell, taste, or of speech perception, color categories cannot always be said to mark out biologically or socially important kinds. Not all red things are dangerous or poisonous, nor do they have one socially governed significance. Categorization—at either the low or high levels— can be thought of as the *warping of perceptual space* (Kuhl et al. 2008). An "unwarped" perceptual space treats all stimuli as equally salient and discriminable. A warped space results in clusters of similar appearing stimuli that in turn have salient dissimilarities from other clusters.

5.3.2 Categorization and Antirealism

Antirealist philosophers of color have taken categorization effects to be conducive to their theory, and have been keen to emphasize their centrality.[30] The idea is that our primary experience of color is of certain hues that are marked by lexical categories and appear to bear obvious relationships of similarity and difference to each other. Such relationships are commonly represented in color spaces, and it seems obvious to us that green is more similar to blue than it is to red, and so forth. These are defining characteristics of color, and we therefore expect a philosophical theory of color to account for them. Yet, if we define colors as physical properties, we get no purchase on such phenomena. The spectrum of visible light is a physical continuum, and yet we perceive it as banded by a small number of distinct hue classes.

The antirealist then claims that if we look to our internal neurophysiology, we do get an understanding of these defining phenomena. According to (Hardin 1993, xxi), the outline of an explanation of color spaces and

---

29. Interestingly, the operational definition of high-level conscious color categories is still a matter of dispute. Davidoff (2001) takes *categorical perception* (CP) effects to be the criterion for a color category boundary. This is where discrimination thresholds are lower across a category boundary than within a category. Yet Hanley and Roberson (2011) have shown that these can occur within a color category. Thus Jraissati et al. (2012) argue for psychological saliency, operationalized with consistency and consensus measures, as the criterion for color categories.

30. See Hardin (1993, xx), quoted in section 2.4.

categorizations has already been given to us by opponent-process theory in psychophysics and physiology:

Given what is known about the processes of color perception it is quite plain that the basic structure of opponent color space is founded on the biology of the visual system. One would be able to answer questions about the relations that colors bear to each other by appealing to the color-relevant features of physical objects only if the structure of color space had its analog in those features. That condition is not satisfied.

Given there are many reasons for skepticism about the sufficiency of low-level physiological explanations for high-level color categorizations (see note 28), it is worth highlighting the fact that all the antirealist needs to show is that an explanation that refers to internal mechanisms—at any stage in the perceptual-cognitive hierarchy—is more likely to yield an understanding of color spaces and categorizations than an explanation put exclusively in terms of external physical stimuli. Pautz (2013) presents examples along these lines for smell, taste, audition, and pain, and in all such instances we would be wrong to think of sensory experiences as simply representing or tracking physical stimuli. But what are we to conclude about the fundamental nature of sensory experiences of color, taste, and smell, given the failures of correspondence to external stimuli? For both Pautz and Hardin, the failure of correspondence leads them to conclude that colors are not instantiated in ordinary physical objects. Furthermore, they argue, it is metaphysically problematic to say instead that the brain, or some psychological state, is the bearer of color. So they are forced to conclude that there is simply no such thing as color: a correct account of the world is one that says that no items, either mental or physical, are actually colored. Ordinary human perceivers are victim of a lifelong and systematic illusion.

It is strange to think that animals could survive in such epistemically shaky circumstances. As Hardin (1992, 371–72) writes, "[w]e must explain how it is that, paradoxically, configuring an animal so that it represents the world as being composed of colored objects—even though it isn't— gives the deluded creature an advantage in coping with its environment." And, if the antirealist is serious in her view on categorization, it must follow that all perceiver-dependent contributions to sensory experience are to be considered erroneous, and that for a perceiver not to be subject to any error he or she must resolve all physical stimuli equally well, with no response nonlinearities or subjective categorizations anywhere in the sensory system. In other words, all perceptual spaces must be unwarped. This is a non-naturalistic way of thinking about perception, for it sets up as a paragon of perception a system of response mechanisms that no animal could possibly have.[31]

All who have studied the perceptual systems of humans and other animals would agree that they do a remarkable job of conveying a rich and varied banquet of information about the surrounding world, and yet they do this in a selective and often idiosyncratic way—what Akins (1996) calls the "narcissism" of sensory systems. Human trichromacy is just one example of a sensory idiosyncracy: our color vision allows us to see a myriad of things around us, yet we cannot see ultraviolet light and we cannot help but see certain colors as more similar or different from each other even though the physical stimuli do not mirror this state of affairs. The perceptual pragmatist does not hold this against perceptual systems, but accepts it as a fact. Indeed the mistake is to think that a mirroring of physical stimuli to perceptual states, analogous to the correspondence of physical quantities with states of a measuring instrument, is an appropriate goal for biology. The antirealist's talk of "pervasive illusion," with its insistence on the incompatibility of the real with the subjective, can be diagnosed as an imposition of a correspondence epistemology that is inappropriate to the topic of biological perception. Yet this assumption is shared by most realists.

5.3.3   Categorization and Realism

Because of their adherence to the detection-correspondence model, color realists soon run into trouble when they consider categorization. The arguments from color similarity and categorization have often been taken as devastating objections against color physicalism, but of course, there have been responses. According to Byrne and Hilbert, both higher level color categories ("determinable colors") and specific metameric (i.e., matching) shades ("determinate colors") are identified with sets of SSR functions. Byrne and Hilbert (2003, 11) insist that color categories are not unreal or subjective:

31. See the "truisms" of section 5.2.

Surfaces with grossly different reflectances can perceptually match even under fairly normal illuminants. So the reflectance-types that we identify with the colors will be quite uninteresting from the point of view of physics or any other branch of science unconcerned with the reactions of human perceivers. This fact does not, however, imply that these categories are unreal or somehow subjective.

The assertion that color categories are not subjective amounts to saying just that they can be described in terms of physical properties. The category 'red' is a heterogeneous set of SSRs, but it can be given an (incomplete) physical description in terms of all the SSRs known to belong to the set. However, the realist's problems are compounded when one moves from considering just the existence of color classes to reckoning with similarity judgments about those categories. It is a commonplace observation that broad color categories can be arranged in a color space, and some classes are nearer neighbors than others: green is closer—more similar—to blue than it is to red. Likewise we readily make similarity judgments about specific shades: peacock blue is more similar to navy blue than it is to saffron yellow. Now one argument that has been raised against color physicalism, the thesis that colors simply are SSRs (or sets of SSRs) is that this implies that perceptual similarity judgments are open to empirical disconfirmation (Johnston 1992). If colors are these physical properties, it could well turn out that physicists will discover that saffron yellow should be classified as a shade of blue, or that green is more similar to red than it is to blue, whatever the psychophysical data.[32]

These examples highlight the fact that realists have divorced color ontology from the psychology of color: being red has nothing intrinsically to do with looking red. But the source of their troubles is the correspondence-detection model. It follows from this model that any subjective categorization of external stimuli implies a reduction in the

32. Byrne (2003) offers a complex response to this argument. First, he argues that even though color experiences represent objective color (i.e., SSR), propositions concerning similarities between different colors are not represented in visual experience. Second, Byrne explains our tendency to make similarity judgments as being a result of our representing each shade as having proportions of primary-like colors called "hue magnitudes." Not coincidentally, the hue magnitudes R, G, B, and Y are naturally associated with the unique hues of opponent coding theory (Byrne and Hilbert 2003, 14). While this interpretation of the hue magnitudes is not obligatory, if it is not employed, the hue magnitudes are left hanging as unexplained primitives in the theory. I thank Christopher Hill for discussion of this point.

tightness of correspondence, and hence a failure of the system to convey external realities with full verisimilitude. In order to be a color realist, one is better off embracing the interaction-utility model and accepting the relationist thesis that colors are in some sense perceiver-dependent.

5.3.4 Relationism and Categorization: Perception for Limited Beings

It is instructive to think of perceptual categorization as just one instance of a general rule about perceptual systems, which is that all discrimination functions come with peaks and troughs. Human observers are best at discriminating achromatic contrast at levels around the absolute detection threshold, and most sensitive to changes in wavelength in the 500 nm range. Many other animals perceive changes in UV reflectance and polarization of light, to which we are completely oblivious. The point is that no animal needs to see all stimuli equally well. Categorization is just one kind of mechanism for highlighting the stimulus differences that are important to the animal, and eliding others (Prete 2004, 3). It is worth pointing out that although color may be perceiver-dependent, and color categorizations subjective, these still provide information about what can be claimed to be more objective. In chapter 4 I emphasized the fact that color vision is integrated with nonchromatic visual processing. This means that color perception is part and parcel of the mechanism for perceiving numerous different properties of objects—shape, distance, lightness, and material composition. Thus a natural way to think about color is as a means by which we see these other, perceiver-independent, properties of objects.

For example, color vision serves to disambiguate the form of some purple flowers from the shadows cast on them. So one's perception of their color is a way of seeing their shape. Likewise Kingdom's demonstration of the color-as-material assumption shows the close connection between perception of color differences and perception of changes in material substance. Changes in color are readily interpreted as alterations in a material surface rather than mere optical effects. This makes adaptive sense, given that in our environment color differences are usually the result of a material change, whereas changes in achromatic luminance, unaccompanied by color shifts, are normally due to shadows or shading. My perception of color is a way of seeing material change and stability. Consideration of the many uses of color vision helps us see how visual experiences involving subjective perceptual categorizations need not be illusory. The category itself may not map on to any objective physical property, but it may still contribute to the discrimination and re-identification of objects.

At the same time many of the external properties that are selectively highlighted by perceptual mechanisms for discrimination and categorization have their special status because of the particular interests and needs of the animal. It is not as if color vision is a means to an unbiased picture of objective stimulus properties. For instance, if Mollon's hypothesis that primate trichromacy evolved to aid foraging turns out to be true, then we see ripe red fruit as saliently different from a background of leaves not because the fruit is, objectively speaking, so very different but because in our evolutionary history it was advantageous to treat the colors of fruit and leaves as categorically distinct (Mollon [1989] 1997).[33]

Finally, the order that arises with perceptual categorization is extremely advantageous to limited beings like ourselves. Compare the phenomenology of color with that of pitch. For those not endowed with perfect pitch, one note does not have any categorical quality that makes it saliently different from other notes. For this reason most of us cannot recognize or classify a note, when heard, as C, D#, E, and so on. Thus pitch is a difficult quality to remember. With color, however, it is easy to classify a shade, and remarkably easy to recall what that color was from one view to the next. On seeing a persimmon for the first time, a viewer will probably notice and remember that it is an orange fruit. This knowledge will make it easy to recognize a persimmon the next time around. In order to learn to identify a persimmon, no one need register the exact shade of the skin, whether it is closer to the color of an orange or a mango. Indeed that there are only a handful of color categories makes them more useful in such situations—it is easier to remember what color category an object belongs to if there are only 10 options, not ten thousand. It is not simply that colors can be equated with our hue categories, and are therefore subjective; or that categorization is merely a distraction from the essential business of perception that is to recover objective physical properties. For categorization—the warping of perceptual space—does help us keep track of what is there in external reality.

---

33. I do not claim that all instances of color vision have this feature. For example, my experience of the spectral bands of a rainbow does not yield any obviously practical information.

The main point of this chapter can be summarized quite succinctly. The debate over color has had a governing assumption lurking in the background, namely that the reality or unreality of color is a matter of how closely perceptual states involving color approach a "God's-eye view" of the mind-independent world. This is the key thought behind both realist and antirealist theories of color, and once it is dropped, both views appear unmotivated. By replacing it with a pragmatist understanding of perceptual systems, color relationism turns out to be the theory that is well motivated and consistent with a naturalistic picture of perception by limited creatures in real environments. In the next chapters I present and defend a novel theory of color that shares much with mainstream relationism while also pursuing the interactionist line introduced here.

6 Active Color

6.1 The Promise of Relationism

As we saw in sections 1.4 and 3.1.3, the emergence of comparative and ecological vision science as a topic for debate in the philosophy of color gave a significant boost to relationist ideas. The significance of these empirical findings was that they introduced a new desideratum to the theoretical debate: it became a requirement on any theory of color that it accommodate the fact that other animals have color visual systems vastly different from the human one, and hence discriminate, and presumably categorize color stimuli in ways that are peculiar from the human perspective. No one species could plausibly claim to have a uniquely correct view of color (as old-fashioned realists had presumed for human trichromacy), while at the same time the significance of color vision in guiding animals around their environments would tell against the eliminativist doctrine that color is *pure* perceptual falsity. Relationism stood out as a viable *via media*.

A theme of this book is that much can be said in favor of relationism even when we restrict our focus to human vision. At the end of the last chapter I argued that relationism is the general approach that best meshes with a scientific understanding of perceptual utility and success. In this chapter I develop a more specific account, asking what vision science would want from a relational philosophy of color. I propose that the best way of thinking about color is one that satisfies these interconnected desiderata:

1. A view that accommodates the inner-relatedness and outer-directedness of color (its "Janus-facedness").

2. A monistic approach—a way of thinking about color that does not pre-suppose a problematic subject–object dichotomy.

3. A means to avoid any contentious reification of color.

In this section I discuss the importance of each of these points and say why existing versions of relationism go some way toward addressing them but have unfulfilled promise. In section 6.2 I argue that a new theory—*color adverbialism*—is best able to deliver on these points.

6.1.1 "Janus-Facedness" and Monism

It should be clear by now that object color is not physical light radiation itself, that it is not something that inheres in objects, having to do exclusively with the chemical makeup of the object, nor is it only the nervous excitation that occurs in the eye and brain of an observer. In our perception of object color all these elements are involved. (Hurvich 1981, 52)

Undisputedly, the concept of human color vision involves both a subjective component, as it refers to a perceptual phenomenon and an objective one…We take this subtle tension to be the essential ingredient of research on color perception. (Mausfeld et al. 1992, 47)[1]

Later in the same article Mausfeld, Niedere and Heyer call this quality the "Janus-facedness" of color: color points out to the world of objects, and at the same time it draws us inward to examine the perceptual subject. This is a common thread in scientific writing on color vision. More recently Hurlbert (2013, 375) has written,

This view, that color is neither purely subjective nor purely physical, sounds like a convenient halfway-house, placed in between extreme positions for the comfort of people who like to look both ways. But it is more than that, being a view for people who like to look in depth and detail at how and why color comes into being, not just what color is. It is a view of color that is neither novel nor unique, but becomes ever more entrenched the more knowledge becomes available about the physiology and phenomenology of color vision.

---

1. These two passages are quoted by Cohen (2009) as epigraphs to chapter 3 of *The Red and the Real*. As I mention in a review of this book (Chirimuuta 2011b), it strikes me that these passages embody an important motivation for relationism that is not developed by Cohen, who instead concentrates on the argument from perceptual variation. The material presented in this chapter is my attempt to make good on this line of thought. See Thompson (1995, 140).

It has always struck me that the "Janus-facedness" of color is its most beguiling quality, philosophically speaking. These scientists are gesturing at an important insight into the nature of color. The challenge is to work this insight into a theoretical account. Hurvich makes the relationist claim that both physics and physiology, objects and subjects, are needed for a viable conception of color, but then resorts to a mereological analysis of the situation: the objective and subjective are "elements" or "components" of color. Thus it is easy to slip into thinking of color as a chimerical beast, part physical, part psychical. Once this move is made conceptual clarity recommends fission (Maund 1981) and the dual-reference approach (Brown 2006), or either one of the procrustean "solutions." Mausfeld (2010) himself has recently advocated a purely "internalist" approach to color. Likewise Hardin (1993) makes a pure internalism out of Hurvich's opponent theory.

This, however, is not what we were after. As I argued in section 3.4, the Procrustean solutions leave one with the feeling that something important is left out. The initial insight was that color is a hybrid, something that somehow spans and encompasses our conception of the perceived object and seeing subject, or even undermines our assumption that these are conceptually distinct. Previous versions of relationism have held out unfulfilled promise here. Because they have remained beholden to correspondence thinking, relationists have continued to treat perceptual states in terms of in–out matching. For example, Thompson does acknowledge "Janus-facedness" as an important requirement of a color ontology, but his account inherits the same conceptual dualism found in other theories, since the contrast between physical properties, on the one hand, and color looks, on the other, is built into his explicit definition of color (Thompson 1995, 245).

Another way of putting this is to say that ontologies of color have difficulty arriving at a view that is both inclusive and *monistic*. As we saw in chapter 2, the problem of color ontology is symptomatic of the famous dichotomies that came to prominence with the seventeenth-century scientific revolution: physical vs. psychical; objective vs. subjective; quantitative vs. qualitative; body vs. mind. Each dichotomy institutes a conceptual dualism, a tendency to divide up the world and its properties according to these binaries, which make it near impossible to consider a connection between both sides of the divide to be anything more than a superficial correlation. Hence the failure of most theories of color to accommodate, or even acknowledge the "Janus-facedness" of color.[2]

Many have observed that the science of psychology has been unfairly burdened by the seventeenth-century legacy, and that success in the material sciences has been bought at the expense of having a conceptual repertoire apt for the sciences of the mind. For instance, Burtt ([1932] 2003, 320) writes that the "Newtonian scientists" managed "to further their own conquests of external nature by loading on mind everything refractory to exact mathematical handling and thus rendering the latter still more difficult to study scientifically than it had been before." As he puts it, "mind was to them a convenient receptacle for the refuse, the chips and whittlings of science, rather than a possible object of scientific knowledge." Thus, whether they know it or not, scientists of the mind have a vested interest in revisionary metaphysics.[3]

Ecological psychology was a movement dedicated to displacing the Cartesian influence from psychology, and as such was consistently distrustful of the seventeenth-century dichotomies, especially the primary–secondary quality distinction, and the distinction between the objective and subjective (Costall 1984). As Gibson ([1979] 1986, 129) famously said with regard

---

2. Jones et al. (1943, 544) provide a nice example of the difficulties raised for psychologists by the hybrid nature of color once the quantitative-qualitative distinction has been instituted: "Brightness is the attribute of color sensation which is most distinctly quantitative....In the sense that it varies in the same manner as the proportion of the chromatic component in the stimulus, saturation may be considered a quantitative attribute of color sensation. Hue is rarely considered to be a quantitative attribute of color sensation." We are not told how it is that quantitative saturation and brightness are integrated with qualitative hue to yield the one quality, color. Another passage illustrates the more general problem of understanding the mind-body connection within the science of perception, "This response [the visual sensation] is of an *entirely different nature* from the nerve impulses themselves. Whereas the nerve impulses are the physical (specifically, physiological) aspects of the total response, the sensations are subjective, or psychical aspects of the response." (p. 549; emphasis added).

3. The difficulties with the conventional, seventeenth century metaphysics are particularly apparent in the *mind-body problem* or *problem of consciousness*, which has only been given serious scientific consideration in the last 25 years. The problem can be stated very simply: *how can the human brain, which is a physical object bearing only quantitative properties, also be the seat of the mind, which is a psychical subject bearing qualitative properties—feelings, emotions, sensations, and perceptions?* Or as McGinn (2000, 13) memorably put it, "[h]ow did evolution convert the water of biological tissue into the wine of consciousness?" See also section 1.3.

to his affordances, "an affordance is neither an objective property nor a subjective property; or it is both if you like. An affordance cuts across the dichotomy of subjective–objective and helps us to understand its inadequacy. It is equally a fact of the environment and a fact of behaviour. It is both physical and psychical, yet neither." Perhaps the same ought to be said for color; the challenge is to put that thought on a sturdier metaphysical footing.

Historical Digression: Monism and Ecological Psychology

If one considers how psychology and perceptual science are fundamentally shaped by metaphysical assumptions, for better or worse, it becomes natural to think that the philosophy of color should have something to offer the science of color, at the very least, to draw attention to the array of concepts that may be innocuous for the physical sciences but have pathological consequences for the sciences of the mind. The relevance of metaphysics to psychology was more readily accepted in the past than it is now, as can be seen if we consider the historical connections between William James's monism and ecological psychology.

There would seem to be a dualism written into the DNA of psychophysics, resting as it does on the contrast between *physis* and *psyche, stimulus* and *response*. Interestingly, the founding father of the discipline, Gustav Fechner, recognized the centrality of this metaphysical issue and himself proposed a monistic, dual-aspect solution to the mind–body problem (Heidelberger 2004). Likewise the William James of the *Principles of Psychology* grudgingly accepted a Cartesian framework, only to repudiate it shortly afterward and at the turn of the twentieth century to concentrate his theoretical efforts on the development of a non-Cartesian metaphysics.[4] With his philosophy of "radical empiricism" James sought to resolve the metaphysical issues hampering psychology by replacing the Cartesian framework, and its later Kantian reconstruction, with one more congenial to the nonphysical sciences.

---

4. See Perry (1935) and Heft (2001, 19–20). As James wrote in *Psychology: The Briefer Course*: "When, then, we talk of 'psychology as a natural science,' we must not assume that that means a psychology that stands at last on solid ground. It means just the reverse; it means a psychology particularly fragile, and into which the waters of metaphysical criticism leak at every joint." (James [1892] 1985, 334; quoted in Heft 2001, 19).

The essay "Does Consciousness Exist?" is of particular interest to our current study. James explicitly rejects the reification of consciousness and moves to an activity view. 'Consciousness' is said to stand for a *function* and not for an *entity* (James 1904, 478). This is followed by an assertion of ontological monism and statement of the relational character of *knowing*, which is the primary example of a function, but the same could equally be said for *perceiving*:

> My thesis is that if we start with the supposition that there is only one primal stuff or material in the world, a stuff of which everything is composed, and if we call that stuff "pure experience," then knowing can easily be explained as a particular sort of relation towards one another into which portions of pure experience may enter. The relation itself is a part of pure experience; one of its "terms" becomes the subject or bearer of the knowledge, the knower, the other becomes the object known.

Below I will propose, in a Jamesian vein, that colors should be thought of as properties of the activity of perceiving, though I opt to remain agnostic about the nature of "primal stuff." As a consequence of his monistic outlook, (James 1904, 480) urges us to consider "experience" as both objective and subjective. In a radical overhaul of traditional ontological categories, our understanding both of the external object and inner thought are to be revised in terms of this Janus-faced notion of experience.

William James is celebrated for his contributions both to American pragmatist philosophy and to the emerging science of psychology. What is not so well known is that the strand of philosophical inquiry initiated by James's radical empiricism came to have a scientific presence in the ecological psychology movement of the twentieth century. J. J. Gibson is the figure most associated with ecological psychology, and he was keen to present the philosophical implications of his work throughout his career (e.g., Gibson 1967). Edwin Holt, James's student at Harvard and Gibson's mentor at Princeton, is the individual who forms the historical connection between ecological psychology, American pragmatism, and radical empiricism. At the end of this chapter I will return to discuss some of Holt's speculations about the nature of perceptual consciousness, discussing the lesson for contemporary theorists.

6.1.2 Dissolving Reification: The Science of the Unlocated

Jackson (1998) defines the problem of color ontology as a location question. Not *"what* is color?" but *"where* is color? inside the mind or out there in objects?" To most people, these two ways of framing the problem are interchangeable. For, if color is reified, it is perfectly natural to ask where it can be found.[5] What is intriguing about the quotation above from Hurvich, and the notion of "Janus-facedness," is the claim that we should not try to pin color down in any of the standard places. And indeed what is curious about all the various disciplines of color science is that researchers who observe very different corners of the world, and very different kinds of things, are *all* considered to be specialists in color. To illustrate the point, here is a list of different branches of color science, ranked in rough order of nearness to visual experience[6]:

- Colorimetry and appearance modeling (Fairchild 2013; Wyszecki and Stiles 2000)
- Psychophysics (Hurvich 1981; Kaiser and Boynton 1996; Gegenfurtner et al. 2001)
- Computational modeling of constancy or discrimination (Gegenfurtner et al. 2001)
- Neurophysiology (Gegenfurtner et al. 2001)
- Genetics (Gegenfurtner et al. 2001)
- Optics (Wyszecki and Stiles 2000)
- Chemistry of colored materials (Nassau 2001)
- Physics of colored materials (Nassau 2001)

One influential textbook is *Color Vision: From Genes to Perception* edited by Gegenfurtner, Sharpe, and Boycott. This text spans at least four of the disciplines listed above. The point is not just that color science is interdisciplinary or "multi-level" (Craver 2007) but that laboratories do not even have to be studying the same corner of the world to all be working on color.

---

5. Specifically, this is a question about where color is *instantiated*. If colors are given a standard Platonic treatment, whereby properties are universals, then strictly speaking colors do not have spatial or temporal location. However, according to this treatment one can still ask where colors are instantiated—in external physical objects or in the head. This is the question at issue here, for instance, Jackson (1998, 87) "The colours must, if they are instantiated anywhere, be findable somehow...."

6. References in parentheses are to key textbooks in the field. The selection of disciplines is not comprehensive, to say the least. For the sake of simplicity of discussion, it misses research in color and cognition (Davidoff 1991), such as color naming and comparative linguistics (Biggam et al. 2011), as well as technologies of color production.

Yet the relevance of each discipline to the others is acknowledged, as demonstrated by the frequent production of textbooks and hosting of conferences that aim at cross-disciplinary synthesis and integration.

Note that no one discipline is held up as the core, the *sine qua non* of color science—the area of study that examines "actual" color, with the rest just studying "background conditions." And there is a striking absence of antagonism between advocates of these very different approaches to color. This is in striking contrast to the kind of winner-take-all rivalry that Longino (2006) observes between advocates of the different methodologies employed in the scientific study of human behavior, such as genetics, social and developmental psychology. Curiously, scientists do not spend time worrying about how properly to locate color, and quarrelling with those who locate it differently. It seems to be tacitly accepted that genuine color science involves the ecumenical study of the various parts of nature that are all relevant to color. This fact is problematic for the physicalist, for, if color really *is* a physical property, its core science should be a physical science. It is hard for the physicalist to account for the fact that the majority of the color sciences are biological and psychological.

But is it actually implied that color is multiply instantiated—somehow present both in the extra-dermal objects and in the seeing brain, or smeared out between these two? The conclusion reached by eliminativists like Hardin (1993) is that color cannot be located in any kind of object. Eliminativism tells us that nothing is actually colored (color is never instantiated), and hence color is nowhere. Yet insistence on the nonreality of color is problematic for reasons of its own (see section 3.4 and section 5.3.2), and it is difficult to square with the fact that scientists do take themselves to be studying a genuine subject matter when they do color science.

Relationism offers a more promising way to make sense of the idea that color is unlocated. A prediction of relationism is that we can have *color science* without there being a *science of color*. In other words, there can be a science of the unlocated. If you accept relationism, it makes sense to say that you do not need to locate color in the world in order to study the interactions that give rise to or constitute color. Instead, we can understand the different parts of nature examined in color science as being the various *relata* that are, in combination, definitive of color. However, most previous relationist theories have an unfulfilled promise here (see section 3.4.3). In particular, the dispositionalist views that have been most influential in relationist thinking all assume that color *is* located in external objects as a dispositional property, and Cohen (2009, 226) shares this supposition.

6.2   Color Adverbialism

Color is a *psychological* property of our visual experiences when we look at objects and lights, not a *physical* property of those objects or lights. The colors we see are based on physical properties of objects and lights that cause us to see them as colored...but these physical properties are different in important ways from the colors we perceive. Color is more accurately understood as the result of complex interactions between physical light in the environment and our visual nervous systems. (Palmer 1999, 95)

This passage from the influential textbook *Vision Science* has often been referred to by philosophers as an expression of scientific orthodoxy. On the basis of quotations that are more selective than mine, Palmer is frequently interpreted as claiming that colors are merely sensations (see Noë 2004, 148; Byrne and Hilbert 2003, 4). Following Giere (2006, 32), however, I think that the word "interaction" is crucial to an understanding of Palmer's intent and that his view is in sympathy with a version of relationism. The idea is not that colors are just in the head but that, to understand color, one must consider the interplay between brain and stimulus, animal and environment. In a similar vein Wolfe et al. (2006, 97) write that, "color is the result of the interaction of a physical stimulus with a particular nervous system." The question now is what to take, philosophically, from such statements. A simple analysis of the message here is that the "interactions" are perceptual processes and that colors are properties of those processes. This is the essence of the ontological theory that I call *color adverbialism*.[7]

7. In section 5.1.1 I discussed how the range of theoretical claims expressed by scientists means that no one statement can be taken as scientific orthodoxy. So, in presenting color adverbialism, my claim is not that this is the only ontological theory that can be said to mesh with current science but that it is an important undercurrent to scientific thinking that has been neglected by philosophical discussion. The quotations from Palmer and Wolfe should be taken as a starting point, or a way in to the theory I develop.

So what are the colors according to this new account? Following David-son (1970), I will assume an event predicate theory of adverbs, such that adverbs are adjectives that apply to events.[8] On the current analysis, colors are not properties of things (minds or extra-dermal objects) but of specific kinds of events, namely perceptual interactions:

Colors are properties of perceptual interactions involving a perceiver (P) endowed with a spectrally discriminating visual system (V) and a stimulus (S) with spectral contrast of the sort that can be exploited by V.

Who is P? Any sighted animal with the right kind of visual system. Must P be conscious? Not necessarily. For the central and introspectively salient cases of human vision, consciousness seems important to color. But this theory of color is meant to extend beyond these cases—to blindsight, to insects where it is perhaps unlikely or at least unknown whether or not they are visually conscious. Moreover action-implications—what the per-ceptual interaction allows individuals[9] to *do*—are very important to my view. Since there is evidence that perceptual processes that guide action "online" are not conscious (Gray 2007) to require that a perceiver be con-scious to be seeing with color would rule out many action-guiding percep-tual processes from being color-involving. I will return to the question of qualitative color in section 6.4.3.

V, the definition of a spectrally discriminating visual system, is intended to rule in the visual machinery of all creatures conventionally classified as having color vision proper, but not those with just the capacity to perform reflexive behaviors in response to stimulation with specific wavelengths of light.[10] This requires opponent processing and some degree of color con-stancy. The sensory mechanisms responsible for "wavelength-specific

8. Tye (1984) argues that the most promising version of adverbialism is one that construes the properties picked out by adverbs not to be properties of events but to be predicates that apply to the perceiving subject. For example, "perceives greenly" is taken to be a predicate that applies to *me* when I gaze at a bowl of pea soup. I reject this option because Tye's main concern, that the Davidsonian analysis allows for the metaphysical possibility of perceiving events detached from perceivers, is simply not a concern in a naturalistic enquiry such as this. Furthermore, by Tye's definition, color adverbialism would have none of the advantages that accrue from moving to an activity focus, as will be discussed below.

9. As with "perceiver," I intend "individual" to refer to human and nonhuman animals.

10. Section 4.2.2; also see Skorupski and Chittka (2011) and references therein.

behaviors" are like isolated detectors, and the behaviors are simple reflexes. I opt to exclude these mechanisms from my category of spectrally discriminating visual systems because they really do appear to be independent sensing modules, whereas on my view the integration of color vision with the rest of vision is fundamental.

The primary restriction on the stimulus is that it should bear *spectral contrast*. That is, it must reflect or generate patterns of light with wavelengths in the discriminable range of at least one kind of visual system. I stipulate that S has spectral contrast if it induces differential responses across the photoreceptor array in at least one of an animal's different photoreceptor types.[11] It is implicit in the definition of "having spectral contrast" that background lighting conditions are such that spectral contrast is present. In other words, light levels must be high enough, and the ambient light must be of a broad enough spectrum to support spectral contrast.[12] Whether or not a stimulus has spectral contrast depends also on the visual system of the animal in question. For example, UV reflective patterns bear no spectral contrast for humans but are color stimuli for other animals with visual UV sensitivity.

Stimuli are most readily thought of as objects with their physical properties such as SSR. But it pays also to include events, like the play of light on back of CD.[13] In my view, nothing is gained by the restriction of color stimuli to either objects or events, material surfaces or lights. Cases may be

11. The definition of spectral contrast is inspired by the more precise notion of *cone contrast*. Brainard (1996) defines cone contrast as the vector of differences between the cone excitation values for background and target, divided by a background value. This kind of metric is valuable for calibrating simple stimuli in psychophysics experiments but hard to apply to complex natural images where the target and background are undefined. The notion of spectral contrast does not have the same technical virtues; it is intended to be intuitively applicable to real world stimuli.

12. Under scotopic conditions, or when there is only monochromatic lighting, there is no spectral contrast. This leads to interesting consequences in the discussion of perceptual error. See section 7.4.1.

13. Pasnau (2009) argues astutely, with reference to physics and chemistry of color, that the most relevant physical stimulus for color is a particular kind of event—the interaction between ambient light and electrons in a material substance. He points out that his "event physicalism" avoids the problems accommodating colored light sources that befall the standard "object physicalism" (i.e., reflectance realism). Non-object stimuli have been a particular focus of attention in recent philosophical discussions of sound. Note, however, that O'Callaghan (2007) and Casati and Dokic (2012) all argue that sound is an event rather than a property of an event.

taken on an individual basis, and the stimulus specified according to the most appropriate analysis in those circumstances. Thus the term "stimulus" is intended to include all visible optical phenomena, including the sky, rainbows, and human-made patterns of light.

This pair of definitions is a formulation of the adverbialist idea that is essentially equivalent to the previous one, but with a more intuitive feel:

Colors are ways stimuli appear to certain kinds of individuals.

Colors are ways that individuals perceive certain kinds of stimuli.

One may choose to focus on either the first or the second of these sentences, depending on the case at hand, but ultimately perceiving and appearing should be thought of as a mutually dependent pair of activities that together make up the perceptual interaction. Thus colors can be treated as modes of appearing-and-perceiving. For example, when a person looks at the sky on a cloudless afternoon, the expanse above her appears to her (shows up for her) in a blue way, and likewise she is perceiving it in a blue manner.[14]

Color adverbialism can be thought of as a species of color relationism because colors are not defined absent a correct alignment of perceiver, object, and viewing circumstances. As with standard versions of relationism, it follows that an object may appear in as many different colors as there are different kinds of perceivers and kinds of viewing circumstances adequate for the stimulus to have spectral contrast. This is what allows for an ecumenical resolution of the problem of conflicting appearances.

---

14. On some interpretations of *De anima*, my account bears a similarity to the Aristotelian theory of perception. For example, Prindle et al. (1980) presents an interpretation whereby perceivers and objects of perception bear complementary "potentialities" that are "actualized" in the perceiver–object interaction. As Prindle et al. (1980, 396) write, "[c]onsider the state of affairs termed 'sourness'. On the assumption of a logical independence of animal and environment, sourness might be ascribed to the object being tasted but, more likely, would be ascribed to the animal doing the tasting (probably to the activity of some of its neural fibers). Herein lies the perennially popular story of secondary qualities. Aristotle, assuming a logical dependence, told a quite different story: Object X has the 'potential' to taste sour to animal Z…while animal Z has the 'potential' to taste, as sour, object X…and in the mutuality of these two potentials, 'sourness' is actualized." (quoted by Thompson 1995, 245). According to the orthodox interpretations discussed in chapter 2, Aristotle is closer to a contemporary primitivist or naïve realist, but see note 4, section 2.1.1.

However, there is a crucial difference. Color adverbialism *does not claim that colors are relational properties of perceiver–stimulus–conditions triads;* instead, we must focus on the interaction occurring between perceivers, objects, and the like, and take that to be the bearer of chromatic properties.[15]

Aside from the work of Giere (2006, ch. 2),[16] the existing theories most closely related to color adverbialism are those of Sellars and McGilvray. Sellars (1971) holds that red sensations have an adverbial status in the current manifest image, though this is set to be revised with the development of a scientific image for sensory experience. In contrast, Sellars (1981) comes to the view that color sensations in an advanced scientific image (not the current one that is bound to a mechanistic view of causality) will be "absolute [i.e. not object bound] processes." In a similar vein McGilvray (1983) writes that colors are properties of "constructings"—sensing events that are internal to perceivers. Such events serve the perceivers' interests in getting them around the external world because ultimately physical objects are causes of the sensing events. Thus colors are to be thought of as "modes of sensing" or "event-properties," with the verb "to color" taking a preeminent position over the noun "color" in McGilvray's analysis.

So while my view has in common with Sellars (1981), McGilvray (1983), and Pasnau (2009) the thesis that colors are properties of processes rather than objects, the key difference is those theories locate the relevant events

---

15. Arguably, color adverbialism does fulfill Cohen's criterion for color relationism, whereby colors are "constituted in terms of a relation between (*inter alia*) objects and subjects" (Cohen 2009, 8). Everything turns on how "constituted" is understood. If colors, as properties of a perceptual interaction, are constituted by that interaction, then they are constituted in terms of a relation (interaction) between objects, subjects, and so on.

16. To my knowledge, Giere is the only other philosopher committed to the view that I call color adverbialism and he calls "perspectivism." He writes: "I claim that colors are best thought of as neither completely objective nor purely subjective, neither as properties of either parts of the material world or of subjective experience, but as a property of an interaction between the material world and human observers" (Giere 2006, 39). I do not believe that the restriction here to human observers is pivotal to Giere's view. See Giere (2006, 32): "Perspectivism also makes good sense of comparative studies of color vision. If humans have a particular colored perspective on the world, so do monkeys, birds, fish, cats, and dogs." Interestingly, Giere's specialty is in the philosophy of science rather than the philosophy of mind or perception, and his focus, like mine, is on the conceptual underpinnings of color science.

as either exclusively internal or external to the perceiver. As such, they can be classified either as species of antirealism or realism, according to the taxonomy of chapter 3. On my view, the relevant events—perceptual interactions—involve both perceiver and the extra-dermal environment. Hence I emphasize the connections with relationism.

One of the central attractions of adverbial approaches is that they allow for a deflationary response to the problem of color. As Boghossian and Velleman (1989, 82n4) write in a thought-provoking footnote:

One might be tempted to dissolve the conflict between the Galilean [antirealist] view and the charitable [realist] view of colour experience by rejecting a presupposition that they share. Both sides of the conflict assume that the properties mentioned in our descriptions of visual experiences are properties that such experience represents objects as having. The only disagreement is over the question whether the colour properties that are thus attributed to objects by visual experience are properties that the objects tend to have. One might claim, however, that visual experience does not attribute properties to objects at all; and one might bolster one's claim by appeal to a theory known as adverbialism. According to adverbialism, the experience of seeing a thing as red is an event modified by some adverbial property—say, a seeing event that proceeds red-thing-ly.... [A]dverbialism would enable one to say that the phrase "seeing a thing as red" describes a seeing event as having some adverbial property rather than as having the content that something is red. One could therefore contend that the question whether things really have the colour properties that they are seen as having is simply ill-formed, since colour properties figure in visual experience as adverbial modifications of the experience rather than as properties attributed by the experience to an object.

Thus the problem of color can be dealt a swift blow. Indeed it is surprising that adverbialist theories have not had more popularity. The reason Boghossian and Velleman give for the neglect of adverbialism is that any such position is ruled out by visual phenomenology, and that adverbialism, "does unacceptable violence to the concept of visual experience." As they go on to claim, color experiences have truth conditions, and hence must be representational. I will address the complex matter of how we should draw lessons from visual phenomenology in chapter 8, and in the next chapter I will show how color adverbialism is consistent with some kinds of representational theory. First, though, I will bracket these worries in order to present the adverbial theory of color and show how it makes good on the desiderata listed above. The material in this chapter should be understood, first and foremost, as a proposal for color ontology in the "scientific image."

Three important features of color adverbialism are:

Activity and occurence Color is primarily to be analyzed in terms of processes occurring, not things subsisting. The idea of perception as an activity is central.

Relationality The processes in terms of which color is to be analyzed relate perceivers to their environment. They are not the internal sensing events of traditional adverbial theories.

Attribution Color adverbialism introduces a very different notion of color attribution. Strictly speaking, color is not a property that can be attributed to extra-dermal objects or to perceivers.

In the remainder of this chapter I will discuss the first two of these aspects, and along the way I will say how the view satisfies the desiderata listed above. While color adverbialism is presented primarily as an ontological position that a color scientist would be best off committing herself to, the theory does have interesting implications for how we should understand perceptual experience. I will discuss these in the following chapters when I take up the complex issues of color attribution, perceptual error, and phenomenology.

6.3   Activity and Ontology

The current wave of color relationism began with the insight that the understanding of the perceptual environment and activity within it is crucial to advancing color ontology.[17] The primary effect of the work of Evan Thompson and his collaborators was the introduction of the literature on visual ecology and comparative color vision to the philosophical community—things have not been the same (i.e., so anthropocentrically blinkered) ever since. Interestingly, in his explicit definition of color Thompson (1995, 245) does not mention perceptual activity at all.

Action in Perception by Noë (2004) is a particularly influential presentation of the enactive approach to perception, and it includes an entire chapter devoted to color. Yet he commits himself to color realism, arguing that colors are perceiver-independent, and is critical of relationism, taking any

17. See Thompson (1995, 244), quoted in section 3.4.3.

such theory to be assuming a problematic identification of colors with inner sensations. On his view, "colours are objective but nonphysical ways that objects affect their environment" (Noë 2004, 155), that we learn about through coming to grips with the ways in which appearances alter as a result of environmental changes (illumination) and changes within a (e.g., position of stimulus on the retina).[18]

Proponents of the enactive account of color, like Noë and O'Regan, focus on perceptual activity understood literally as bodily movement and do not make the connection between their activity focus and any revisionary metaphysics that breaks with the traditional emphasis on substance and stasis. In other words, they concentrate on the continuity between perception and action without considering the ontological implications of this approach. But as I argued in chapter 5, just thinking about perception as interaction, aside from actual bodily movements and sensory-motor loops (important though those are), can motivate a revision of the metaphysics of perceived qualities. So color adverbialism may usefully be thought of as an ontological adjunct to enactive approaches. It is now time to say something about the ontological picture that comes into focus here.

6.3.1   Substance and Process

General substance ontologies make the claim that continuants (objects, substances, entities, etc.) and their properties are the basic ontological categories. This view is dominant in contemporary philosophy (e.g., see Heil 2012). In contrast, general process ontologies make the claim that occurents (activities, events, processes, performances, actions, etc.) and their properties are the basic ontological categories.[19] Now, my proposal that colors are properties of perceptual activities is consistent with a substance ontology, so long as it is *not* supposed that perceptual processes and colors

---

18. See Broackes (1997), O'Regan (2011, ch. 11), and Gert (2012a). Gert classifies his version of this theory as a kind of dispositionalism, hence a kind of relationism. Perhaps this is the correct classification of Noë's theory as well, despite his criticism of relationism. Note that he posits "nonphysical ways" because what is crucial to him is the effects of objects on a Gibsonian optic array, which is not the neutral physical surroundings but the environment *for* an animal. Schellenberg (2008, 60n) holds this reading. She proposes an analysis of color in terms of situation-dependent properties that are decidedly not perceiver-related.

19. See Simons (2000) on the continuant–occurent distinction, and Whitehead ([1929] 1979) and Rescher (2000) for examples of systematic process metaphysics.

are somehow ontologically basic. The most I need from a general ontology is the assumption that processes exist in some sense alongside the entities that they are associated with. This could mean that the ontologically basic entities "make up" the less fundamental processes. As long as processes bear properties of their own not attributable to entities, this would be compatible with my view. It is comparable to the situation in which one says that pure water has a property (wetness) that is not attributable to its fundamental constituents (H_2O molecules), even though pure water is by hypothesis the aggregate of water molecules.

My view is, of course, more suggestive of an ontology in which processes are ontologically basic. This could either be a dualism of the sort articulated by Machamer et al. (2000), where both entities and activities are fundamental ontological categories, or a pure process ontology. Thus I remain noncommittal over the choice between a substance and dualist or process ontology as this larger ontological issue is not relevant to my discussion of color, and because any satisfactory argument for or against any one of these ontologies is far beyond the scope of this book. What I will say is that the substance focus of most of the metaphysical background assumed in the philosophy of perception seems to have made many philosophers somewhat oblivious to the possibility that colors could be properties of processes rather substances. This is a widespread tendency in the philosophy of mind. As Figdor (2014, 38) notes, there is "a kind of inattentional blindness philosophers of mind have shown when it comes to conceiving of their explanandum as a kind of complex activity."

So what is to be gained by treating color in a processual fashion? Shortly I will argue that this approach gets us traction with the issues stated above as requirements on a color ontology friendly to perceptual science. But one thing first to point out is how well the process approach fits itself into a neuroscientific framework. The genuinely explanatory (as opposed to merely descriptive) models in neuroscience are models of processes—neural processing. For example, an account of the early stages of color vision describes light being absorbed and selectively reflected from a material surface, photons hitting the retina and being selectively absorbed by cone cells, these cells transmitting electrochemical signals to other retinal neurons, leading up to the important stage of opponent coding by retinal ganglion cells, and further (not yet well understood) stages of processing in the thalamus and cortex.[20] In this, and in other textbook mechanistic neuroscientific explanations, the activities can be said to play a starring role alongside the entities (Machamer et al. 2000, 8). One might even claim that the substance (anatomy) of neurons is significant just insofar as it allows them to do particular things—fire action potentials, activate or inhibit other neurons, and so forth.[21] In sum, the major subject matter of neuroscience is neural processing, and likewise visual processing and perceptual activity are the primary explanatory targets for vision science. From the point of view of these sciences, it is fitting that color should turn out to be a property of a process, not of a substance.

6.3.2 Color Unlocated and Insubstantiated

Section 2.2 dwelled on the ontological anxieties that have long been caused by the reification of color—its being treated not only as a property of substances but almost as a substance in itself. Above in section 6.1.2 I pointed out that the theories most symptomatic of reification—versions of color realism, with their commitment to color being somewhere locatable—stand at odds with the current situation of color science whereby there is no one thing, or type of thing, or part of the world, that experimenters study in order to find out about color. I pointed out that all versions of relationism have an advantage here because they can posit that each branch of color science is actually focusing on one particular relatum, among the many that together constitute color.

It is worth emphasizing that the adverbialist position stands at the farthest possible distance from reified notions of color, for color is not even to be thought of as a property of material substances. It also bears emphasis that adverbial properties of perceptual interactions are just not the kind of thing that could enter into an ontology derived from physical science, whereas properties of material substances are. So for the adverbialist it comes as no surprise if physicists and chemists have not (and almost

20. This is a simplified version of an account such as Martin (2009).

21. To date, overt links from neuroscience to process metaphysics seem to be confined to consciousness science—one of the more speculative branches of neuroscience (e.g., Weber and Weekes 2009; Barrett and Seth 2011). However, there is currently something of a wave of process metaphysics in the philosophy of biology. Dupré (2013) argues that standard accounts of mechanistic explanation, even of the dualist Machamer et al. (2000) sort, are too thing-focused and that processual ontologies afford greater understanding of biological systems. See also Dupré (2012).

certainly will not) discover chromatic properties of matter that correspond to any perceptually derived notion of color. Yet this is the failure that haunts the color realist.

Like one view in the vicinity of relationism, the *relativism* of Brogaard (2010), color adverbialism posits that actual instantiations of color are dependent on there being the right configuration of object, viewing circumstances, and perceiver. In other words, it follows that in the absence of all perceivers (e.g., the dark side of the moon) nothing is colored. Cohen (2009, 226) finds this "implausibly idealistic," and ensures that this is not a consequence of his own role functionalist version of relationism. However, as Brogaard (2012, 315) observes, the perceiver-dependence of color instantiations also explains why colors simply have no place in physical theories, ones that aim to describe what is there in the world independently of thinking and perceiving subjects. Moreover it is entirely consistent with scientists' claims that colors are a result of animal–environment interactions.[22]

6.3.3   What Stays the Same?

Of course, this consequence of color adverbialism would seem to intensify a concern about relationism—that colors become a Heraclitean flux and the color of an object, like a flowing river, is not something that can ever stay the same (Cohen 2009, 125). This sits uneasily with the apparent stability of colors (even as viewing circumstances change), and the fact that one of the functions of color vision is to aid the re-identification of objects. So what must be pointed out is that even for the adverbialist something *does* stay the same: the stimuli and the perceivers that engage in perceptual activities may themselves be largely unchanged from one occasion to the next. This explains why it is natural to speak of "the same color."

An analogy is helpful here. Imagine a series of performances of a particular musical score, such as a keyboard prelude by J. S. Bach. There are sets of performances that are quite different from one another because they are played on different instruments (harpsichord, clavichord, and modern piano). Some are more similar to each other: the series of different pianists' performances on a modern instrument, or the various interpretations of one musician. Some are perceptually indistinguishable from one another: as can be achieved by a professional musician aiming at exact replication of

22. Palmer (1999, 95) and Wolfe et al. (2006, 97), quoted at start section 6.2.

a previous performance. Each performance is an event brought about through the interaction of a player, an instrument, and a score. As an event, each performance is unique because it occurs in different stretches of time. Yet the properties of different events may be more or less similar to one another. Because they all involve the same score, all the renditions have some harmonic, melodic, and rhythmic properties in common. Thus one can say, "it's the same piece of music," even though the music itself is the acoustic event, not the score. And one may say this even for acoustic events that are not perceptually indistinguishable. For the indistinguishable performances it seems legitimate to say that the events instantiate exactly the same acoustic properties, even though they occur at different times and the entities giving rise to the event have changed slightly—the instrument and the player will have aged, just a little bit, from one performance to the next.

The score is to the musical performance as the stimulus is to the color. When one has roughly constant color perceptions of a material object it makes sense to say "it's the same color" because each perceptual experience is shaped by the same physical stimulus. When I now have experiences of the colors of a painting that are absolutely indistinguishable from one moment to the next, I might as well say that the colors instantiated in my perceiving are the same each of the different times, even though, as time passes, the paint will be bleached slightly (imperceptibly) more, and the lenses of my eyes will have yellowed just a little.

A similar worry about Cohen's relationism is that it is the height of ontological profligacy to posit that each object bears an infinite number of colors, all indexed to different perceivers and circumstances (Hardin 2004). The adverbialist is in a good position here because this multiplicity of color is most counterintuitive when one supposes that colors are always there instantiated in things. It is natural to be concerned about how so many rednesses could all be clustered on to one small cherry at once. But for the adverbialist all these colors are *not* instantiated all the time. They need a perceiver to "make them happen."

6.3.4 Back to Primitivism

As discussed in section 3.1.2, primitivism is usually defined by its commitment to the thesis that colors are the properties revealed to us in ordinary experience. But as Watkins (2010, 123n) observes, "[a]s 'Primitivism' is commonly used in the color literature, to be a primitivist is to hold only that colors are not reducible to other properties." Another way of putting this commitment is to say that colors are emergent properties of physical systems, where emergent properties are novel, unpredictable, "higher level" attributes that are not explainable in terms of "lower level" properties, and they have their own causal powers (Kim 1999). One interesting feature of color adverbialism is that on this second, more liberal definition of primitivism it might turn out to be a primitivist theory, as I will now explain.

Arguments that make trouble for emergence, and nonreductive physicalism in general, assume what Mitchell (2012) has called a "static mapping picture" whereby the functional properties of higher level entities are fully cashed out in terms of the stable microphysical properties of lower level entities in the supervenience base. Since the only ontological categories in play are entities and their properties, all characterized in a snapshot view without consideration of their evolution in time, this mapping picture presupposes a general substance ontology.

Mitchell (2012, 177) writes:

If we take a snapshot view of the higher and lower levels, then the dynamics of *how* the higher level is constituted and stabilized is lost. Contemporary sciences show us that there are processes, often involving negative and positive feedback or self-organization, that are responsible for generating higher-level stable properties, and these processes are not captured by a static mapping.

This implies that in order to evade the pull of reductionism the advocate of color as an emergent property would be wise to look for parallels with canonical scientific examples of emergent behavior, such as flocking. What is typical of such cases is the presence of a feedback loop that stabilizes an emergent property, for example, the V shape of a flock of birds or the density of a school of fish. In other words, the lower level components of the system (the birds or fish) are sensitive to the presence of the higher level property (shape of formation), and they modify their behavior in order to maintain it. So the higher level property can be said to exert downward causation.

Mitchell's point is that a reductionist *could* take a snapshot view of a flock of birds or school of fish and say that that shape is merely a property of the aggregate of lower level components. But that would be to miss the scientifically interesting thing about the system: how simple low-level properties can give rise to it, and how once arisen, a system's very stability is due to the dynamism of low-level components—their sensitivity to environmental perturbations so as to stabilize the emergent feature. I would add further that to treat the system in the way encouraged by substance ontology (as one that can be fully characterized without any reference to the temporal dimension) will obscure what is made salient by a treatment encouraged by a process ontology—that the system is one that requires changes through time in order to be what it is (Dupré 2013, 30).

Thus a genuinely dynamic mapping picture will be one in which the higher level property is not just an aggregate of lower level ones (be they entities or activities) but something more like an attractor for the system as a whole—a feature that the system as a whole works to maintain in the face of external perturbations. Whether the properties of perceptual processes can be characterized in this way is a matter for empirical investigation. Moreover the emergent status of chromatic properties will also depend on the general ontological picture—whether or not one is committed to processes and substances as basic categories. Needless to say, the claim that there can be a primitivist twist on color adverbialism is a highly speculative one. But primitivists who are keen to satisfy their nonreductionistic inclinations about color while looking to place these intuitions on a firmer naturalistic footing, may well find it advantageous to pursue this line of inquiry.

6.4   Relationality

The reader might be puzzled by the fact that I have claimed the name "adverbialism" to label my theory, while at the same time eschewing a characteristic feature of that view, namely its rejection of any relational (i.e., act-object) analysis of perception in general. My theory is relational in two important senses—it links colors both to stimuli and to perceivers, and it treats vision as fundamentally a process that connects a perceiver to some sort of extra-mental object.[23] Importantly, the traditional versions of adverbialism denied relationism in both senses. For instance, McGilvray's (1983) theory has it that the adverbial modifications that are definitive of color

---

23. I say "fundamentally" because the connection is not merely a causal one. That is, one could deny the thesis that perceptual experience is constituted by the perceiver's relation to an extra-mental object but still accept that those objects are the causes of experience. Thanks to Craig French for raising this issue.

are properties of "seeing events" that are unambiguously "in the head," as McGilvray (1994) would later put it.[24]

One reason for my departure from this standard tenet of adverbialism is that my motivations are very different. The original adverbialism was a reaction against sense-data theories of perception.[25] The sense-data theory is known as an *act-object* theory because it treats perception as requiring the correct combination of an act (perceiving) and an object (sense-datum). The first adverbialists were concerned to depart from the act-object approach because of the troubling ontological status of sense-data. Since the threat of having to posit mysterious sense-data is not a current concern, I propose to shift adverbialism back into the orbit of act-object theories, and below I will say more about how I understand the object of perception.[26]

However, both traditional adverbialist and sense-data theories can be understood as responses to arguments from illusion and hallucination.[27] Put bluntly, the argument states that since in my veridical perception of a banana and my hallucination of one I have indistinguishable experiences of yellowness, curvedness, sweetness, and the like, I cannot suppose that an ordinary material banana serves as the actual object of my experience, even when it is veridical. For the sense-data theorist, veridical, illusory, and hallucinatory experiences are all presentations of sense-data, proxies for the actual properties of the banana, whereas for the classical adverbialist there is simply no object in either the ordinary or non-ordinary situations—all we must posit to describe perceptual experiences are the internal sensing events. Since I eschew both the sense-data and classical adverbialist accounts of illusion and hallucination, I will shortly say something about how these

---

24. Conduct (2008) is an exception here. See Crane (2000) and Fish (2010, ch. 3) for discussions on the early adverbialists.

25. That is to say, the idea that the actual objects of our perceptual experience are not material things but immaterial (but also extra-mental) *sense-data*, from which we infer the presence of ordinary objects (e.g., Russell [1912] 1980).

26. Because I reinstate the object of perception, my version of adverbialism does not fall foul of the standard objection to classical adverbialism, the "many properties problem" of Jackson (1975). See Fish (2010, 39–44) for discussion of Jackson's objections to adverbialism and the responses of Tye and Sellars.

27. See Smith (2002) and Fish (2009) for recent analysis and responses to these arguments.

are to be handled in my theory. Before that I will say something about the advantages of combining relationism with adverbialism.

6.4.1 Adverbialism and the Inner-Outerness of Color

Early in this chapter I argued that the "Janus-facedness" of color—the way that the study of color directs us both to perceivers and to things perceived—is an important signpost toward improved theorizing in this area. While this desideratum has been noted on a number of occasions by perceptual scientists, it has made comparatively little impact on the philosophical debate. On consideration of this point, relationist ontologies come out in front compared to their realist or antirealist rivals. Color adverbialism shares this advantage with other versions of relationism.

Yet adverbialism has an additional feature in its favor. This book begins with a quotation from James (1904, 481), who writes that "the whole philosophy of perception from Democritus's time downwards has been just one long wrangle over the paradox that what is evidently one reality should be in two places at once, both in outer space and in a person's mind." Now this paradox is no less manifest in the standard forms of color relationism. For example, a dispositionalist holds that red, as instantiated in external objects, is a dispositional property of the thing to have a particular chromatic effect on a trichromatic person, under normal conditions. The chromatic sensation that the person undergoes in response to the standard symbols of love and communism are the psychical corollaries of the physical dispositions. So there is no "one reality" for color, as the dispositionalist sees it, and she would most likely dispute the claim that it is "evidently" the case that there should be. But for the adverbialist, there is no color-in-the-object, on the one hand, and color-in-the-mind, on the other; there is just one color—the property of a perceptual process. Thus color adverbialism is uniquely positioned to articulate the "Janus-facedness" of color.

More fundamentally, the reason why color adverbialism is able to avoid this troublesome duplication of color is that the origin of the theory is in the idea that perception should be thought of in terms of interaction and not correspondence. The correspondence framework, which is presupposed by other versions of relationism brings with it the notion that there are two ontologically disparate realms to be matched together in the process of perceptual judgment, the inner and the outer. Thus it becomes impossible to resist the idea that whatever external property we identify as red (be it a dispositional or a perceiver-independent one) finds its corollary inside the mind of a perceiver as, for example, "the sensation of red." Within the interaction framework, and the adverbialist theory that flows from it, there is no reason to pair "actual red," "physical red," or "external red" with "internal red" or "sensation of red." There is just red, which is not simply inner *or* outer. Now this position itself raises a pair of questions. The first concerns the status of color-involving experiences that are apparently unrelated to external objects. The second asks whether or not color is to be treated as a *qualitative* property. I will now address both of these in turn.

6.4.2 Hallucination, etc.

It seems that we have color experiences in the absence of any external object—for example, in dreams, hallucinations, and when the visual cortex is stimulated directly to induce flashes of colorful light known as phosphenes.[28] Yet, on my view, color is a property of a perceptual interaction involving both a perceiver and a stimulus that lies beyond the eye. So, if these other experiences genuinely involve color—of the same kind as in the ordinary perceptual cases—then they stand as clear counterexamples to my view.

Imagine that I have a full-blooded, 3D, technicolor hallucination of an emperor butterfly fluttering before my eyes. Let us assume that by visual cues alone I would not be able to tell the hallucinated butterfly apart from a real one. I think I see a pair of wings red-ly, gold-ly, and black-ly, and yet there is nothing actually there to see. Whatever these colors are, they cannot be properties of a perceptual interaction between myself and a pretty invertebrate because no such creature is present in my vicinity. So my response to this case is simply to say that the "colors" I associate with the butterfly hallucination are not colors in the usual sense, but they are derivative of them. It is quite straightforward to say that these *H-colors* (let us call them) are properties of another kind of process—not a perceptual one but a hallucinatory one. That is, they are a property of the series of neural events inside my brain that gives rise to the hallucinatory experience. This experience can be analyzed in the following way:

I hallucinate H-red-ly, H-gold-ly, and H-black-ly.

---

28. I do not here consider the colors of after-images or the colorful haze that one sees through closed eyelids. I would argue that these still arise from a perceptual interaction that involves an extra-ocular object.

The hallucinatory events may well have a lot in common with ordinary perceptual events—for instance, they might show similar visual cortex activiations on an fMRI scan—but there would still be differences, such as in the patterns of pre-cortical activation. One could think of H-colors as properties of sensings or neural firings, not perceivings. They are "truncated colors" because they lack any link to an extra-ocular stimulus.

This response is a *disjunctivist* one, for it denies that there is a fundamental, chromatic common factor shared between my veridical and hallucinatory experiences involving color.[29] Still H-colors *are* relatives of ordinary colors. It is likely that some of the same neural events occur in both the hallucinatory and veridical experiences. Thus it is not surprising that the hallucinatory colors could be manifest in such a way that I might fail to distinguish them from ordinary colors. But what I want to emphasize is that the H-colors are parasitic on the ordinary ones. It is because I have seen real butterflies, with real red, gold, and black manifestations that my drugged or diseased brain fires off in such a way that I experience mirage-like replicas of these original encounters.

Similarly phosphene colors—*P-colors*—are properties of the particular neural firings that are generated by transcranial magnetic stimulation (TMS). These neural firings bear even less resemblance to the pattern of activity that occurs in response to an actual visual stimulus, and P-colors are less likely to be mistaken for ordinary colors. *D-colors* are properties of the neural activity patterns characteristic of dream states. Even on introspective evidence these are revealed to be quite different from ordinary perceptual colors (Schwitzgebel 2011). It bears emphasis that P-, H-, or D-colors should never be thought of as elements of ordinary colors. I am consciously breaking away from the tradition in the philosophy of mind that understands neural processing in the visual cortex as the last stage as a series of events leading to visual experience, and hence a "common factor" in veridical, hallucinatory, and illusory experiences.[30]

---

29. See articles in Haddock and Macpherson (2008) and Byrne and Logue (2008) for further reading on disjunctivism. Importantly, this passage is not intended to address the epistemological worry of how ordinary visual experience of a butterfly can justify belief that there is a butterfly, given the possibility of a subjectively indistinguishable hallucination. My point is rather that from a third-person, scientific perspective the two states *are* distinguishable.

30. See, for example, Fish (2010, 3–5) on the "common factor principle." Disjunctivism is just the denial of this assumption.

6.4.3   Adverbialism and Consciousness

The last point raises the question of how to handle the qualitative nature of color. As I state above in the definition of perceivers relevant to the adverbialist theory, these individuals are often conscious and the conscious phenomenology of color would seem to be quite integral to what color is (for those perceivers). So my position is that color must be considered a qualitative, and not purely quantitative, property when it is a property of perceptual processes involving conscious perceivers. But as I have emphasized, color cannot be analyzed down into physical and psychical components, or color perception thought of as the representation of the correspondences between these two. So an implication is that if color is indeed a qualitative property, then its phenomenological what-it's-like-ness is also not confined to the mind of the perceiver.

In the recent history of the color debate, before the current popularity of primitivist views, if one wanted to claim that color is a qualitative property, one would have to have conceded that it is a mental one, instantiated only in the minds or brains of individuals. So those who wanted to deny that color is instantiated purely in the mind-brain would also have to deny its qualitative nature. But as Byrne (2006) and Kalderon (2007) observe, this tendency to treat the problem of consciousness as the problem of the mind-brain relationship is an arbitrary response to the more general problem of how there can be *any* qualitative properties in a physical world. The qualitative is really a bump that can be shifted around under the worn rug of materialism. Most bet that the neuroscience of the future will eventually smooth out the wrinkles (and properly clean out the dirt that has been tucked under there). Hence the current preference is to keep the lumps underneath the mental area of the rug. Yet, in principle, nothing should prevent us from shifting the wrinkles over to the physical side, or indeed spreading them evenly between the two sides.

The claim that consciousness is not confined to the brain and is somehow "in between" mind and the physical world has recently been advocated by Alva Noë, and he emphasizes that consciousness must be understood in terms of activities. For example, Noë (2009, xii) writes that "[c]onsciousness is not something that happens inside us. It is something we do or make. Better: it is something we achieve." Interestingly, this claim has a precedent in early ecological psychology most influenced by James's radical empiricism. Holt wrote, for instance, that "[c]onsciousness is not a substance but a relation—the relation between the living organism and the environment to which it specifically responds" (Holt 1915, 96, quoted in Heft 2001, 87).

The problem is that in the absence of further metaphysical articulation, such claims are quite perplexing. Color adverbialism is one way to make sense of the notion of qualitative properties "out of our heads," and a move to a processual ontology would be a clear way to articulate the idea that consciousness is not something in us (an entity) but something we do (an activity). All this is of a piece with the idea that properties of consciousness— qualitative chromatic properties and other *qualia*—are adverbial properties of processes. A line of philosophers, including James (1904), Whitehead ([1929] 1979), and Sellars (1981) took the move toward a process ontology to be the most promising route to a resolution of the mind-body problem,[31] though their path has been underexplored in recent philosophy of mind. In this chapter I hope to have conveyed the benefits of the adverbial approach to color, with or without any wider commitment to process metaphysics. Any success here would suggest that a similar strategy could be useful in addressing the other problems of the qualitative.

31. Also relevant is Seibt's (2012) exposition of Bergson: "As long as we understand conscious experience as a subject–object relation we merely follow the theoretical habits in which we have been conditioned by the substance-metaphysical tradition. However, when we carefully attend to what we take in during conscious experience and who we are, without forcing a conceptualization of that experiential content or the act of experience, we find not a relation and ready-made relata but an interactivity or ongoing interfacing with the world."

7 True Colors

Overview

In the previous two chapters I presented arguments in favor of general color relationism, and the more specific adverbialist thesis. In chapter 5 I encouraged a break with realism and antirealism, arguing that the problem of color should no longer be framed as an inquiry into whether any properties outside the mind correspond to the properties we experience as the colors. In chapter 6 I took a yet more radical step, arguing that we should no longer think of colors as properties instantiated in extradermal objects, or somehow inside the mind, but as modifiers of perceptual processes or interactions.

The motivation for this rather different theory of color comes largely from consideration of the theoretical commitments and conceptual needs of perceptual science. As such, color adverbialism is not intended as an exposition of the ontology assumed by ordinary color discourse, or as an analysis of color visual experience. However, it is still beneficial to see how this theory stands with respect to the dominant theories of visual experience within the philosophy of perception—representationalism and naïve realism. So in this chapter I will argue that color adverbialism is compatible with versions of representational and naïve realist theories. Along the way I will address a number of potential objections to my position, concluding with a discussion of how the adverbialist should analyze cases of perceptual error.

By the end of section 7.3 the reader will have before her a smorgasbord of the more general theories of perception that are hospitable to color adverbialism, and she is free to select the one most palatable to her taste. By a large degree, the reader's evaluation of these different theories will be guided by her prior theoretical affiliations. The choice of any such theory may seem like a recherché philosophical issue, but I would like to assure the reader who has less patience for the abstractions of the philosophy of perception that the matter does have some bearing on the concerns of perceptual science. For instance, there has been a long-standing controversy within perceptual science between Gibsonians, who hold that perception is direct and presentational and Marrians, who take perception to be or indirect and representational. While the material presented here is by no means intended to resolve this debate, it does aim to shed new light on the pro's and con's of each position.

7.1   The Issue of Attribution

A central and distinctive feature of color adverbialism is that it does not take color to be the kind of property that is instantiated in ordinary physical objects. Instead, it posits that color properties modify perceptual processes—interactions that involve perceivers and physical objects. This peculiarity of the adverbial theory is what allows it to deflate the problem of color: our visual system does not mask external reality from us by painting it in false color, for visual experience should not be thought of as attributing colors to external objects; colors are, contrary to expectation, just not that kind of property.[1]

Boghossian and Velleman (1989, 82n4) immediately raise an object to adverbialism, which they believe removes it from contention:

Seeing something as red is the sort of thing that can be illusory or veridical, hence the sort of thing that has truth-conditions, and hence the sort of thing that has content. The content of this experience is that the object in question is red; and so the experience represents an object as having a property about which we can legitimately ask whether it is a property that objects so represented really tend to have.

The quick way with this objection is to point out that it begs the question against adverbialism. Boghossian and Velleman are simply asserting

---

1. Note that an adverbialist need not deny that color perception represents colors as being properties of objects. For instance, James McGilvray is an adverbialist but also an error theorist: he claims that color experience *does* represent colors as being properties of objects. Since this position does not allow for a deflation of the problem of color, I do not discuss it further. The question of which theory of color gets the phenomenology right will be left for the next chapter.

what adverbialism most typically denies—that visual experience is subject to accuracy conditions. This denial is not peculiar to adverbialists but is common ground with naïve realists such as Travis (2004) and the anti-representational account of Gupta (2006). Furthermore, in presenting the case against the simplistic, detectionist approach to color perception (chapters 4 and 5), I have already given reason to doubt Boghossian and Velleman's claims.

Still, it is worth noting that the assumptions that Boghossian and Velleman bring to their objection are common within the philosophy of perception. Most color theorists in fact do subscribe to them, and so would be predisposed to rule out color adverbialism. So I will now spell out the "simple Russellian representational theory" that Boghossian and Velleman assume, and that is hostile to adverbialism. I will show that this account of the content of perceptual experience is itself made vulnerable by consideration of the interconnectedness of color with other visual modalities that was first introduced in chapter 4, and then continue by sketching out an alternative representational theory that is friendly to adverbialism and which blends harmoniously with the *coloring for* model of that chapter.

7.1.1 Preliminaries: A Simple Representational Theory

Boghossian and Velleman (1989) subscribe to a representational view of visual experience. On their particular account, when you see an everyday object, for example, a turquoise sock cast aside on a beige rug, your color visual experience can be analyzed just in terms of an attribution of the property 'turquoise' to the sock and 'beige' to the rug. In psychological terms, the attribution of properties by one's color visual experience is equivalent to the process of color recognition. Likewise your form experience is analyzed in terms of one attributing the geometric property of 'rectangularity' to the rug and, perhaps, 'crumpled irregularity' to the sock. Visual experience is representational in that it has phenomenal or experiential contents that can be glossed as propositions such as 'the sock is turquoise'.[2] Furthermore Boghossian and Velleman's account is consistent with the idea that visual experience can be analyzed in an atomistic or modular manor—that

---

2. The controversy over conceptual and nonconceptual content can be ignored for the purposes of this discussion.

the total experiential content is a simple conjunction, a linear sum, of all the separate property attributions. It is a *simple* theory.

The other distinctive feature of their theory is that it is *Russellian*. That is, it makes the assumption that visual experience is entirely a matter of *what* is represented, and not of *how* it is represented. In other words, visual experience can be fully analyzed in terms of the properties attributed to objects in the visual field.[3] The Russellian commitment is expressed very clearly in Boghossian and Velleman's assertion that "[t]he content of this experience [of seeing red] is that the object in question is red" (Boghossian and Velleman 1989, 82n4). It is implicit that the content of an experience of seeing red is exhausted by the attribution of redness: *the content of this experience is that the object in question is red, and that's all there is to it.*[4] This is an expression of atomism with regards to perceptual contents. Thus I call the theory of visual experience in play behind Boghossian and Velleman's objection to color adverbialism the "simple Russellian representational theory."

This same account is also presupposed by Averill (2005, 217) in his defense of projectivist antirealism:

In this paper, seeing is assumed to be a matter of visual representation. Thus, seeing something as having a color is a matter of visually representing it as having a color. Here 'color', and the more determinate terms 'red', 'orange', 'brown', 'white', and so on, are used to refer to properties we visually attribute to things.

And it is also endorsed by Pasnau (2009, 358) and Frank Jackson in their expositions of physicalism. Jackson's "prime intuition" about red "is simply that red is the property objects look to have when they look red" (Jackson 1998, 89).

Most tellingly, this view has found favor with color relationists. For instance, Thompson et al. (1992, 62) state, "[t]hat color should be the

3. This characterization borrows from Thompson (2009, 100): "For any experience (that has phenomenal content) with phenomenal character r [e.g., qualitative redness], there is some property p_r [i.e., the property 'red'] such that, necessarily, if an experience has phenomenal character r then it attributes p_r [to some object]." This amounts to the claim that there is a one-to-one correspondence between phenomenal character (the qualitative feeling of redness) and the represented properties attributed to objects (the property 'redness'; Thompson 2010, 150–51). Shoemaker (2006) calls this the "Ways = Properties principle." It is a commitment common to representationalists such as Dretske (1995) and Tye (2000).

4. Compare Boghossian and Velleman (1991, 68): colors "are the properties that objects appear to have when they look colored."

content of chromatic perceptual states is a criterion of adequacy for any theory of perceptual content." This is most readily interpreted as a claim for Russellianism and simplicity—that the content of color visual experience is, exclusively, the color attributed to an object, and that the color visual experience has no bearing on the attribution of nonchromatic properties. Similarly, when Cohen (2009, 21) analyses a situation in which the same reflectance stimulus appears as variable shades of gray (simultaneous surround contrast effect), he writes that:

In each case of variation considered, there is variation in the way that the stimulus looks (in respect of color) to a single subject. On a more or less standard view of the visual system as visually representing the world, this entails that, in each case, there is a set of variant representations of the color of the stimulus. (see Cohen 2007, 349n2)

Again, this is consistent with the simple Russellian theory, and it should be noted that Cohen (2009, 89–94) explicitly rejects an alternative Fregean analysis. Thus Cohen never considers the possibility that content of chromatic experience should be analyzed in terms other than the attribution of colors to stimuli.

7.1.2 The Complexity of Color Experience

My dispute, at this point, is not with the representational theory more generally but with the particular assumption of simplicity—that the content of chromatic perceptual states is *uniquely and exhaustively* color. If one takes any actual visual experience, color is always there among a complex of other material qualities (e.g., glossiness), geometric properties (e.g., shape and distance), as well as the play of light and shadow. The argument of chapter 4 was that *color vision* makes a contribution to our perception of all of these other properties/qualities, and that the perception of other visual qualities also informs color vision. Hence one cannot *presume* that the way something looks (in respect of color) can just be reduced down to being the color it is represented as having. Given the interplay of visual submodalities, a likely scenario is that the way something looks, colorwise, is also a representation of how it looks shapewise, texturewise, lightingwise, and so on. Any simple parsing of a scene into representation of color, representation of shape, representation of texture, representation of lighting, could well be theoretical prejudice disguising itself as introspective report. Of course, however, one could claim that the nonmodular, subpersonal visual processing that was described in chapter 4 gives way to a modular representation of object properties at the personal, experiential level. I will now present an example to illustrate that the complex, holistic, and "non-modular" interpretation of experience is more compelling than the simple, atomistic, and "modular" one.

I call color experience "complex" or "rich" because it tells us so much more than just what the colors of things are. The idea that the content of chromatic perceptual states is simply color is an impoverished view, both from the point of view of phenomenology and from the third-personal, functional perspective of chapter 4. In order to develop the complex account, it is necessary to sketch a new framework for analyzing visual experience that does not presuppose atomism. One way to do this is to invoke the perceptual pragmatism of chapter 5. Rather than determining the content of a perceptual representation by assessing how things would have to be in the world if the representation is to be deemed accurate (correspondence model), one determines the content by assessing which discriminations, identifications, judgments, are made possible by this perceptual state (pragmatic approach). This can be done either introspectively, from the first-person perspective or observationally, from the third-person perspective.

Consider the following scenario:

I see a green bus trundling down the road. Color is a salient part of my experience but not the only part. If I were to describe the perceptual state verbally I'd start by saying "I'm seeing a bottle green double-decker, it's not full but it's accelerating...."

Having learned the lesson of chapter 4, I can say that this perceptual state allows me to:

1. Discriminate an object from its background. (State affords scene segmentation.)

2. Run for the bus. (State enables object pursuit.)

3. Know a bus is there. (State facilitates judgment about presence of an object.)

4. Surmise that the bus exterior is painted with a matt paint that absorbs a large proportion of incident light. (State facilitates judgment about physical properties surfaces.)

5. Say "that bus is green." (State affords application of color word.)

6. Recognize it as one of the fleet of the usual company. (State enables object identification.)

Each of these points alludes to one aspect of the content of the perceptual state/representation. Color vision plays a part across the board, and as follows from the material of chapter 4, the contribution of color vision cannot be described in isolation from the contribution of other visual modalities (e.g., processing of form). In this example, motion and color perception work together for very efficient scene segmentation. I have not given an exhaustive characterization of the contents of this state. Perhaps there can never be one. Our introspective and scientific, third-person access to the information is incomplete. This does not matter for my purposes because all I want to say is that the color-involving contents of visual experience go beyond the aspects of the experience that are implicated in hue recognition. That is what I mean by the richness or complexity of color perceptual states. Color recognition is just one facet of color vision, and color vision cannot be disentangled from perception in general.

I envisage that a proponent of the simple representational view will say that even though the contents of the entire perceptual state encompass all of the above points, the *color* content is only the aspect associated with the attribution of the color to the bus. In other words, one might argue that while many kinds of visual information *fix* the content of a color-involving experience, the chromatic content itself is just the color attribution: does not color content, by definition, specify only color despite depending in various ways on achromatic properties?[5] One thing first to note is that the language we use to describe perceptual experience is already biased toward atomism. Just because we talk of "(pure) color content," it does not follow that there is such a thing. It is helpful to employ more neutral language, which is why I urge that we speak instead of "color-involving content". It should then become clear that in asserting that the content of this color-involving experience is simply a color attribution, the Russellian is begging the question against my view. What ground does she have for thinking that the contents of color-involving experiences are delimited in this way?

When philosophers use oversimplified toy examples, such as a visual representation of a red ball on a table, it is tempting to analyze

5. I thank Shivam Patel for his formulation and discussion.

them atomistically. The chromatic, spatial, and geometric might be taken as distinct and fully separable. Moreover the viewer is assumed to be a passive spectator who is not at all inclined to interact with what she sees. However, if we move to realistically complex perceptual encounters with the world, such as searching for a chipmunk scuttling under a pile of fallen leaves, the separation between the chromatic, the spatial, and indeed the cross-modal contents is not so clear cut. In a realistically challenging perceptual task the different senses must work together—bootstrap across one another—in order to find the sought-for object. It does not make sense to analyze each sensory contribution in isolation from the others. And introspectively these contributions are bound together so tightly that they cannot so obviously be unwoven. Rather than enforce an atomistic decomposition on the experience as a whole, it is preferable to analyze the perceptual state in terms of what it enables the perceiver to *do*. And if one declares that "the content of this experience is 'seeing a brown chipmunk-shaped thing scuttling around in the right hand side of the pile of brown leaf-shaped things,'" this should be taken as nothing more than shorthand for what would be a richer and far longer description.

With a more complex picture in place we can call into question something as seemingly obvious as Jackson's "prime intuition." My claim is that when objects look red, they also, for example, look to have a material presence, a three-dimensional shape, and a surface texture. When objects look red, I may also be able to recognize them as familiar, to track them as they move, to plot a course toward them. All of these looks, and all of these potential actions, are both inseparable from and in virtue of those things looking red. Looking red cannot be reduced to the mere having of a putative redness property.

One might raise the objection that when a collection of objects differ *only* their colors, we have strong ground for saying that color is a separable visual attribute, and that the atomistic analysis is on target.[6] But this simply ignores the fact that a chromatic change also entails changes in the object's contrast with its background, which in turn affects scene segmentation, and it alters our notions of the material constitution of the object. This much we know about the functional or informational implications of chromatic changes. From the first person perspective, these nonchromatic

6. Thanks to Carrie Figdor for raising this example.

changes *do* make a difference to our experience of the object and how we would interact with it. For example, as raspberries on a bush ripen and turn from pale green to dark red, my experience of their shapes also changes because those shapes now pop out and no longer merge into the shapes of the background leaves. The redder they are, the easier it is for me to pick them.

7.1.3 A Complex Representational Theory

As an alternative to the simple Russellian representational theory, which is widely assumed within the philosophy of color but contested elsewhere, I will now outline a complex Fregean account. The basic idea of the Fregean theories is that contents are a matter of *how* the world is represented, not just *what* is represented.[7] As such, experience must be analyzed in terms of "modes of presentation," not just in terms of properties attributed to objects.[8]

One important feature of Fregean accounts is that they break with the assumption of attribution that was crucial to Boghossian and Velleman's objection to adverbialism. For example, on Brad Thompson's Fregean account, "The colour phenomenal properties that characterize a subject's perceptual experience are not...properties that the experience attributes to the external object of perception" (Thompson 2009, 113).[9] So from this standpoint it is simply false to assert, as Boghossian and Velleman (1989)

7. Or to put it more formally: "According to Fregean theories of phenomenal content, the phenomenal content that is shared by any two phenomenally identical experiences is a matter of *how* the world is represented, and need not involve sameness in *what* is represented" (Thompson 2009, 101). For important discussions of the Fregean theory, see Chalmers (2004, 2006), Shoemaker (2006), Thompson (2009, 2010), and Schellenberg (2011).
8. The view I outline here borrows heavily from Brad Thompson's expositions. As Gert (2012b, 321) notes, there is no consensus theory of Fregean "sense," but modes of presentation can be employed within the philosophy of perception as "ways of appearing."
9. Matthen (2009) also gestures in this direction in his analysis of variation in perception of unique blue: "Unique-blue variation is not substantive; it is a difference in the 'how' not the 'what' of sensory representation," and he goes on to call this an "an adverbial aspect of perceptual representation." Note that the application of the sense-reference distinction by contemporary philosophers of perception is different from Frege's own presentation in that modes of presentation can be employed in a way that does not entail reference to any external property. For example, when discussing an example of color constancy Siegel (2013, §3.3) writes:

do, that color is the property that visual experience attributes to objects, and that adverbialism is thereby refuted. Adverbialism is only vulnerable to Boghossian and Velleman's objection if one assumes a particular theory of the contents of visual experience. The rejection of a Russellian theory in favor of a Fregean one is not a devastating cost to any color adverbialist who is also committed to the representational framework. Even though Fregean accounts of color such as Thompson's are not immediately suggestive of adverbialism, they do contain the raw materials for such a view. This is the "complex Fregean representational theory," which I will briefly sketch in the remainder of this section.

The view is "complex" because it is grounded in the holistic, nonmodular conception of vision and visual experience.[10] The other basic commitment of the view that I am sketching out is the Fregean idea is that color experience "is a matter of *how*" the world is represented. Here is the complex Fregean view in outline:

1. Experiences involving color are elicited by configurations of numerous kinds of properties in the environment—spectral ones like SSR and wavelength of light, and nonspectral ones like texture, shape, and motion.

2. Phenomenal contents of an experience involve modes of presentation (MOPs) of ascribed properties.

One attempt to account for the variation in these cases is to invoke Fregean modes of presentation of the constant features. In the case of color, such a Fregean proposal would say that experience represents the brownness of the table under modes of presentation that vary with the variations in lightness and darkness. The appeal of this strategy is that it does not treat the constant property and varying ones on a par: the constant feature is represented at the level of reference; the varying features at the level of sense. The table does not look to be both brown and shiny white or grey; it looks to be brown, by looking shinier or brighter in some parts than it does in others. In this case no attribution of shiny-whiteness or grayness is made to the table itself. Thanks to Ori Beck for raising this issue.

10. Interestingly, holism is one element of Brad Thompon's account of color, and he writes that "[u]p until now, it has been assumed that the phenomenal content of colour experiences is atomistic. That is, it was assumed that phenomenal colour properties represent the properties that they represent independently of other phenomenal properties (such as spatial phenomenal properties or other phenomenal colour properties instantiated in the visual field). But there is another possibility.... [Namely] the possibility that what property is represented by a phenomenal colour property depends on these other features of the phenomenal character of the total visual experience (including spatial features and what other phenomenal colour properties are instantiated in the experience)." (Thompson 2009, 113–12).

3. MOPs were originally introduced to convey the different cognitive roles played by different semantic descriptions. Analogously, chromatic MOPs capture the different perceptual and behavioral roles played by different color perceptual states.

4. Chromatic phenomenal modes of presentation are associated with nonchromatic property attributions in complex, color-involving visual representations.

5. For example, when I see an object commonly referred to as a "red ball," the redness I experience is a mode of presentation of its spectral and non-spectral properties. In other words, the redness is one of their ways of appearing.

6. That is, I see its sphericality and smoothness redly; I see its SSR redly; I see its bouncing motion redly.

It should be clear that this Fregean account is compatible with the adverbialist ontological position whereby redness is a property of a perceptual process that allows for seeing the ball's shape, material stability, SSR, and the like. The difference from other Fregean accounts of color, in particular those of Brad Thompson and Joshua Gert, is that I do not isolate one property type that appears under the color modes of presentation. Whereas Thompson (2009) argues that chromatic phenomenal modes of presentation are associated with spectral properties like SSR, and for Gert (2012a) the property that the MOP picks out is just a color, conceived as a complex dispositional property, I hold that there is not one property appearing under the different color modes of presentation. What is presented is a complex of spatial, spectral, and material properties.

Let us reconsider one of the examples from chapter 4 (section 4.2.1), where hue and saturation gradients, in combination with a texture gradient, form a powerful cue for distance. Figure 4.3 is a photograph of the Blue Mountains near Sydney, which demonstrates how the color of the distant mountains, due to atmospheric scattering, indicates their distance from the perceiver. In such a case it is natural to say that *we see distance bluely*. In other words, the blueness in our perception of the mountains is a way that their distance appears to us, it is a mode of presentation of their distance.

The appeal of the complex Fregean representational theory (aside from its impressive sounding name) is that it makes the representational framework hospitable for color adverbialism. This framework is favored by the majority of philosophers writing on color, and so it is an important result that such readers are not forced to make an invidious choice between adverbialism and their prior commitment to representation.[11] One disadvantage of the complex Fregean representational theory is that the correspondence approach to perception threatens to re-colonize the discussion. This is because the theory sets up a stark division between the actually representing contents of experience, which can be analyzed in terms of correspondence with external physical properties, and the subjective, modes of presentation that do not correspond to anything in the world. As a consequence we are left still in the grip of the seventeenth-century dichotomies (physical vs. mental, objective vs. subjective), and the modes of presentation themselves look to weave together into a "veil of perception." For it is hard to see, on this view, how the subjective components of sensory experience do anything other than stand in the way of our apprehension of the objective properties of things. If the reader is unconcerned by such matters, then this species of representational theory should be adequate to her needs. In the next section I will show how color adverbialism is compatible with a species of direct realist theory and is thus suited to those more bothered by this set of issues.

7.2   Color Relationism and Relationism in General

Next to the representational account of perception, the other dominant theory is *naïve realism* (aka *direct realism, disjunctivism,* or *(perceptual) relationism*).[12] Instead of thinking of perceptual states as representational states

---

11. It is also worth mentioning that the theory developed here allows us to bypass a new objection to color relationism. In a review of *The Red and the Real,* Pautz (2010) argues that visual experience cannot plausibly be said to represent the fine-grained relational properties that Cohen has identified with the colors. Again, this objection is only damaging on a Russellian theory of visual experience (the sort assumed by Cohen). According to color adverbialism, and the Fregean theory of visual representation, color experiences are *not* thought to represent the fine-grained, adverbial properties that have been identified with the colors; if they serve to represent anything at all, it is the nonchromatic properties of objects.

12. *Perceptual* relationism, as opposed to *color* relationism, is the thesis that perception must be understood in terms of a relation between a perceiver and a perceived object; perception is not to be understood in terms of the representation of one's surroundings. For an extended defense of the position; see, for example, Campbell (2002), Fish (2009), and Brewer (2011). Beyond the color debate, this view is usually referred to as "relationism," but to avoid confusion, I refer to it as "perceptual relationism."

that attribute properties to external objects, philosophers in this camp take perceptual states to be *presentational* ones—states that bring an object and its qualities into view. The key idea is that perception *acquaints* us with the objects around us, and is never mediated by proxies such as representations.[13] Theorists of this stripe would have no time for the objection raised against color adverbialism by Boghossian and Velleman (1989) because they reject the assumption that perceptual experience is representational and attributive. But at the same time it has typically been assumed that the only color ontology consistent with direct realism is primitivism. So I will now show that a particular version of naïve realism is compatible with my adverbialist theory.

One central charge against naïve realism is that it is not compatible with the known facts of perceptual processing. The amount of neural processing that occurs in the brain and sensory periphery, and the subtle ways in which alterations of brain states apparently affect perceptual states, seem to belie the direct realist claim that the brain makes a minimal contribution to perceptual experience.[14] Interestingly, the variety of naïve realism that I argue is compatible with color adverbialism is not vulnerable on this point as it accommodates the fact that perceptual experiences are substantially shaped by neural workings.

7.2.1   The Access Intuition

Regardless of longstanding controversy over its ontological status, color has often been used to illustrate the idea of perceptual acquaintance. In a famous passage, Russell ([1912] 1980, 25) states:

The particular shade of colour that I am seeing may have many things said about it. I may say that it is brown, that it is rather dark, and so on. But such statements,

---

13. Most advocates of the representational view now deny that they are committed to the indirectness of perception. As Hatfield (2009, 350) puts it, "representations…are not *that which* we see, but *that by which* we see" (emphasis original). But see Fish (2004) and Kriegel (2011).

14. See, for example, Pautz (2011) and Nanay (2014). This relates to objections made by Marr (1982) against Gibson's version of direct realism (Gibson 1967; also see Smythies 1999). Another important objection is that direct realists cannot handle cases of misperception. The standard reply is *disjunctivism*—the denial of a common factor between subjectively indistinguishable veridical and illusory (or hallucinatory) states. This response has itself generated a whole literature (e.g., Haddock and Macpherson 2008; Byrne and Logue 2008) and has also drawn charges of inconsistency with scientific facts (Burge 2005).

though they make me know truths about the colour, do not make me know the colour itself any better than I did before: so far as concerns knowledge of the colour itself, as opposed to knowledge of truths about it, I know the colour perfectly and completely when I see it, and no further knowledge of it itself is even theoretically possible.

Since for Russell the bearers of colors are sense data, acquaintance is a mere matter of contact with these nonmaterial entities. Philosophers such as John Campbell, Bill Brewer, and Mark Johnston have sought to develop the Russellian notion of acquaintance but on the assumption that the bearers of colors are ordinary external objects. Thus color vision helps put us in perceptual contact with the world around us. Their primary motivation is the intuition that perception gives us access to external reality. Let us call this the *access intuition*. For example, Johnston (1996, 189) writes that:

My pleasure in seeing color is not simply the pleasure of undergoing certain sensory experiences, it is also the pleasure of having access by sight to the natures of the colors and hence access to part of the nature of colored things.

For Johnston the question of what kinds of properties are thus revealed by sight has been a vexed one. While Johnston (1992) took a dispositional theory to be most conducive to satisfying the access intuition,[15] by 1996 he was hostile to the idea that perception of any perceiver-dependent property can be revelatory of anything more than the idiosyncratic reactions of a perceiver, writing that:

The same perceptual experience is as much a manifestation of my disposition to see the apple as red as it is a manifestation of the apple's disposition to look red to me. So the same response is potentially as much a revelation of a dispositional property of mine as it is a revelation of a dispositional property of the apple. (Johnston 1996, 197)

An instructive way to demonstrate the compatability of color adverbialism with perceptual relationism is to work through Johnston's concerns with color relationism more generally, and showing how adverbialism can address them. I begin by examining the access intuition, as formulated by Johnston (1996). Crucially the phrase "access to part of the nature of coloured things" is ambiguous and can be read in at least two ways: (1) as

15. "When a disposition is the disposition to produce a certain subjective response then a subjective response of the kind in question may indeed reveal the nature of the disposition so long as the subject takes his response to be the manifestation of the disposition" (Johnston 1992, 226).

Figure 7.1
Tree fungus. Photographs of tree fungus among the undergrowth of a north Australian rainforest.

access to, specifically, the colored nature of those things; or (2) access to, simply, those things. In his rejection of color relationism, Johnston (1996) assumes (1). Yet, if we bring to mind the coloring-for-perceiving account that was developed in chapter 4, we see that (2) is a live option. Color vision does not serve us as a means to acquainting us with the colors of things; rather, it helps us to see things. Once one accepts the idea that color vision is integral to the perception of objects—their material boundaries, their 3D structure, and their very there-ness among other objects in space—it becomes intuitive to say that color vision gives us access to the presence of those things.

Figure 7.1 presents images of a tree fungus, one is in black and white and the other in color. In the colored image, the fungus pops out to the viewer, whereas its presence is obscure in the monochrome version. It is natural to say that in the colored image you simply see the fungus better—its boundary with the tree trunk is that much more salient, the fungus is much more *there*. On the adverbial analysis, the idea is that *we see the fungus red-ly*, namely that the redness in our perception of the fungus is the way that this object makes itself present to us. At the same time the redness itself is a property that belongs to the perceptual relation (the perceptual process or interaction) between ourselves and the fungus. This allows the color adverbialist to follow up on a suggestion made by Logue (2012, 222) whereby, "Naive Realism can appeal to *both* relata in accounting for the phenomenal character of veridical experience, as well as to facts about the relation itself."

On the current proposal, the character of "phenomenal redness" is determined jointly by the nature of the object and that of the perceiver.[16]

7.2.2 Two Ancient Metaphors

But how has this anything to do with this naïve realism? I have nowhere
claimed that perceptual experiences involving color grant us access to the
intrinsic nature of things—as Logue (2012, 227) puts it, "insight into what
things in one's environment are like independently of one's experiences of
them." This is a commonly expressed desideratum of naïve realism, and the
adverbialist account clearly does fall short of this mark. In order to show
why the color adverbialist can still claim to accommodate a variant of naïve
realism, I propose that we examine the two foundational metaphors of the
doctrine.

The window metaphor occurs frequently in expressions of naïve realism.
The idea is that the eyes are our window on the world, and we just see
straight out through them in order to apprehend external reality. As Burnyeat (1979, 83) writes, describing its traces in ancient texts, it is "an implicit
picture or model of perception" and "at some level people are powerfully
drawn to the thought that we look through our eyes as through a window."
Among recent authors Campbell (2002, 119) gives an extended discussion
of this often implicit model. He writes that "[o]ne analogy is that the Relational View [naïve realism] thinks of perception as like viewing the world
through a pane of glass," though he also notes that one limitation of the
analogy is that it is homuncular, presupposing a "man in the head" looking
out through the window. Campbell goes on to describe how this analogy
can be extended to accommodate the fact that neural processing occurs

---

16. Note that my proposal differs from Logue's on two of substantial points. First,
on her account color and shape properties are only attributed to objects of perception, even though the phenomenal character of veridical experiences of those
properties may be determined either by the intrinsic nature of the property itself
or by the nature of the perceiver. Second, she posits a bimodal distribution of
"Kantian" properties (e.g., color) and "Berkeleian" ones (e.g., shape). In veridical
experiences of the former properties, phenomenal character is mostly determined
by features of the perceiving subject whereas, in veridical experiences of the latter,
phenomenal character is "mostly determined by the fact that the subject perceives
an instance of that property" (Logue 2012, 226). This distinction appears to map on
to the traditional primary-secondary quality one. I wish to remain agnostic about
the relative proportions of perceiver and object contributions to color and shape
experiences.

whenever we see something—a fact often taken to defeat direct realism in favor of a representational theory:

Suppose we have a medium which, like glass, can be transparent. But suppose that, unlike glass, it is highly volatile, and needs constant adjustment and recalibration if it is to remain transparent in different contexts...The upshot of the adjustment, in each case, is still not the construction of a representation on the medium of the scene being viewed; the upshot of the adjustment is simply that the medium becomes transparent. You might think of visual processing as a bit like that. (Campbell 2002, 119)

So Campbell does not deny that our perceptual window can ever fail to be perfectly transparent—sometimes the neural processing required to achieve transparency does not come up to par. But the problem remaining is that anything the perceiver brings to experience has to be understood as distorting the apprehension of the world itself. The window works best when it makes itself invisible. Any signs of its presence—marks, tints, or irregularities in the glass—can only render the view imperfect in its presentation of external reality. If we embrace this picture or metaphor, then color adverbialism *is* incompatible with perceptual relationism. For according to my account, even the most ideal perceptual encounter will leave traces of its own workings on experience. As I argued in chapter 5, there can be no "God's-eye view" that only gathers objects and properties as they are in themselves. To perceive is to interact, and one never achieves the neutrality of the remote spectator that is assumed on the window model.

Thus the synthesis of color adverbialism with naïve realism requires that we consider an alternative guiding picture. An equally ancient metaphor for perceptual realism is that of the wax and seal. In the *Theaetetus* Plato likens memory to the impression made by a signet ring on wax. In *De anima* (424a, 17–24) Aristotle applies the metaphor to perception: our senses are that which receive the forms of objects without their matter, just as wax receives the form of the seal.[17]

Of the two foundational metaphors for perceptual relationism, the wax and seal picture is the one amenable to my account because it allows for the perceiver to bring something to experience without somehow interfering

---

17. See Caston (2004, 301ff) for an extended discussion of this metaphor. On his account, it is critical that the signet ring is an identifying sign of its wearer, and not any old object that can leave a shape impressed in wax. The issue of interpretation is not critical here, since what follows is obviously my "spin" on the wax and seal picture.

with the result—for perception need not be characterized as a disembodied view. The wax is not a transparent object that, like the window, allows us to see through to the world. Rather, it is a receptive medium suited to have items in the world leave traces on it. It must be granted that there is something about the nature of wax that enables the seal to leave its mark, just as there is something about the nature of our visual system that enables external objects to affect it, through the mediation of light. It is because of the nature of the wax (i.e., its malleability) that the seal's shape can be impressed on it. But its specific type of plasticity also influences the resulting impression, and also what information about the seal can be gathered from it. For example, a very soft and malleable piece of wax will give you a very detailed impression of the texture of the seal but will tell you little about how hard the seal was stamped because it will only receive an impression when pressed very gently. A harder, less malleable piece of wax will give you a less detailed impression of the texture of the seal but will work over a greater range of interactions, also giving information about how hard the seal was stamped.

So any contributions of the properties of the wax to the resulting impressions should not be considered obstacles to seeing the world. Instead, the wax and seal metaphor makes it plain that it is in the nature of the perceptual relation that both object and perceiver influence the resulting perceptual impression. Yet we still have access to objects, in the sense that the perceptual interaction "puts us in touch" with them.[18] Most fundamental, the wax and seal metaphor treats perception as a process of interaction rather than an attempt to arrive at inner mental states that correspond to external states of affairs. Thus the impression on the wax should not be thought of as aiming at a perfect reproduction of the seal, as would be assumed within the correspondence framework, and if our thinking were held captive by the metaphor of the window. The crucial point is that

18. One can think of the wax and seal metaphor as describing a touch-based version of perceptual realism, whereas the metaphor of the window is most naturally associated with vision (see section 5.2.3). Note also that the wax metaphor is itself subject to differing interpretations—one passive, where the wax is a blank substrate waiting to be inscribed by external reality, and the other active, where it is the wax's own qualities and potentialities that enable it to interact with the environment in the right way. I am obviously leaning on the second one. Again, my discussion is not an interpretative one—a claim that this is how we should read Aristotle—but instead I present it as my own elaboration of an ancient picture.

reality makes contact with our perceptual systems, not that our perceptual states somehow replicate perceiver-independent reality.

One interesting feature of this version of color adverbialism, in contrast with the complex Fregean theory sketched above, is that it need not assume any robust distinction between primary and secondary qualities or the objective and subjective "components" of perceptual experience. All such elements are the result of an interaction with the world, and as such they are all informative. Thus we can abandon the correspondence framework, for we need not categorize some elements of the perceptual experience as "matching" their external counterparts and others not. Of course, this raises the worry that on this account there are no resources to deal with misperception. This issue will be the topic of section 7.4.

7.3   Stand-alone Adverbialism

I introduced adverbialism in chapter 6 as a theory just of color, with the implication that it could be naturally extended to the other secondary qualities. One worry that might have occurred in reading this chapter concerns whether I can restrict adverbialism to the secondary qualities, or if it must stand as a general theory of perception.[19] I used the coloring-for-perceiving model to ground adverbial analyses such as "we see the sphericity of the ball redly." Is it not as much an implication of the model that shape modifies perception of color, and "we see the redness of the ball spherically," or rather that "we see the ball redly and spherically"?

I would here note that the complex Fregean representational theory does invite one to restrict adverbialism to color and the other secondary qualities. A robust primary-secondary quality distinction is implicit in the view, since the secondary qualities are the modes of presentation of primary qualities. It therefore follows that we see the sphericity of the ball redly, but not vice versa. However, if one has no antecedent belief in the primary-secondary quality distinction, one will not be compelled by that account.

Stand-alone adverbialism may indeed be attractive to someone suspicious of the primary-secondary quality distinction.[20] The idea here would

---

19. I thank Keith Allen and Bence Nanay for raising this point.
20. See Koenderink (2013) for the case that the perception of shape bears important similarities with the perception of secondary qualities.

be to combine general adverbialism with perceptual relationism, such that when I see a red ball I am perceiving *that object* redly, glossily, spherically (see Conduct 2008). Because the account is relational it bypasses the many-property problem (Jackson 1975) that haunted classical adverbialism: for the presentation of the object unifies the different adverbial modifications. I do not simply see redly, glossily, spherically, and then wonder how these different aspects of visual experience converge on one thing and not another.

At the same time the theory sketched here can comfortably address a logical difficulty presented by Tye (1984).[21] It appeared as a problem for classical adverbialism that one could not infer from a statement that 'X senses redly and circularly' the statement that 'X senses redly'. Tye responds by presenting a yet more refined version of the logical operators involved in adverbialist statements. However, on my holistic account this failure of entailment is entirely to be expected. As I emphasized above, we should *not* analyze complex perceptual experiences as if they were an aggregate of simple ones. Thus we should not assume that the chromatic component of 'seeing redly and circularly' can be abstracted away from the geometric part, such that 'seeing redly' is straightforwardly derivable from the more complex description. Of course, we would expect there to be some relationship between the simple and more complex statements, but if the complex experience is not a straightforward conjunction of simple ones, then that relationship cannot just be conjunction elimination.

Needless to say, I have given just some preliminary pointers toward a general adverbialism. This direction of investigation may be of interest to those dissatisfied with the orthodox representational and naïve realist theories, who therefore wish to expand upon color adverbialism.

7.4   False Color

Even if one is now persuaded that color may not be a property attributed to objects, a more basic objection still stands, one alluded to by Boghossian and Velleman (1989, 82n4) when they write that "[s]eeing something as red is the sort of thing that can be illusory or veridical." The objection is that any theory of color that is ecumenical with respect to variations in

21. I am grateful to Ori Beck for bringing up this objection to adverbialism.

perceivers and viewing conditions cannot account for the fact that some color visual experiences are treated as illusory and others as veridical.[22] On a relational view such as Cohen's, it would seem that there can be no such thing as an illusory color experience because for whatever color you experience, however dysfunctional your visual system and however weird your viewing situation, there is a relational color property there to match it. Yet we often talk of misperceiving the colors of things, and intuitions are fairly robust that on some occasions—such as when color constancy fails dramatically—we are wrong in our color judgments.

In order to address this objection, I will employ a divide and conquer strategy. It has been a common mistake to lump together all candidate cases of misperception. On my view some instances are genuine perceptual errors while some are not. We should be careful to separate the examination of potentially illusory perceptual encounters from the analysis of language where there is disagreement over color ascriptions. Thus I will discussing three separate categories of possible misperception: first "ecologically relevant misperception," then "textbook illusions," and finally "disagreement."

7.4.1 Ecologically Relevant Misperception

Imagine you stumble into the cloakroom of a dimly lit nightclub. It's cold outside and you want to go home. You look everywhere for your burgundy colored coat. But all you see is a dark gray one of a similar fabric and cut. Then you realize that it *is* your coat, and that you have been the victim of a trick of the light—in other words, a failure of color constancy. You walk home, all the time worrying about the readiness with which your eyes can deceive you.

Cohen (2007, 345) discusses an analogous case—failure to recognize a red Chevrolet under sodium vapor lamps—and concludes that the error here comes with your failure to represent the car as gray *only in these peculiar viewing circumstances*. The car *is* gray for you in these lighting conditions, but you misrepresent it as gray for you *simpliciter* (i.e., gray also in more

---

22. See, for example, Hilbert (1987, 88), Watkins (2002, 93), Byrne and Hilbert (2003, 57–58) and Tye (2012, 300–302) for versions of the objection. The objection is not a concern for traditional dispositionalism, which indexes colors to standard observers and standard conditions. Colors experienced by nonstandard perceivers, or in nonstandard conditions, then count as illusory.

standard viewing conditions). On Cohen's account the fault is not with your color visual system, or with color visual experience, but more on the side of your nonphenomenal "taking" of the experience; there is nothing actually wrong with your color visual awareness of things.

In my estimation, however, the most important thing about these dramatic failures of color constancy is that in such cases you are really *seeing less well*. One of the central functions of color vision—object recognition—has gone awry. Moreover a host of other functions served by color, such as scene segmentation, differentiation of shadows from surfaces, and perception of material sameness, will all be underperforming. So we should acknowledge that some kind of genuine misperception does occur, without analyzing it in terms of the attribution of the wrong color to an object. This is what I call *ecologically relevant misperception*.[23] Under conditions that are hostile to our color visual system contributing to all of its usual functions (e.g., at low light levels, or if strong chromatic light leads to failures of color constancy), then we *do* misperceive in a certain sense. What we call "misperceiving the color of things" is better put as, "not seeing things as well as we are accustomed to—not seeing well enough to perform our usual visually guided tasks without difficulty."[24]

23. My notion of ecologically relevant misperception has some relationship to Matthen's *action relative realism*: "If the occurrence of a state in violation of its normal response condition disrupts some innate activity, then we say that there is an environmental feature represented by that state, and that this representation is real in the sense that it is subject to error" (Matthen 2005, 206). A substantial difference is that I do not evaluate perceptual states in terms of functions that they have evolved to perform. For this reason my account, unlike Matthen's, does not invoke hypotheses that are extremely difficult to confirm, such as the conjecture that an evolutionary specified function of human trichromacy is to distinguish ripe fruit from foliage. Even though Matthen does allow also for "developmentally specified" functions, the evolutionary element leads to consequences that differ from my account. For example, he takes it that human dichromats (but not canine dichromats) misperceive colors because their visual system is less able to aid in certain functions such as fruit picking. On my account, human dichromacy is just a different way of seeing things. Since dichromats can perform most color-involving visual functions as well as trichromats (see Broackes 2010 and references therein), their own normal capacities are the standard against which ecologically relevant misperceptions are compared.

24. This account of error is of a piece with the perceptual pragmatist shift from analysis in terms of correspondence to a utility-based evaluation; see section 5.2.1. One consequence of this account is that if your practical aims shift radically, this can change the criteria for misperception. Imagine that you are tired of your burgundy coat and wish you had bought a more neutral looking one, for example, a conservative dark gray. But because you are too law-abiding to deliberately go home with

Furthermore under scotopic conditions (where the illumination is so dim that we must rely on rod-based vision) or if the lighting is monochromatic, there is no spectral contrast, according to the definition of section 6.2. So it is an implication of color adverbialism that in these extreme viewing circumstances—where everything takes on a grainy colorless tone or is washed out to the same hue—we are *not*, strictly speaking, seeing with color. This may seem a counterintuitive result, but we can appreciate that it brings us to another important way in which color adverbialism is able to ground the notion of color misperception. If you walk into a room lit by a monochromatic green lamp, and everything looks either black or a lighter or darker shade of green, the adverbialist can literally say that those greens and blacks are not the "real colors" that we associate with those things. We can think of them instead as pseudo-colors. Likewise the strange tones that objects take on at night, which are often described as "grays," but to me are unlike any of the daylight colors, can be thought of as pseudo-colors. More formally, pseudo-colors are properties of perceptual interactions that bear some phenomenal similarity to ordinary colors but occur when the lighting conditions are such that no stimulus bears spectral contrast.

In sum, there are two substantial ways in which the color adverbialist can speak of genuine misperception involving color. Of course, cases such as these are only a subset of all the scenarios that have been characterized as "illusions of color." I will now discuss why in these other cases it is misleading to talk of misperception.

7.4.2 Textbook "Illusions"

There is a large area of murkiness around the use of the word "illusion" in vision science and psychology, and this tends to infect philosophical discussion. As became apparent in section 5.2.3, many textbook illusions, such as the Adelson checkerboard, can only be deemed instances of misperception under the particular assumption that the visual system should be compared with a physical measuring instrument.[25] For example,

---

another person's coat, it serves your unconscious desires if you find yourself in a situation in which your coat is indistinguishable from a conservative, gray-looking one and you make an "honest mistake" in swapping coats. Relative to your idiosyncratic interests, your failure to visually discriminate the coats would not count as a case of misperception.

25. A point also made by Schwartz (2006, 225).

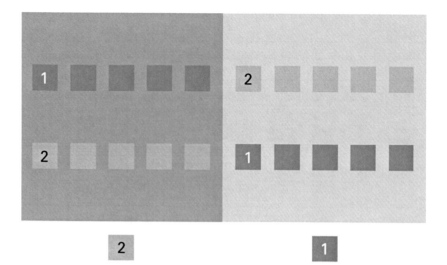

Figure 7.2
Color contrast effect. Squares in the top row all appear as roughly the same grey color. However, squares on the top left have the same physical spectral values as the other squares labeled 1, which appear mushroom pink in other contexts, and squares on the top right have the same physical spectral values as the other squares labeled 2, which appear sage green in other contexts. Image adapted from website of Akiyoshi Kitaoka, reproduced with permission.

if one takes it that the task of the visual system, when confronted with the Adelson checkerboard, is to act like a photometer and detect the amount of light emitted from each pixel of the image, or to give a report on which physical lightnesses (reflectances) are the same, and which are not, then the visual system *does* misperceive. But on any ecologically grounded description of the system, one that takes the relevant features of interest to be objects and surfaces rather than photons and reflectances, and accepts that interpretations of a stimulus configuration affect perceptual experience, then it does not.

Most of the textbook color illusions are analogues to the Adelson example, except that we are dealing with spectral surface reflectance rather than achromatic reflectance. The simplest cases are the surround contrast effects that are often referred to as "illusions," though I have this in scare quotes because I believe it to be a misnomer. For example, in figure 7.2 the squares in the top row all appear as roughly the same gray color, but on a white

Figure 7.3
Color contrast effect and color constancy. The top tiles of Rubik's cube, which appear blue on the left-hand side and yellow on the right-hand side, actually have the same reflectance that appears gray if seen against a white background. The equivalence can be demonstrated by viewing these tiles through a paper cutout that masks the surrounding area. Image created by Beau Lotto, reproduced with permission.

background they appear very differently—one sage green and the other salmon pink. On the assumption that the task of the visual system is just SSR matching, an error occurs because perceptually it is not the case that all squares labeled '1' appear to be the same, nor is it the case that all of the squares labeled '2' perceptually match. For the color adverbialist (as for Cohen's ecumenical color relationist) there is no ground to say that the appearance in one context, with the white background, is more correct than the appearance with the colored backgrounds: both ways that the squares appear are on the same footing. Moreover, if we take a slightly more elaborate version of a surround contrast effect, we will see that from an ecological and functional perspective it makes sense to say that neither of these appearances are misperceptions, and that it is no cause for concern if the same reflectances do not look the same in different contexts.

In figure 7.3 the tiles on the top of the Rubik's cube, which appear blue on the left-hand side and yellow on the right-hand side, have the same reflectance, which appears gray against a white background. This is an impressive color contrast effect that, like the Adelson effect, can be explained in terms of the operation of a perceptual constancy. The visual system interprets the image as if it the Rubik's cube were a 3D object bathed in strongly chromatic light. A short wavelength reflecting (blue appearing) surface under medium wavelength (yellow appearing) illumination *would* give rise to a roughly achromatic combined stimulus at the retina. Likewise the proximal stimulus arising from a yellow appearing tile under short wavelength (blue appearing illumination) is also achromatic. So, if we accept that the visual system interprets concrete and pictorial stimuli in terms of layers of surfaces and illuminants (Brown 2014), and is not in the business of just recording the reflectance values of each pixel in a 2D image, then it makes sense that the same physical reflectance can have these various appearances. There is no reason to take one of these to be the real appearance of the physical reflectance, and the others illusory. If we must speak of illusion here, it should be in the general sense that the visual system makes the same interpretative moves when confronted with 2D pictorial representations as it does for 3D arrangements of objects in space. Indeed, if we set up an actual Rubik's cube in these two viewing conditions, the proximal stimuli would roughly match those produced by figure 7.3, and this would just be a straightforward case of color constancy.

7.4.3 Disagreement

Many of the discussions of misperception, however, do not rest on analyses of the actual workings of the visual system but on intuitions based on how we (ordinary folk) would *talk* about cases of conflict in perceptual judgment. For example, Tye (2012, 300) writes:

Suppose that I am viewing a yellow ball that looks yellow to me. I remark, "That ball is yellow." I then leave and you enter. You are shown the same ball. Unknown to you, you have an unusual physiological condition, the result of which is that in certain lighting, yellow things look pink to you, not yellow. The result is that the ball looks pink to you. You are asked whether the ball is yellow. You say, "That ball is not yellow; it's pink."
You and I disagree. What you say contradicts what I say.

Tye presents this case as an objection to Cohen's relationism because on Cohen's view there is no genuine disagreement here: the ball is yellow-for-me and pink-for-you.[26]

---

26. On my account, the pink appearance would count as ecologically relevant misperception if your physiological condition and the strange lighting interfere with the usual color-involving functions. But in what follows I will assume that the relevant cases of disagreement do not come under this heading.

In order to discuss such examples I will have to be quite open about the fact that I do not intend the color properties described by the adverbialist theory to be the referents of the color predicates found in ordinary language. In other words, I am not holding out for a neat "properties = predicates" mapping. Indeed it seems somewhat crazy to expect that the color concepts implicit in our ordinary discourse will simply pick out the chromatic properties investigated by the technical sciences. So if the concept associated with the ordinary word "pink" is of a putative chromatic property instantiated in objects such as flamingo feathers, that is fine. Color adverbialism does not aim to capture the conceptual structure of ordinary language. So on my account, it is simply the case that I perceive the ball yellowly and you perceive it pinkly, and these different ways for the ball to appear are on an equal footing. Just because our ordinary language attributes a quality "yellow" to balls (and not perceptual processes), and the grammatical conventions are such that a ball cannot be both yellow and pink all over and at the same time, should we really be committed to the claim that there is a discourse-independent fact of the matter about what color the ball has, independently of its being perceived (even when nothing in our best scientific account gives us a clue about how to decide on such facts)?

Admittedly this methodological position does go against most philosophy of color, which quite deliberately seeks to analyze color perception and color discourse in a uniform manner.[27] So it is worth saying a little about how I see the relationship between adverbial color ontology and ordinary color language and concepts, even if this is just a preliminary sketch. I take it that words like 'pink', 'mauve', 'purple', are labels we associate with categories of perceivings—ones that occur when we see objects pinkly, mauvely, or purplely. In our ordinary discourse these predicates are taken to pick out properties of objects that those objects do not actually bear (speaking from a scientific perspective). Perhaps the best analysis of ordinary language is to say that such predicates purport to refer to coarse-grained relational properties, for example, as Cohen (2009, 108ff) has it, causing

---

27. For example, Cohen (2009, 107–108) writes: "Amongst the views cataloged above, there is only one that I wish to reject…which involves claiming that the relevant predicates (in our case, [ordinary language] color predicates) express non-relational properties. This view, of course, amounts to repudiating color relationism." Brogaard (2010) also takes this methodological position.

pink experiences in standard conditions to creatures like me. Or perhaps (as more philosophers think) speakers take them to pick out a perceiver-independent chromatic property that each object has to the exclusion of other colors. Either way, this would explain why we say such things as "the cocktail looked neon pink but it's really purple," and it explains the robustness of the intuition that there is real disagreement when perceptual reports conflict.

Color visual experience is such that it supports such conceptual and linguistic practices. Because of the phenomena of constancy, and coarse color categorization, it is straightforward for us to label everyday objects with predicates that we associate with certain color experiences. But that does not entail anything about the ontology implicit in perceptual science. Furthermore it is supremely useful to engage in ordinary color discourse when, for example, we need to set up a communal system for labeling objects, for signaling, and for a host of aesthetic activities. Inter- and intrasubjective variation in color vision is normally subtle enough that it does not disrupt these practices. While I do not need to insist that a scientifically based ontology is the *only* ontology—perhaps from the perspective of ordinary discourse there *are* colors (understood as perceiver-independent properties of material surfaces)—I should note that my analysis of these linguistic and behavioral patterns sits well with a fictionalist account, like the one proposed by Barry Maund. To take one of his examples, scientific discourse has retained the concept of Newtonian mass even though, from the perspective of modern physics, this is not a property that objects actually have. Even if (by hypothesis) objects really only have rest mass and relativistic mass, Newtonian mass earns its keep in its usefulness for everyday purposes, in engineering, and in most scientific practices (Maund 2012, 380).

To sum up, we can consider color-involving experience to be one of the raw materials for the elaborate structure that is color discourse. So, while it is a problem for me if perceptual experience by itself is somehow inconsistent with color adverbialism (since perceptual experience is as much raw material for perceptual science as it is for color discourse), inconsistency with ordinary color language is not troublesome. I devote the next and final chapter to the worry that color phenomenology alone can refute my account.

8 Outerness without Ontological Commitment

8.1 The Objection from Phenomenology

An obvious objection to color adverbialism is the thought that *colors simply do not look to be properties of perceptual processes.* The purpose of this final chapter is to convince the reader that this objection is not nearly as effective as it first seems. Importantly, the idea that relationist theories of color can be straightforwardly refuted by the testimony of visual experience is a major thread in the debate over relationism. As Johnston (1992, 226) puts it, "[a] basic phenomenological fact is that we see most of the colors of external things as "steady" features of those things, in the sense of features which do not alter as the light alters and the observer changes position." So in the first part of this chapter I will concentrate on the phenomenological objection to relationism in general. I will show that the objection rests on assumptions that are controversial in the light of the understanding of color science that has been developed in this book. Then in section 8.5 I will examine any particular phenomenological issues surrounding color adverbialism.

In chapter 3 I presented relationism as a viable option for those unconvinced by realism and unhappy with the error theoretic consequences of eliminativism. Between the Scylla of eliminativism and the Charybdis of realism, relationism shines out as a rescue beacon: *colors are real but just not mind-independent.* To many this is no more than a siren song, for if visual experience presents colors as mind-independent, then relationism crashes us as swiftly onto the rocks of error theory as does eliminativism. This is the essence of the *objection from phenomenology*

(OP).[1] Many have found it persuasive, and it is perhaps the primary objection against relationism. In this chapter I will argue that it fails to stand up to scrutiny, both as a general argument against relationism and when directed against color adverbialism. I will ask whether any instances of color experience have a face value that says, as many have claimed, 'this property is not relational'. My message will be that in the case of color and relationality, phenomenology is an unpersuasive witness.

At the outset it is useful state to the various conclusions about this topic that have all been advocated at one time or another. The many different philosophers who have invoked OP all agree that phenomenology is unambiguous in presenting color as a nonrelational property. Other philosophers have argued the exact opposite—that phenomenology presents color as a relational or dispositional property.[2] My claim, however, will be that phenomenology is actually neutral about the relationality or nonrelationality of color. In reaching this conclusion I am in agreement with Levin (2000) and Cohen (2009). Because of the fact that there are these *three* different positions in play, the key proposal that color is not presented as nonrelational cannot be understood as the claim that color *is* presented as relational. The distinction is important because "not being presented as nonrelational" can *mean either that color experience is neutral as to relationality or that color is presented as a relational property (as perceiver-dependent).*[3]

---

1. See Armstrong (1997), Boghossian and Velleman (1989), Johnston (1992), McGinn (1996), Tye (2000), and Chalmers (2006). Many of these authors target dispositionalism in particular. Since the arguments can be generalized to other versions of relationism, I include them in my discussion of OP. For overview, see Cohen and Nichols (2010). They primarily address a close cousin of OP: the objection that pre-theoretical common sense is committed to the nonrelationality of color. (e.g., see Gibbard 2006). The supposed warrant for commonsense antirelationism is the authority color experience. So, if OP is rejected, this argument is severely weakened as well.

2. Dummett (1979), Evans (1980), McDowell (1985), and Langsam (2000); see Byrne (2001) and Allen (2007) for criticisms. Due to restrictions of space I will not discuss these arguments further.

3. It is tempting to avoid use of the double negative by using "intrinsic" as synonymous with "nonrelational," and stating my main claim as to show that color is not presented in experience as a property intrinsic to external objects. See Cohen (2009, 8) on problems with this use of terminology. As before, I use the terms "perceiver-dependent" and "relational" interchangeably (likewise "perceiver-independent" and "nonrelational").

My first task will be exposition of the objection from phenomenology. The aim of section 8.2 is to introduce two criteria that any successful version of the objection from phenomenology should satisfy. First, it should be obvious what it is about color phenomenology that is incompatible with relationism, and second, a convincing case ought to be made that the offending phenomenological datum is actually a *perceptual* experience, not a theoretically motivated interpretation of experience. In section 8.4 I discuss the Chalmers (2006) version of OP. This formulation, which I take to be the strongest in the current literature, rests on the observation that we experience color as out there in the world; unlike pain, color does not seem to depend on states of the body. This is a phenomenological datum that is hard to dismiss. Yet in section 8.3, by employing the two criteria I show that the simple outerness of color, and the obvious phenomenological differences between color and pain, do not entail that color is presented in experience as a nonrelational, perceiver-independent property of objects.

8.1.1   Presenting the Objection

There are numerous versions of the objection from phenomenology in the current literature. The objection takes its most complete form in the following passage from McGinn (1996, 541–42):

But surely [relationalism] misrepresents the phenomenology of color perception: when we see an object as red we see it as having a simple, monadic, local property of the object's surface. The color is perceived as intrinsic to the object, in much the way that shape and size are perceived as intrinsic. No relation to perceivers enters into how the color appears; the color is perceived as wholly *on* the object, not as somehow straddling the gap between it and the perceiver. Being seen as red is not like being seen as larger than or to the left of. The "color envelope" that delimits an object stops at the object's spatial boundaries. So if color were inherently relational,...then perception of color would misrepresent its structure—we would be under the illusion that a relational property is non-relational. Contraposing, given that perception is generally veridical as to color, colors are not relational....

Here is a reconstruction of McGinn's version of OP:

I. Colors are presented[4] in our visual experience as nonrelational properties of external objects. (*Basic Phenomenological Fact*)

---

4. This locution is intended to serve as a placeholder for whatever account of perceptual presentation the particular author would endorse—some kind of representational theory, a version of naïve realism, and so forth.

II. If colors were relations, and color vision were veridical, then colors would not be presented in our visual experience as nonrelational. (*Perceptual Relevance*)

III. Either colors are nonrelational, or color vision leads us to systematically misperceive the nature of color.[5] (from I and II)

IV. We do not have reason to think that color vision systematically misleads us about the nature of color. (*Veridicality of Color Perception*)

V. *Conclusion*: Colors are not relations.

Assumption *I* frequently stands alone as a charge against color relationism. Some of the passages cited by Cohen and Nichols (2010) as instances of the objection from phenomenology are simply expressions of *I*. But why should we expect ordinary visual appearance to have any bearing on obtuse questions about the nature of perceived properties? By comparison, a scientifically informed philosopher would not now assume that if speed is a relational property, and motion perception is veridical, that speed would not be presented as a nonrelational property. That is because we do not commonly take ordinary visual experience, even when veridical, to speak to the relationality or otherwise of the property speed. So something like assumption *II* is called for in order to assert the relevance of experience here. Although it is required for the move from *I* to *III*, it appears to have been assumed without comment by McGinn.[6]

It is highly implausible that any of the advocates of this objection would not assent to *II*. Indeed it is integral to the case being made against relationism that the relationality or otherwise of color is just the sort of thing that a veridical perceptual experience is able to present; moreover that it is the

---

5. Or equivalently: *If colors are relational, then perception is not veridical regarding color* and *if perception is veridical regarding color, then colors are not relational.*

6. Similarly Tye (2000, 152–53) passes from *I* to *III* without articulating *II*: "Still, it may be insisted, the relational view of color (or at least some colors, e.g., the achromatic ones) surely goes against ordinary color *experience*. When, for example, a rubber ball looks blue to me, I experience blueness all over the facing surface of the ball. Each perceptible part of the ball looks blue to me. And none of these parts, in looking blue, look to me to have a relational property. On the contrary, it may be said, I experience blueness as intrinsic to the surface, just as I experience the shape of the surface as intrinsic to it [*I*]. This simple fact is one that relational approaches to color cannot accommodate without supposing that a universal illusion is involved in normal experiences of color [*III*]—that colors are really relational properties even though we experience them as nonrelational."

kind fact about properties in the world that a perceptual system is able to recover. But since *II* is assumed only tacitly, it may be contentious for me to direct all my fire on it.[7] So the obvious strategy is to challenge the opening premise *I*. Importantly, *I* is the assumption shared by all versions of OP, so a successful rebuttal of *I* will undermine the different varieties of the objection.

8.2   The Two Criteria

8.2.1   Criterion 1: The Descriptive Question

In order better to understand what claim is being made in assumption *I*, the statement that colors are presented in visual experience as nonrelational properties, it is instructive to have an answer to the following question:

What would our color phenomenology have to be like such that people would say that color is presented as a relational property (or at least not presented as nonrelational)?

There is need for such questions because they give substance to the objectors' claims. Common sense does not give me a pre-theoretical handle on the claim that "red looks nonrelational," as it does for the claim that "tomato ketchup looks red." But such notions become more transparent when it is spelt out how color experience would have to be in order not to fall victim to objections grounded in visual phenomenology. Thus I will be making it a criterion for a successful presentation of OP that it be obvious that a particular aspect of color phenomenology is at fault, and that we have some hints as to how things would have to be for the phenomenology to be consistent with relationism. Furthermore it is desirable if the objector can flesh out a notion of relationality-in-experience that is at least conceptually possible. Without this substance behind it, the objection from phenomenology is just bald assertion and empty rhetoric. This brings us to the first criterion.

Criterion 1 *Any formulation of the objection from phenomenology should make it clear what aspect of color experience is inconsistent with relationism; it should*

---

7. One philosopher who has challenged *II* directly is Sellars (1981, 19): "Thus, we must not suppose that if the true theory of the status of expanses and volumes of color stuff is one according to which they have categorical status C, then they present themselves phenomenologically *as having this status.*"

not presume bizarre or impossible requirements for what it would take for color experience to be consistent with relationism.

In presenting his version of OP, Johnston (1992, 226) gives a clear answer here. It is the steadiness of the colors of ordinary objects that is problematic for the relationist:

Thus there is some truth in the oft-made suggestion that (steady) colors don't look like dispositions; to which the natural reply is "Just how would they have to look if they were to look like dispositions?"; to which the correct response is that they would have to look like colored highlights or better, like shifting, unsteady colors, e.g. the swirling evanescent colors that one sees on the back of compact discs.[8]

Both Levin (2000) and Cohen (2009) have published rebuttals of OP that focus on Johnston's version, and it is worth going through their points. First, Johnston is acknowledging that the relationality of a property cannot be "given" in one single instant. Levin and Cohen note this and specify the circumstances in which the relationality of color *could* be manifest. As (Levin 2000, 157) writes:

[O]rdinary perception must be regarded as neutral between such a [nonrelationist] view and dispositionalism. Ordinary perception of color may seem to reveal colors to be simple monadic properties, just as a quick glance may seem to reveal an object with color highlights to be an object that is "steadily" striped. But in both cases, the "glances" are too quick to be definitive, given the sorts of experiences required for making the distinction; in neither case can these judgments be expected to reflect what perception in the proper circumstances would in fact reveal.

Thus, while ordinary, inattentive perceptual experience may not be of the right sort to provide phenomenological evidence, the carefully calibrated experiences that are made possible in a psychophysics lab would be:

[T]here is both a good sense in which phenomenology can speak to the question of whether colors (steady and unsteady alike) are relational or not.... The sense in which it will is the sense in which phenomenology includes systematic comparisons

8. The majority of the colors of ordinary physical objects would be classified as "steady colors"—ones that do not undergo obvious or dramatic change with a shift in viewing angle or angle of incident light. Boghossian and Velleman (1989, 86) offer a version of OP that also turns on the apparent stability of colors: "If colours looked like dispositions, however, then they would seem to come on when illuminated just as a lamp comes on when its switch is flipped. Turning on the light would seem, like simultaneously, turning on the colours; But colours do not look like that; or not, at least, to us."

of the sort made available by psychophysical methods, combined with ratiocination. (Cohen 2009, 159–60)

Second, Johnston makes a gift to the relationist in telling us that to observe whether or not a property is relational we need to have a way of wiggling one of the relata and seeing how this effects the relation. We can call this the "interventionist prescription." So it turns out that we *cannot* observe the perceiver-dependence of color by putting ourselves in place of different perceivers (because we cannot get inside other people's heads), but we *can* see how changing things about our visual system does alter perceived color in ways that conform to Johnston's interventionist prescription. For example, by adapting to tinted lenses and then observing how objects differ from their normal hues when the lenses are removed. That is enough to say we can—in those circumstances—experience the perceiver-dependence of color. And so it ceases to be a problem for the relationist that colors often, or even in the majority of cases look stable. This is because the relationist only need predict the appearance of perceiver-dependence in cases where something about the perceiver is changing enough to influence experience. And such changes may well be rare occurrences.

If she considers Johnston's version of OP alone, the relationist now has the resources to deny the first premise of the argument, yielding the alternative postulate:

I*. Colors are not presented in our basic or ordinary visual experience as either nonrelational or relational properties of external objects.

This would seem to be happy news for the relationist but there is a problem with only addressing the steadiness version of OP because, as we will see in section 8.3, it fails to capture the supposed phenomenological facts that are most damaging for the relationist. Moreover others pressing OP will note that even in cases where the interventionist criterion is satisfied (an external condition changes and the apparent color of an object changes), the object's color can fail to look to be dependent on that external condition. Here is an example from Allen (2007, 144):

[T]urning on a desk lamp in an already day lit room brings about a very noticeable change in the appearances of the objects it illuminates. But we do not ordinarily think that turning on a desk lamp actually changes the colours of the objects it illuminates. The objects' colours appear to remain constant throughout the change in the illumination.

If this is so, then there is more to assumption *I*, more to the basic phenomenological facts, than Johnston, Levin, or Cohen have acknowledged. Before moving on to consider other versions of OP, I will consider a rejoinder to the Levin–Cohen argument because it brings to light the second important criterion.

8.2.2   Criterion 2: Perception or Reflection?

Levin and Cohen's response to OP rests on the idea that the objector is mistaken in equating the absence of an appearance of relationality in visual experience with an appearance of nonrelationality. As Cohen (2009, 159) writes:

[S]ince the manipulations required to bring out the relationality of steady colors do not occur "all by themselves" in ordinary perception, subjects are left without the phenomenological evidence they would need to come to a suitable conclusion on this matter. But since they lack the requisite evidence, and also (wrongly) believe they would possess such evidence if it existed, they have concluded (wrongly) that steady colors are phenomenally presented as non-relational. Which is to say that, after having looked for phenomenological evidence in the wrong place, such thinkers have compounded their error by mistaking an absence of evidence for evidence of absence.

However, a couple of examples of quite ordinary perceptual judgments show that this conception may not be such a mistake. Consider the following rejoinder to the Levin–Cohen position *I**:

You're watching the hour hand of a clock. The hand itself is moving, but so slowly that your visual system cannot integrate over the extended period of time that it takes for the hand to have a noticeable change in position. So the hand does not look to be moving. It looks static. No one has committed an error by "mistaking an absence of evidence for evidence of absence," even though the experience was not of a sort that could have yielded evidence one way or the other for the motion of the hand (cf. Levin's color "glance"). Evidence had nothing to do with it; phenomenology was *not* neutral. The hand just *looked* static. That's just what my experience is like. Likewise my experience of color is just that it's nonrelational, an intrinsic property of objects, as stated in *I* and not *I**.[9]

9. Following the examples of failure to detect motion the objector now needs to deliver some additional support for *IV*, veridicality, in order to make OP go through. For if the analogy is left as it stands it could turn into an argument for error-theoretic relationism: colors are relational but our visual system fails to perceive them as such.

A similar point could be made about a failure to detect motion under inappropriate stroboscopic viewing conditions. The stroboscopically lit people *do* look static. Your experience is not of a scene neutral between presenting motion and stillness, as Cohen and Levin would have it for color glances. If these examples stand up, they suggest that the proponent of OP has the phenomenology right, after all.

The natural reply in support of *I** is to flag up the disanalogy between motion and color relationality. Two points can be made here. One is physiological, the other phenomenological. First, while the motion of an experienced object can make a claim to be a basic perceptual property or quality, relationality cannot. Scientists talk of neurons being "motion detectors," and region MT being a "motor area." In addition motion experiences can give rise to adaptation effects, the kind of effects that Block (2010) employs as the hallmark of genuinely perceptual processing. (Has anyone ever heard of a "relationality adaptational effect"?) Where is the "relationality detecting neuron," and the "relationality region"? If these are to be found anywhere it will not be in the visual cortex, or any dedicated sensory region. Second—and more important, since OP turns on phenomenology—our experiences of motions are so much more *concrete* in nature than our experiences of relationality. There is something so *abstract* about relationality—it is a rarefied philosophical notion after all—that assertions of it being simply given in experience, in the way that motion (by hypothesis) is, should be met with default suspicion.

What we now see is that the objection from phenomenology relies on the notion that there is some quality of relationality or nonrelationality that may figure in perceptual experience in a way analogous to the experiences of uncontroversially perceptible properties, like motion. This leads to an important pair of questions, ones that the proponents of OP have never to my knowledge addressed:

(a) What grounds are there to say that we simply *see* as opposed to judge, infer or *surmise* that color is a perceiver-independent (or otherwise) property?

(b) And even then how could we be sure that "seeing" perceiver-independence is encapsulated from thoughts about the intrinsic nature of color?

If the proponent of OP cannot supply an answer here, then her argument is in trouble because *I* and *II* can be rejected. The assumed phenomenological fact of *I* may very well be either (a) some nonperceptual interpretation of an experience as presenting a nonrelational property when in fact the experience is neutral; or (b) some perceptual experience that has been cognitively influenced by a prior belief in the nonrelationality of color. Thus the basic phenomenological facts are at best biased witnesses. And if it turns out that beliefs are influencing experience and/or interpretation of experience, then there is no reason to think that colors that are actually relational would not appear as nonrelational. So *II*, the assumption of perceptual relevance, is false.

I will focus on question (a), since if there is a case of cognitive penetrability, as alluded to in (b), it is likely to be introspectively and empirically indistinguishable from the case alluded to in (a) where belief affects interpretation of experience. Both (a) and (b) place a burden of proof on the objector to relationism, and introspective evidence is likely to be inadmissible; the authority of introspection is precisely what is in question here.[10] The proponent of OP has to make a plausible case that the supposed phenomenological fact is perceptual and not cognitive in origin.[11] I do not intend to raise the bar too high here. I will not be more stringent about what counts as a perceptual experience of relationality than I would be about what counts as a perceptual experience of motion.

These questions bring our attention to another important criterion for a successful presentation of OP.

Criterion 2 *It should be possible to show that the putative phenomenological facts are indeed grounded in visual perceptual experience rather than theoretical reflection; it should be demonstrable that we see, and do not surmise, that color is a nonrelational property.*

10. Note also that none of the disputants in the debate over cognitive penetration seek refuge in the authority of introspection. It is conceded that whether perceptual states are or are not encapsulated from beliefs is not something that can be read off from experience.

11. Note that if she does concede that it is cognitive in origin, she can still run an argument similar to OP, based on what "common sense" tells us about color and the need for philosophy to conform to pre-theoretical opinion. I think this argument is weaker than OP because of the mutability and historical contingency of any such opinions, as I discuss in chapter 2 and in Chirimuuta (2011a).

A further analysis of McGinn's version of OP is instructive at this point. Some parts of his description of color experience can be seen to address criterion 1. He does indicate how colors would have to look in order to appear as relational properties, that is, they would appear:

i. Not to be intrinsic to the object—unlike shape and size.

ii. As though a relation to a perceiver enters into the appearance.

iii. Not wholly on the object.

iv. But as somehow in between the object and the perceiver.

v. Like some examples of canonical relational properties (e.g., larger than and to the left of).

vi. As an envelope that extends beyond the object's spatial boundaries. (Based on McGinn (1996, 541–42), quoted at start §8.1.1.)

It is not clear at the outset what (ii) could amount to, or what the similarity with shape and size alluded to in (i) could really be. The only problem with (iii), (iv), and (vi) is that the examples of canonical relational properties given in (v) cannot satisfy them! (For how does a desk lamp's being to the left of my laptop look like it's spread out between the lamp and the computer? How does my desk's largeness, relative to the book, fail to be contained by its perceived contours?) Items (iii), (iv), and (vi) could be satisfied if taken in a much less literal way. In some abstract sense the lamp's being to the left of my computer does point beyond the lamp to the neighboring object. But if this is McGinn's way of meeting criterion 1, then he cannot meet criterion 2 because this very abstract sense of a relational presentation could not plausibly be taken as a perceptual given.

One charitable (probably too charitable) reading of McGinn is that he is just gesturing to the outerness of color. That is to say, that his sketch just amounts to the common observation that colors are "out there" on objects, at a distance from us. Then, if one equates this "outerness" with the perceiver-*independence* of an apparent property, it would follow that a perceiver-*dependent* property would have to appear as not at a distance away but somehow smeared out across space. As we will now see, such thoughts about outerness are of considerable importance to the debate.

8.3   Color, Pain, and Body-Relatedness

One of the tasks of Chalmers' (2006) landmark paper on perceptual experience is to argue for an error theory of color. He describes a hypothetical Edenic world where ordinary objects bear mind-independent, qualitative properties. He believes that we ordinarily experience colors as mind-independent, qualitative properties, and that in Eden, but not in our actual world, ordinary color experiences would be "perfectly veridical." "Perfect veridicality" and "perfect color" are technical notions introduced by Chalmers to convey the precise claims about states of affairs that are made by perceptual experiences. If the perfect veridicality conditions of color do not require a state of affairs in which the color is experienced by a subject, then it follows that the perfect color is not perceiver related. Thus Chalmers (2006, 76) writes:

[I]t seems that an object can be perfectly red without anyone experiencing the object as perfectly red. The phenomenology of color does not seem to be the phenomenology of properties that require a perceiver in order to be instantiated. (The phenomenology of pain is arguably different in this respect, . . .).[12]

For Chalmers, the primary phenomenological datum is the supposed perceiver-independence of color. Yet it is not obvious what this observation amounts to until it is specified how perceiver-dependence could be packed into sensory experience. The comparison between color and pain experiences serves to satisfy criterion 1. Perceiver-(in)dependence is cashed out as body-(in)dependency. Anticipating criterion 2, the comparison also shows how sensory experience itself, and not our theoretical interpretation of it, could convey perceiver-relatedness as body-dependency. So unlike the

---

12. Arguably, in Cohen's (2009) *role functionalist* theory, objects instantiate colors whether or not any perceiver currently views them. So role functionalism would not be vulnerable to Chalmers's version of OP. However, it should be noted that role functionalism then becomes quite a watered-down version of relationism, in that colors are not literally perceiver-dependent properties. Even for the classic dispositionalist, perceivers are required for the standing color dispositions to be manifest. It is this aspect of dispositionalism that the steadiness version of OP takes issue with: even if the disposition *is* a stable property of objects, the objection is that the instability (perceiver and situation dependence) of the manifestation ought to show up in experience, if dispositionalism is true. According to color adverbialism, colors do require perceivers in order to be instantiated. Hence I do take Chalmers's objection seriously.

other versions of OP, it comes ready prepared with means to address both criteria, making it the most serious challenge for the relationist.

Pains and other bodily sensations *are* readily analyzed as presentations of states of the body, and so one could go further than Chalmers and make the case that the properties such states present are obviously *body-dependent*. Thus, insofar as colors are experienced differently from bodily states, they are not experienced as relational; they are instead experienced as perceiver-independent. (According to Chalmers' account, the only options for color are that it might appear perceiver-independent or perceiver-dependent. He does not consider any claims for the neutrality of color phenomenology.)

It is worth comparing this line of thought with the Lockean idea that for color to present itself as a kind of disposition it would have to seem as if its experiential manifestation is in the body, as we feel with pains:

[H]e that will consider that the same fire that, at one distance produces in us the sensation of warmth, does, at a nearer approach, produce in us the far different sensation of pain, ought to bethink himself what reason he has to say—that this idea of warmth, which was produced in him by the fire, is actually in the fire; and his idea of pain, which the same fire produced in him the same way, is not in the fire. Why are whiteness and coldness [thought to be] in snow, and pain not, when it produces the one and the other idea in us; and can do neither, but by the bulk, figure, number, and motion of its solid parts? (Locke [1690] 1993, bk. II, ch. 8, §16)

Given that Locke is the supposed father of the dispositional theory of color, we now see that he has left the color relationist with a troubling legacy: either colors, when thought of as relational, are to be felt as having their manifest effects in the body or we are to say that we experience them as perceiver-independent properties, and we are guilty of a projective error.[13]

One concern about this line of thought, however, is that it risks setting us out on a hunt for impossible comparisons. Vision is an *exteroceptive* modality, and pain sensitivity is *interoceptive*. This is the difference between modalities that take their objects from the external world, and those whose objects are in the body. The exteroceptive–interoceptive distinction is a fundamental fault line across sensory modalities and experiences (Craig 2002). Arguably, for an exteroceptive modality to yield usable perceptual

---

13. In the paragraph before the passage quoted above, Locke describes how the commonsense view, which he rejects, is guilty of this mistake.

experience, it has to look as if it has a source in the external world, not only inside you—it has to be "outer-directed."[14] For an interoceptive modality to function properly it must appear that any warnings it flags up are associated with one's own body parts, not someone else's, and not with the external causes of bodily damage.[15] In short, the case against OP is doomed if the relationist is required to demonstrate that the phenomenology of color is like that of the interoceptive modalities.

So the challenge for the relationist is now to reconcile the idea that color experience is outer-directed, since it is bound up with an exteroceptive modality, with the idea that color is in some sense perceiver-dependent. It will not be necessary to go so far as to argue that color manifests itself as obviously perceiver-dependent—it will be a victory for the relationist just to make the case that visual phenomenology is neutral about the relationality of color. What the relationist must now provide is a means to reconcile the outer-directedness of experiences involving color vision, due to vision being an exteroceptive modality, with the thesis that colors do *not* appear as perceiver-independent.

8.4   On Outer-Directedness

In the previous section I presented a new version of OP that is inspired by Chalmers and apparently meets the two criteria delineated above. The analysis of this objection unearthed an important assumption concerning the nature of exteroceptive sensory states: the outer-directedness of experiences involving color is generally taken to entail that colors are presented as nonrelational, perceiver-independent properties. I will now argue that such a line cannot be taken without over-intellectualizing perceptual experience—in other words, without failing to satisfy criterion 2.

Then in section 8.4.2, by way of a final answer to those nonrelationists who cling stubbornly to the supposed testimony of their experience of color despite all the discussion above, I point out that it remains to

14. Below I use the terms "outer-directedness" and "outerness" interchangeably. These terms are related to the technical idea of transparency of experience, in particular what Block (2010, 26) calls the positive claim in Moore's idea of diaphanousness, meaning that perceptual experience is purely one of openness to the world.

15. This is a point articulated by Descartes and his followers, Malebranche, and Arnauld; see Gaukroger (2006, 336).

be shown that it is color experience by itself that is the basis of their key phenomenological datum, and not some more complex, multimodal experience of the scene. The recalcitrant nonrelationist is left with an as yet unaddressed burden of proof, and thus fails to meet criterion 1.

8.4.1 Phenomenology or Theory?

In this section I challenge the assumption animating Chalmers' and the body-relatedness version of OP—that the outer-directedness of color experience entails that colors appear to be perceiver-independent. I aim to refute the idea that the *appearance* of (and not the thought of or inference to) perceiver-independence always accompanies experiences such as these. My goal is to create space for the idea that we can experience the outerness of the visual world without accepting that that very experience burdens us with ontological commitment to colors being nonrelational, perceiver-independent properties. The strategy will be to show that equating outerness with perceiver-independence amounts to a theoretical adherence to specific accounts of perceptual experience, rather than something just given in experience itself.

Criterion 2 was presented above to highlight the difference between the putative perceptual manifestation of relationality, and the perceptual presentation of ordinary perceived qualities, such as motion. I reintroduce it here as a challenge to those who assume that the very nature of representations of pain or color determines that we experience those qualities as perceiver-dependent or independent, respectively.

Criterion 2 *It should be possible to show that the putative phenomenological facts are indeed grounded in visual perceptual experience rather than theoretical reflection; it should be demonstrable that we see, and do not surmise, that color is a nonrelational property.*

The first thing to do is this: consider with a fresh mind, unjaded by years of the debate over intentionality and transparency, whether or not there is a gap, however slight, between the (content of) perceptual experience's looking to concern something outside yourself and the far more abstract notion of the properties thus attributed being entirely perceiver-independent. I do hope you will agree that it is not a nonnegotiable position, that it is not irrational or introspectively dishonest for me to claim, for myself, that the outer-directedness of my experience is perceptual in a way that claims for the perceiver-independence, or otherwise, of properties thus experienced are not.

As in the comparison with motion and relationality above (section 8.2.2), there is a purely perceptual gloss on the outerness phenomenon—in that it marks out sensations arising from exteroceptive as opposed to interoceptive modalities—but it is not obvious how a perceived property can simply appear relational or nonrelational without cognitive elaboration. Furthermore the interoceptive–exteroceptive distinction is marked anatomically by different sensory pathways, as is the distinction observed in the anatomy of the visual system between areas specialized for moving stimuli, and those that are not. This raises the suspicion that the claim that the outer-directedness of a perceptual experience entails that perceived properties appear to be perceiver-independent is an interpretive overlay on an experience that is itself neutral about relationality.

In presenting his distinction between Edenic and Fregean content of perceptual experiences, Chalmers (2006, 76) basically concedes this very point:

The phenomenology of color vision clearly makes claims about objects in the world, but it does not obviously make claims about ourselves and our perceptual relation to these objects. As theorists who introspect and reflect on how our phenomenology seems, we can say that on reflection it seems to us (introspectively) as if we are acquainted with objects and properties in the world. But it is not obvious that perceptual phenomenology itself makes such a claim: to suggest that it does is arguably to overintellectualize perceptual experience.[16]

I understand "introspection," when contrasted with "perception" in this way to be some kind of interpretive take on perceptual experience—what we gather from our experience on the basis both of phenomenology and related theoretical commitments. It cannot be insignificant that this concession is made in one of the strongest cases yet presented for the nonrelational character of color phenomenology.

Still, a proponent of OP might still want to claim that her *theoretically informed* take on color experience is the only one that is compatible with the phenomenology of outerness. Strong representationalist theories of perceptual consciousness purport to be motivated by the phenomenological observation of *transparency* or *diaphanousness*, which states that

16. Compare Chalmers (2006, 77): "Even if perception makes no claims about our perceptual experiences and our perceptual relation to the world, introspection does."

experience reaches all the way out to the object represented, including no intrinsic qualities of experience (e.g., see Tye 2003). As such, they are also committed to a Russellian theory of perceptual content. So, if the proponent of OP combines the transparency observation with a strong representationalist thesis that perceptual consciousness is exhausted by representational content—by the representation of how things stand in the external world—then she must inevitably conclude that colors are represented as perceiver-independent properties. But, of course, there are alternatives to strong representationalist theories of perceptual consciousness. If it turns out that color relationism is not compatible with strong representationalism, that is not a devastating cost. We have already seen that color adverbialism must reject Russellian theories in favor of Fregean accounts of perceptual content (section 7.1). If the relationist must subscribe to an account that posits either nonintentional aspects of experience, awareness of perceptual modes of presentation, or body-related elements of perceptual content, she is doing no more than following in the footsteps of many renowned philosophers of mind. She may propose, for example, that objects' colors look to have an ultimate origin in something "out there," but nonetheless colors as we experience them are colors-as-perceived, rather than colors-in-themselves.[17] What is there, just in the experience, that can separate this from the account given by the proponent of OP?

I can now draw together the threads of my response to this new version of OP. It is fairly uncontroversial that pains ("pain properties") do manifest themselves as body-dependent, and that this is not a theoretical gloss on actual pain experience. The obstacle to colors manifesting this kind of body-dependency is that they are associated with vision, an exteroceptive modality, not an interoceptive modality that informs the subject about

17. Or as Chalmers (2006, 76) himself puts it, "One *could* hold a view on which, for an experience to be perfectly veridical, a subject must perceive the relevant perfect colors. On such a view, the character of visual experience is such that in addition to representing the presence of colors, visual experiences also represent the *perception* of colors. If one held this view, one would hold that no such experience is perfectly veridical unless the relevant perfect colors are perceived by a subject (the subject at the center of the relevant centered world....)." If the perfect veridicality conditions of color require a state of affairs in which the color is perceived by a subject, then it follows that the perfect color is perceiver-related. Chalmers (2006, 76) goes on to write that, "I am inclined to think that the character of visual experience is not like this," but this remark leads on to the passage quoted above to the effect that it is introspective reflection, rather than experience per se, determining the outcomes here.

bodily states. It has seemed to many that the outer-directedness of color rules out apparent body-dependency, *and thus rules in apparent perceiver-independence*. But it seems that the move from the outerness of color to the interpretation of color experience as presenting perceiver-independence is a theoretically informed gloss on visual experiences that are actually neutral on this issue. This much has been conceded by Chalmers in his account of color phenomenology. Unless it can be demonstrated otherwise, the relationist is left free to conclude that visual experience alone makes no claims either way as to the relationality of color. This result gives the relationist grounds for rejecting *I*, the first assumption of the objection from phenomenology, since the claim that color is presented as a nonrelational property appears actually to be a theoretically motivated interpretation of visual experiences which are themselves neutral on the issue.

8.4.2 Objects, Outerness, and Sensory Complexity

The intended outcome of the above discussion is that the proponent of OP withdraws her claim that basic color phenomenology presents colors as nonrelational, perceiver-independent properties (assumption I). For she has reason to worry that her cherished phenomenological facts originate not from color experience, which is itself neutral about the relationality or nonrelationality of color, but from her own theoretical commitment to nonrelational accounts of color, or to a particular theory of visual representation. But she may still cling on, asserting that she cannot help but see colors out there in the world as perceiver-independent properties of objects, and that she is compelled to give this intuition weight in her theorizing about color, even if it turns out to be some undisclosed mix of interpretative introspection and theoretical deliberation. So, if the discussion above did nothing to loosen the grip of such intuitions, consider next my final challenge to the thesis that the outer-directedness of visual experience implies the perceiver-independence of color.

The thesis that appearances of outerness entail appearances of nonrelationality is not only vulnerable to a challenge from criterion 2, which questions what sort of claims can be made on the basis of perceptual experience alone, but also from criterion 1, which questions what it is about color experience that leads to the familiar claim that colors are presented as perceiver-independent.

Criterion 1 *Any formulation of the objection from phenomenology should make it clear what aspect of color experience is inconsistent with relationism; it should not presume bizarre or impossible requirements for what it would take for color experience to be consistent with relationism.*

Up until now, I have not called into question the phenomenological datum of outerness. But now I emphasize that this datum is always described to us in the context of a normal perceptual event (e.g., Wittgenstein pointing to the sky, Tye gazing at the ocean, Eloise admiring a tree), involving not only color vision but other visual and nonvisual modalities, jointly apprehending a complex scene. It remains an open question whether or not the supposed outerness of color is actually the outerness of the complex, multimodal, experience of the scene. So I will now ask whether the manifest outerness of color is due to how we experience color per se or if it actually results from the bundling of color with nonchromatic perceptual qualities when we look at objects around us.

In this section I will suggest that the supposed outerness of color *may not* be just there in color experience, but that it is a product of your perception of the entire scene (the simultaneous interpretation of achromatic, spectral and nonvisual cues). It is common methodology in the philosophy of perception to take an atomistic approach to experience, considering one component of it in isolation (e.g., the color, but not the shape, distance or motion of one object alone), even though we never actually experience anything like that; then it is just assumed that the qualities of the complex experience are just the total of qualities of the experiential atoms.[18] But may it not be that some of the most striking features of perceptual experience, such as its outer-directedness, emerge in the complex perceptual Gestalt, and that it is a mistake to posit such features ready formed in the hypothetical experiential atoms? The lesson of chapter 4 was that we should not presume to analyze color in isolation from the rest of visual perception, so it now behooves us to consider an anti-atomistic alternative to the standard account of visual phenomenology.

---

18. Consider Chalmers (2006, 52): "For simplicity, I will focus just on the experience of color at a specific point: for example, the experience of a book's being a specific shade of blue at a specific location on its surface. The conclusions generalize, however, and I will discuss the generalization later in the chapter."

It may not be commonplace to think like this, but consider how unnatural it is to draw all our conclusions about perceptual experience from the kind of perceptual encounter that we never have—like the gaze, for an instant, on a motionless universe containing only one object. We see the long influence, I conjecture, of the Lockean tradition that makes "simple ideas" the building blocks of all experience. Whatever the origins of this methodological practice, we can now land the advocate of OP with another burden of proof: I contend that the phenomenology of ordinary perception (i.e., of a complex scene, viewed multi-modally over time) cannot distinguish between the thesis that outerness is (a) a feature of the perceptual Gestalt, or (b) of some putative phenomenological elements (e.g., of color, motion, texture). The formulation of OP that rests on the outer-directedness of color assumes (b) without justification. Some concluding examples suggest that the justification needed for OP will not be forthcoming.

It is no coincidence that we experience color, size, and shape in the same way, as McGinn observes. For we (or our visual systems) need to orchestrate an interpretation of shape and spectral cues in a way that makes for a consistent understanding of the world. As I have argued in chapter 4, color vision is not something that happens independently of the rest of vision, and this is an important empirical finding that the philosophy of color is yet to absorb. Color vision is bound up with our perception of the shape and distance of ordinary objects. When this is considered, it begins to seem plausible that the extradermal appearance of a colored object is a function of its being perceived *as an object*, something with a shape, a size, a distance from you, as well as a material surface that interacts with the spectrum of ambient light.

To make this case compelling, it would be helpful to have an example of a color experience occurring without any perception of an external object. Since we cannot transport ourselves to the possible world containing chromatic properties but no spatial ones, I will refer to one readily available example that I think closely approximates this case, in that we encounter a color experience not readily associated with an extradermal object. This is the "color Ganzfeld." Look at the orangy field that you experience when you close your eyes and orientate yourself toward a bright light. Is it near or far, does it appear to belong to anything, or is it simply some meaningless expanse? Most important, does it look to be out there in the world, or belonging to the body, or neither of these? The most that I can make of my phenomenology is that it looks to be both or neither. It is, I contend, an uninterpretable sensation, one that is to all intents and purposes neutral about its outerness or innerness.[19]

Another readily observable phenomenon may be instructive here. You are drawing near the end of this book. You are probably feeling quite fatigued; your eyes are weary. Stand up abruptly and stare at some feature of the room around you—a door, for example. Then "zone out"—try to de-focus both your eyes and your attention from the object at the center of your view. What you should find is that you still see that patches of color you identified as surfaces of the object, but you no longer see them as making up a solid object in three-dimensional space. You may also experience a flattening of visual space. How do the chromatic aspects of your experience change, now that you are disrupting their ordinary association with a material body? Do they still look to be out there in space, or is there not now a vagueness about their spatial location? Absent their association with external objects, it is not clear that we can talk of colors themselves being presented as external to me.

We are not in a position to judge that *color* is presented as out there on the surfaces of objects, when what is conveyed by the perceptual Gestalt is always greater than the sum of its experiential parts. This again raises the point made in chapter 7 that questions about color experience, shape experience, or motion experience are all misguided if considered individually. On this view there is no well-formed question about how we experience color in ordinary viewing circumstances; only questions of how we see *things*, objects that happen also to appear as colored. Thus we have an important addendum to the claim that color phenomenology is neutral about the outerness or perceiver-independence of color. We can now cash out the conclusion that color phenomenology is neutral as the thesis that the very question, "does ordinary color experience present me with a body-independent or nonrelational property?" is misguided. We can only ask about what vision, in general, presents us with. And once we move to this level of generality we should not be tempted to say that, "visual experience

19. Colored after images would be another obvious thing to consider, but I will rule them out because these can often be interpreted as looking to be at different distances from the perceiver. This is due to the way we (or our visual systems) associate the color patch with the object it rests on, thus looking small if viewed 'on top of' a close object, and large if viewed 'on top of' a distant one, as described by Emmert's law.

presents color as an external, nonrelational property," because it is not clear that visual experience is presenting the property *color* in any of the relevant ways; for it is simply presenting *things*. Moreover, when we manipulate our visual experience in such a way that we no longer perceive things—in the color Ganzfeld, or by "zoning out"—color is *not* clearly presented as an external, still less perceiver-independent property.

I should emphasize that my use of these examples does not rest on any attempt to extrapolate from unusual to typical color experiences. Of course, it could be that ordinary (object-involving) experience presents color as "out there," but unusual (object-less) experience does not. Rather, I have presented something like an under-determination argument: the experience of complex scenes is compatible with either (1) the outerness of color phenomenology (atomistic interpretation) or, alternatively, (2) the outerness of the perceptual Gestalt. Since ordinary visual experience cannot decide between (1) and (2), and since the unusual cases give reason to doubt (1), we should not accept (1) until further evidence or argument is provided.

I conclude that the supposed outerness of color experience may not be a feature of color phenomenology per se, but a feature of our experience of objects bearing numerous properties, including color. Furthermore, if the psychological story about the complexity of experience is correct, then it makes no sense to ask whether colors are ordinarily presented as relational or nonrelational, inner sensations or external properties. For visual experience is in the business of presenting things, not simple perceptual elements like colors.

Until the proponent of OP can prove otherwise, it is safe for the relationist to assert that color experience by itself is neutral about its being outer-directed or otherwise, and hence the assumed outerness of color cannot be the basis for an argument that colors are manifestly perceiver-independent properties. In other words, we have outerness of the visual world without ontological commitment to colors out there.

8.5   Special Worries for Color Adverbialism?

Color adverbialism has two implications that are highly counterintuitive by traditional lights. First, the idea that colors be attributed not to substances but to activities is not a part of our everyday conception of color, nor is it indicated by our everyday experience of color. Second, the perceptual processes that instantiate the colors are transient, and this goes against the common intuition that colors are "stable" properties. One way to respond to such worries is with a shrug of the shoulders. Here is Sellars (1981, 19):

To put it bluntly, the fruits of painstaking theory construction in the psychology and neuro-physiology of sense perception cannot be anticipated by screwing up one's mental eye (the eye of the child within us) and "seeing" the very manner-of-sensing-ness of a volume of red.

However, what should now be clear is that the verdict of "intuitive" or "counterintuitive" is often used without disclosing whether the source of the intuition is "basic phenomenology," or some undisclosed mix of inter-pretative introspection and theorizing. If color phenomenology itself is incompatible with color adverbialism, then that would be a damaging result for the project set out in this book, since visual experiences are an important source of data for perceptual science. Yet already in this chapter we have seen that the testimony of visual experience is not all that it seems and that phenomenology has less to say about the relationality or nonrela-tionality of color than has been widely assumed. I will now apply these lessons to the special case of color adverbialism. In section 8.5.1, I will address concerns relating to the instantiation of colors in perceptual pro-cesses rather than perceived objects. Then in section 8.5.2, I will show how the instability of color instantiations are still compatible with the phenom-ena of color constancy. Finally in section 8.5.3, I will say a few words about common sense.

8.5.1 Outerness and Adverbialism

One thing clear at the outset is that visual experience does not disclose the adverbial nature of color in any overt way. To borrow again from Sellars (1981, 67), "[i]f there are states of sensing bluely, they obviously do not present themselves as such—otherwise the very existence of a controversy about their existence would be inexplicable." Yet, I suspect, many read-ers on first encountering color adverbialism will have already presumed that visual phenomenology is straight-out inconsistent with the theory. This is, I suspect, because many readers will have assumed that the outer-directedness of visual experience entails that colors be conceptualized as properties instantiated in objects.

However, the arguments presented in section 8.4 give us good reason to believe that the phenomenological datum of outerness saddles us with no specific ontological commitments. For starters, the assumption that the outer-directedness of visual experience entails that colors appear to be instantiated in external objects, like the assumption that their apparent body-independence entails that colors are presented as nonrelational properties, is a theoretical spin on phenomenology. It seems that this problematic overintellectualization (overintepretation) of visual experience has had free reign because alternative proposals, which describe how ontologically uncommitted (neutral) phenomenology is compatible with various ontologies, have not been on the table. That is to say, since no one has sketched a picture that recasts our phenomenology from the perspective of a radically different ontology, it has been all too easy to believe that visual experience presents colors just as the realist believes them to be.

From section 8.4.2 we already have the outlines of such a picture. The crucial thing is to *begin* with the complex perceptual Gestalt, not with any hypothetical experiential atoms. I argued above that it is entirely consistent with visual phenomenology to say that a complex array of objects is presented as out there beyond the body and that this outerness is a feature of the experiential whole but not any of its parts (e.g., color experience per se). Thus visual phenomenology is really noncommittal about the ontological status of any individual kind of perceived property. On this view, the outer-directedness of visual experience is entirely consistent with color adverbialism.

Furthermore the integration of color with the overall experience of objects beyond the perceiver is built into the definitions of color, according to the adverbialist. Colors are both "ways objects appear to us" and "ways we perceive objects." So even though color is treated as a property of a perceptual process, it is integral to its nature that color is a manner of presentation of the extradermal world, when chromatic vision functions alongside the perception of shape, texture, distance, and the rest.

8.5.2 Color Constancy

Similar considerations allow the color adverbialist to address the worry that the transience of the processes that instantiate colors is incompatible with our experience of color as a steady property, in particular the phenomena of color constancy. The most pointed concern is simply this: Can color adverbialism account for color constancy? The basic answer is that the phenomenology of color constancy, like the outer-directedness of visual experience, needs to be understood holistically.

I quoted above a passage from Allen (2007, 144) that noted that in situations of color constancy, an object can look to have a stable illumination and perceiver-independent color even when there are perceptible changes in its surface hue or brightness. This was a strike against Johnston's (1992), Levin's (2000), and Cohen's (2009) idea that any such changes will lead to an appearance of dependency on the factor that has caused the color change (their "interventionist prescription"). Allen argues that in such cases colors are nonetheless presented as perceiver- and illumination-independent properties and that relationism is inconsistent with the phenomenology. My account of constancy provides an alternative that is friendly to relationism in general and color adverbialism in particular.

Color constancy is very much bound up with our perception of colored objects as objects (see section 4.2.2). If visual stimuli are impoverished to such an extent that we can no longer interpret the stimuli as things, not even as two-dimensional shapes painted on a flat surface, then constancy is severely diminished (Hansen et al. 2007). Likewise measures of constancy are highest in real world viewing conditions where perceivers are surrounded by real objects under a natural range of illuminants (Brainard et al. 2003). So given that our impressions of constancy are only robust when we recognize the colored stimulus as some kind of an object or surface, we have an alternative way to understand Allen's observation of stable colors. Namely our apprehension of the sameness of the *object* (with a particular shape, solidity, distance, and color) is part and parcel of our impression that the color is constant, despite the very apparent changes in hue and brightness. If color perception cannot be separated from perception of other properties, there is nothing to persuade us that color experience (plus some attendant ontological commitment to perceiver-independent color), and not *object* constancy, is driving the phenomenology.

This holistic approach to constancy is readily integrated with color adverbialism. Indeed for the adverbialist, color experience (when it is relatively unaffected by changes in illumination) is a manner of perceiving the constancy of objects (their identity over time, the stability of their material composition, etc.). In other words, when we bring our basket of freshly picked strawberries indoors to the kitchen, we see the sameness of their ripe skins redly.

8.5.3   Common Sense

Lewis (1997, 325) writes:

An adequate theory of colour must be both materialistic and commensensical. The former demand is non-negotiable. The latter can be compromised to some degree....But compromise has its limits. It won't do to say that colours do not exist; or that we are unable to detect them; or that they never are properties of material things; or that they go away when things are unilluminated or unobserved; or that they change with every change in the illumination, or with every change in an observer's visual capacities; or that the same surface of the same thing has different colours for different observers. Compromise on these points, and it becomes doubtful whether the so-called 'colours' posited in your theory are rightly so-called. Yet it is a Moorean fact that there are colours rightly so-called. Deny it, and the most credible explanation of your denial is that you are in the grip of some philosophical (or scientific) error.

As will be clear by now, the color adverbialist does compromise common sense far more drastically than Lewis would countenance. Yet she need not deny that there are Moorean colors, for these are just not the colors of perceptual science. The project of color adverbialism, as presented in this book, has been to work out the ontological commitments of perceptual science. What we have learned—and we should not be at all surprised—is that these are not the commitments of common sense. One only has reason to follow Lewis in considering there to be an invidious choice between Moorean colors and naturalized colors if one is in the grip of explanatory monism—the doctrine that science, common sense, and metaphysics must together work toward the one best description of the world. For a pluralist it is a perfectly acceptable result if different domains of enquiry and practice do have their proprietary notions of color. Since perceptual science places perceivers and their experiences in a pivotal role in its account of color, we cannot say either that the colors of *that* branch of science are the colors of physics. This result is consistent with a broader view of science that takes our best empirical knowledge of nature to be unavoidably dappled (Cartwright 1999) and disunified (Dupré 1993), or shaped by distinct theoretical perspectives (Giere 2006). So even *within the scientific image* the Sellarsian synoptic project may well be doomed to failure. I believe we can live with that.

8.6   Conclusions and Directions

In this book I have examined the problem of color in a broad sweep beginning in chapter 2 with a survey of the historical factors that have shaped subsequent debates, and concluding in chapters 6 through to 8 with a series of challenges to the conceptualization of color to which most contemporary philosophy of perception adheres. My central claim has been that a close examination of perceptual science (chapters 4 and 5) provides the motivation and dialectical support for a chromatic ontology that trespasses beyond the traditional confines. Color adverbialism asserts not only that colors are perceiver-dependent properties but that they are properties of perceptual interactions rather than of the perceived object or mind-brain. I have shown that there is nothing fatally implausible or counterintuitive about this claim, so long as color vision is understood within its proper context—as integrated with nonchromatic vision—and not assumed to be some hypothetical color-detecting module.

There are two significant questions that have arisen in the course of the book and deserve more extensive treatment than possible here: first, whether adverbialism is viable as a general theory of perception, beyond the chromatic case; second, the issue of how we should understand color concepts, and the interrelationship of chromatic experience, thought, and language. The home territory for color adverbialism is the study of the visual capacities that humans have in common with other animals. Even though the spectral sensitivities of bees and great apes are quite different, color constancy is understood in analogous terms for both forms of life. Furthermore there is overlap in some of the recognized functions of constant color perception, namely in foraging for food. Via the notion that colors are concurrently ways objects appear and ways individuals perceive certain objects, color adverbialism accounts well for the functional significance and phenomenological salience of color, when considering vision aside from thought and language.

However, in the specifically human context, color names and their associated concepts become a parallel target of enquiry. As I have diagnosed the recent color debate, a central tension and difficulty has been generated by the felt need to reconcile, in one ontology, the divergent requirements both of perceptual science and ordinary language. But even if no ontology can do both, at least potentially a story can be told about how the perceptual one sits with the linguistic or conceptual one. I have left this project for future research because it is so obviously hostage to there being some resolution to the controversy over the role of concepts in human perceptual experience.

In any case, I have aimed with this book to show the utility of placing within the frame of history and philosophy of science, topics typically classified as belonging to the philosophy of mind and perception. And as I argued at the outset, color is a microcosm for broader debates concerning the place of mind in nature and the ever recalcitrant problem of the qualitative. Thus I also hope to have offered the patient reader a variety of materials and suggestions for approaching this range of interconnected questions in somewhat novel ways.

References

Akins, K. 1996. Of sensory systems and the "aboutness" of mental states. *Journal of Philosophy* 93 (7): 337–72.

Akins, K. 2001. More than mere coloring: A dialog between philosophy and neuroscience on the nature of spectral vision. In *Carving our destiny: scientific research faces a new millennium*, ed. J. Fitzpatrick and S. M. Bruer. Washington, DC: Joseph Henry Press.

Akins, K., and M. Hahn. 2014. More than mere colouring: The role of spectral information in human vision. *British Journal for the Philosophy of Science* 65: 125–71.

Alexander, P. 1985. *Ideas, Qualitities and Corpuscles: Locke and Boyle on the External World*. Cambridge, UK: Cambridge University Press.

Allen, K. 2007. The mind-independence of colour. *European Journal of Philosophy* 15:2 15 (2): 137–58.

Allen, K. 2009. Inter-species variation in colour perception. *Philosophical Studies* 142: 197–220.

Allen, K. 2010. In defence of natural daylight. *Pacific Philosophical Quarterly* 91 (1): 1–18.

Aquinas, T. 1945. *Commentary on Aristotle's* De anima. London: Routledge.

Aristotle. 1993. *De anima*, ed. M. Durrant. London: Routledge.

Armstrong, D. 1968. *A Materialist Theory of the Mind*. London: Routledge.

Armstrong, D. 1969. Colour-realism and the argument from microscopes. In *Contemporary Philosophy in Australia*, ed. R. Brown and C. Rollins. London: George Allen and Unwin.

Armstrong, D. 1987/1997. Smart and the secondary qualities. In *Readings on Color: The Philosophy of Color*, vol. 1, ed. A. Byrne and D. Hilbert. Cambridge: MIT Press.

Atherton, M. 2003a. Asking about the nature of colour. In *Colour Perception: Mind and the physical world*, ed. R. Mausfeld and D. Heyer. Oxford: Oxford University Press.

Atherton, M. 2003b. How Berkeley can maintain that snow is white. *Philosophy and Phenomenological Research* 67 (1): 101–13.

Averill, E. 2005. Toward a projectivist account of color. *Journal of Philosophy* 102 (5): 217–34.

Backhaus, W., and R. Menzel. 1992. Conclusions from color-vision of insects. *Behavioral and Brain Sciences* 15 (1): 28.

Barlow, H. B. 1953. Summation and inhibition in the frog's retina. *Journal of Physiology* 119 (1): 69–88.

Barrett, A. B., and A. K. Seth. 2011. Practical measures of integrated information for time-series data. *PLoS Computational Biology* 7 (1): e1001052.

Bennett, J. 1971. *Locke, Berkeley, Hume: Central Themes*. Oxford: Oxford University Press.

Bergstrom, S., C. Frey, and B. Allander. 1974. *Om du skall gora en riktig dåligbild, då racker det inte med svartvitt, då måste du ha farg*. Stockholm: Sveriges Radio.

Berlin, B., and P. Kay. 1969. *Basic Color Terms: Their Universality and Evolution*. Berkeley: University of California Press.

Biernoff, S. 2002. *Sight and Embodiment in the Middle Ages*. Houndmill: Palgrave Macmillan.

Biggam, C., C. A. Hough, C. J. Kay, and D. Simmons, eds. 2011. *New Directions in Colour Studies*. Amsterdam: John Benjamins.

Block, N. 2010. Attention and mental paint. *Philosophical Issues* 20: 23–63.

Bloj, M., D. Kersten, and A. Hurlbert. 1999. Perception of three-dimensional shape influences colour perception through mutual illumination. *Nature* 402: 877–79.

Boghossian, P., and J. D. Velleman. 1989. Colour as a secondary quality. *Mind* 98: 81–103.

Boghossian, P. A., and J. D. Velleman. 1991. Physicalist theories of color. *Philosophical Review* 100 (1): 67–106.

Boyle, R. [1666] 1979. The origin of forms and qualities according to the corpuscular philosophy. In *Selected Philosophical Papers of Robert Boyle*, ed. M. A. Stewart. Oxford: Manchester University Press.

Bradbury, J., and S. Vehrencamp. 2011. *Principles of Animal Communication*, 2nd ed. Sunderland, MA: Sinauer Associates.

Brainard, D. 1996. Cone contrast and opponent modulation color spaces. In *Human Color Vision*, 2nd ed., ed. P. K. Kaiser and R. M. Boynton. Washington, DC: Optical Society of America.

Brainard, D., J. Kraft, and P. Longère. 2003. Colour constancy: developing empirical tests of computational models. In *Colour Perception: Mind and the Physical World*, ed. R. Mausfeld and D. Heyer. Oxford: Oxford University Press.

Brewer, B. 2011. *Perception and its Objects*. Oxford: Oxford University Press.

Broackes, J. 1997. The autonomy of color. In *Readings on Color 1: The Philosophy of Color*, ed. A. Byrne and D. Hilbert, 191–225. Cambridge: MIT Press.

Broackes, J. 2010. What do the color-blind see? In *Color Ontology and Color Science*, ed. J. Cohen and M. Matthen, 291–405. Cambridge: MIT Press.

Brogaard, B. 2010. Perspectival truth and colour primitivism. In *New Waves in Truth*, ed. C. Wright and N. Pedersen, 249–66. New York: Palgrave Macmillan.

Brogaard, B. 2011. Centered worlds and the content of perception. In *Blackwell Companion to Relativism*, ed. S. D. Hales, 137–58. Hoboken, NJ: Wiley-Blackwell.

Brogaard, B. 2012. Colour eliminativism or colour relativism? *Philosophical Papers* 41 (2): 305–21.

Brouwer, G., and D. Heeger. 2009. Decoding and reconstructing color from responses in human visual cortex. *Journal of Neuroscience* 29: 13992–14003.

Brown, D. 2006. On the dual referent approach to colour theory. *Philosophical Quarterly* 56 (222): 96–113.

Brown, D. H. 2014. Colour Layering and Colour Constancy. *Philosophers' Imprint* 14 (15)

Bruce, V., P. R. Green, and M. A. Georgeson. 1996. *Visual Perception: Physiology, Psychology, and Ecology*. Hove, UK: Taylor and Francis.

Burge, T. 2005. Disjunctivism and perceptual psychology. *Philosophical Topics* 33: 1–78.

Burge, T. 2010. *Origins of Objectivity*. New York: Oxford University Press.

Burnyeat, M. 1979. Conflicting appearances. *Proceedings of the British Academy* 65: 69–111.

Burnyeat, M. 1992. Is an aristotelian philosophy of mind still credible? a draft. In *Essays on Aristotle's* De anima, ed. M. Nussbaum and A. Rorty. Oxford: Oxford University Press.

Burr, D. C., and M. C. Morrone. 2004. Visual perception during saccades. In *The Visual Neurosciences*, ed. L. M. Werner and J. S. Chalupa, 1391–1401. Cambridge: MIT Press.

Burtt, E. A. [1932] 2003. *The Metaphysical Foundations of Modern Science*. Mineola, NY: Dover.

Byrne, A. 2001. Do colours look like dispositions? Reply to Langsam and others. *Philosophical Quarterly* 51: 238–45.

Byrne, A. 2003. Color and similarity. *Philosophy and Phenomenological Research* 66 (3): 641–65.

Byrne, A. 2006. Color and the mind-body problem. *Dialectica* 60 (2): 223–44.

Byrne, A., and D. R. Hilbert. 2003. Color realism and color science. *Behavioral and Brain Sciences* 26: 3–64.

Byrne, A., and D. R. Hilbert. 2007a. Truest blue. *Analysis* 67 (1): 87–92.

Byrne, A., and D. R. Hilbert. 2007b. Color primitivism. *Erkenntnis* 66: 73–105.

Byrne, A., and H. Logue, eds. 2008. *Disjunctivism: Contemporary Readings*. Cambridge,: MIT Press.

Campbell, J. (1993). A simple view of colour. In *Reality, Representation, and Projection*, ed. J. Haldane and C. Wright. Oxford: Oxford University Press. Reprinted in Byrne and Hilbert (1997), vol. 1.

Campbell, J. 2002. *Reference and Consciousness*. Oxford: Oxford University Press.

Campbell, K. 1969. Colours. In *Contemporary Philosophy in Australia*, ed. R. Brown and C. Rollins. London: George Allen and Unwin.

Campenhausen, C. 1986. Photoreceptors, lightness constancy and color vision. *Naturwissenschaften* 73: 674–75.

Campenhausen, C., and J. Schramme. 1995. 100 years of Benham's top in colour science. *Perception* 24: 695–717.

Cartwright, N. 1999. *The Dappled World*. Cambridge: Cambridge University Press.

Casati, R., and J. Dokic. 2012. Sounds. In *The Stanford Encyclopedia of Philosophy*, ed. E. N. Zalta. http://plato.stanford.edu/archives/sum2013/entries/scientific-realism/.

Caston, V. 2004. The spirit and the letter: Aristotle on perception. In *Metaphysics, Soul and Ethics: Themes from the Work of Richard Sorabji*, ed. R. Salles, 245–320. Oxford: Oxford University Press.

Chakravartty, A. 2013. Scientific realism. In *The Stanford Encyclopedia of Philosophy*, ed. E. N. Zalta. http://plato.stanford.edu/archives/sum2013/entries/scientific-realism/.

Chalmers, D. 2004. The representational character of experience. In *The Future for Philosophy*, ed. B. Leiter. Oxford: Oxford University Press.

Chalmers, D. 2006. Perception and the fall from eden. In *Perceptual Experience*, ed. T. Gendler and J. Hawthorne, 49–125. Oxford: Clarendon Press.

Chang, H. 2012. *Is Water H_2O? Evidence, Realism and Pluralism*. Dordrecht: Springer.

Chirimuuta, M. 2008. Reflectance realism and colour constancy: What would count as scientific evidence for hilbert's ontology of colour? *Australasian Journal of Philosophy* 86 (4): 563–82.

Chirimuuta, M. 2011a. Touchy-feely colour. In *New Directions in Colour Studies*, ed. C. Biggam, C. A. Hough, C. J. Kay, and D. Simmons. Amsterdam: John Benjamins.

Chirimuuta, M. 2011b. Review of "The red and the real: An essay on color ontology." *International Studies in the Philosophy of Science* 24 (3): 339–42.

Chirimuuta, M. 2014. The metaphysical significance of colour categorization: Mind, world, and their complicated relation. In *Colour Studies: A Broad Spectrum,* ed. W. Anderson, C. P. Biggam, C. A. Hough, and C. J. Kay. Amsterdam: John Benjamins.

Chirimuuta, M., and I. Gold. 2009. The embedded neuron, the enactive field? In *The Oxford Handbook of Philosophy and Neuroscience*, ed. J. Bickle. Oxford: Oxford University Press.

Chirimuuta, M., and M. Paterson. 2014. A methodological molyneux question: Sensory substitution, plasticity and the unification of perceptual theory. In *Perception and its Modalities*, ed. D. Stokes and M. Matthen. Oxford: Oxford University Press.

Chirimuuta, M., and D. J. Tolhurst. 2005. Does a Bayesian model of V1 contrast coding offer a neurophysiological account of human contrast discrimination. *Vision Research* 45: 2943–59.

Chittka, L., and A. Briscoe. 2001. Why sensory ecology needs to become more evolutionary: Insect color vision as a case in point. In *Ecology of Sensing*, ed. F. Barth and A. Schmid. Berlin: Springer-Verlag.

Churchland, P. M. 1981. Eliminative materialism and the propositional attitudes. *Journal of Philosophy* 78: 67–90.

Churchland, P. M. 2007a. On the reality (and diversity) of objective colors: How color-qualia space is a map of reflectance-profile space. In *Neurophilosophy at Work*, ed. P. M. Churchland. Cambridge, UK: Cambridge University Press.

Churchland, P. M. 2007b. Chimerical colors: Some phenomenological predictions from cognitive neuroscience. In *Neurophilosophy at Work*, ed. P. M. Churchland. Cambridge, UK: Cambridge University Press.

Churchland, P. M., and P. S. Churchland. 1981. Functionalism, qualia and intentionality. *Philosophical Topics* 1: 121–45.

Clark, S. 2007. *Vanities of the Eye: Vision in Early Modern European Culture*. Oxford: Oxford University Press.

Clifford, C., B. Spehar, S. Solomon, P. Martin, and Q. Zaidi. 2003. Interactions between color and luminance in the perception of orientation. *Journal of Vision (Charlottesville, VA)* 3: 106–15.

Cohen, J. 2003. Perceptual variation, realism, and relativization, or: How I learned to stop worrying and love variations in color vision. *Behavioral and Brain Sciences* 26 (1): 25–26.

Cohen, J. 2004. Color properties and color ascriptions: A relationalist manifesto. *Philosophical Review* 113 (4): 451–506.

Cohen, J. 2007. A relationalist's guide to error about color perception. *Noûs* 41 (2): 335–53.

Cohen, J. 2009. *The Red and the Real*. Oxford: Oxford University Press.

Cohen, J. 2010. It's not easy being green. In *Color Ontology and Color Science*, ed. J. Cohen and M. Matthen. Cambridge: MIT Press.

Cohen, J. 2012. Redder and realer: Responses to egan and tye. *Analytic Philosophy* 53 (3): 313–26.

Cohen, J., C. L. Hardin, and B. P. McLaughlin. 2006. True colours. *Analysis* 66 (4): 335–40.

Cohen, J., C. L. Hardin, and B. P. McLaughlin. 2007. The truth about "the truth about true blue." *Analysis* 67 (2): 162–66.

Cohen, J., and S. Nichols. 2010. Colours, colour relationalism and the deliverances of introspection. *Analysis* 70 (2): 218–28.

Conduct, M. D. 2008. Naïve realism, adverbialism and perceptual error. *Acta Analytica* 23:147–159.

Conway, B. 2009. Color vision, cones, and color-coding in the cortex. *Neuroscientist* 15 (3): 274–90.

Costall, A. P. 1984. Are theories of perception necessary? A review of Gibson's "The ecological approach to visual perception." *Journal of the Experimental Analysis of Behavior* 41: 109–15.

Craig, A. D. 2002. How do you feel? interoception: The sense of the physiological condition of the body. *Nature Reviews. Neuroscience* 3: 655–66.

Crane, T. 2000. The origins of qualia. In *The History of the Mind-Body Problem*, ed. T. Crane and S. Patterson. London: Routledge.

Crane, T., and D. H. Mellor. 1990. There is no question of physicalism. *Mind* 99: 185–206.

Craver, C. F. 2007. *Explaining the Brain*. Oxford: Oxford University Press.

Croner, L., and T. Albright. 1997. Image segmentation enhances discrimination of motion in visual distractors. *Vision Research* 37: 1415–27.

Cropper, S. 2006. The detection of motion in chromatic stimuli: Pedestals and masks. *Vision Research* 46: 724–38.

Cropper, S., and A. Derrington. 1996. Rapid colour-specific detection of motion in human vision. *Nature* 379: 72–74.

Danilova, M., and J. D. Mollon. 2012. Cardinal axes are not independent in color discrimination. *Journal of the Optical Society of America. A, Optics, Image Science, and Vision* 29: 157–64.

Davidoff, J. 1991. *Cognition through Color*. Cambridge: MIT Press.

Davidoff, J. 2001. Language and perceptual categorisation. *Trends in Cognitive Sciences* 5 (9): 382–87.

Davidson, D. 1970. The individuation of events. In *Essays in Honor of Carl G. Hempel*, ed. N. Rescher, 216–34. Dordrecht: Reidel.

De Valois, R. L. 1965. Analysis and coding of color vision in the primate visual system. *Cold Spring Harbor Symposia on Quantitative Biology* 30: 567–79.

Dedrick, D. 2006. Explanation(s) and the patterning of basic colour words across languages and speakers. In *Progress in Colour Studies: Psychological Aspects,* vol. 2, ed. N. Pitchford and C. P. Biggam. Amsterdam: John Benjamins.

Dennett, D. 1987. *The Intentional Stance*. Cambridge: MIT press.

Derrington, A., J. Krauskopf, and P. Lennie. 1984. Chromatic mechanisms in lateral geniculate nucleus of macaque. *Journal of Physiology* 357: 241–65.

Des Chene, D. 2006. From natural philosophy to natural science. In *The Cambridge Companion to Early Modern Philosophy*, ed. D. Rutherford. Cambridge, UK: Cambridge University Press.

Des Chene, D. 2008. Aristotelian natural philosophy: body, cause, nature. In *A Companion to Descartes*, ed. J. Broughton and J. Carriero, 17–32. Hoboken, NJ: Wiley-Blackwell.

Descartes, R. 1985. *The Philosophical Writings of Descartes*. vol. 1, ed. J. Cottingham, R. Stoothoff, and D. Murdoch. Cambridge, UK: Cambridge University Press.

Dominy, N. 2004. Fruits, fingers, and fermentation: The sensory cues available to foraging primates. *Integrative and Comparative Biology* 44: 295–303.

Dretske, F. 1995. *Naturalizing the Mind*. Cambridge: MIT Press.

Dummett, M. 1979. Common sense and physics. In *Perception and Identity: Essays Presented to A.J. Ayer*, ed. G. F. MacDonald. London: Macmillan.

Dummett, M. 1993. *The Logical Basis of Metaphysics*. Cambridge: Harvard University Press.

Dupré, J. 1993. *The Disorder of Things*. Cambridge: Harvard University Press.

Dupré, J. 2012. *Processes of Life*. Oxford: Oxford University Press.

Dupré, J. 2013. Living causes. *Proceedings of the Aristotelian Society Supplementary* 87: 19–37.

Durrant, M., ed. 1993. *Aristotle's* De anima *in Focus*. London: Routledge.

Eddington, A. [1928] 2012. *The Nature of the Physical World*. Cambridge, UK: Cambridge University Press.

Egan, A. 2012. Comments on Jonathan Cohen's *The Red and the Real*. *Analytic Philosophy* 53 (3): 306–12.

Evans, G. 1980. Things without the mind. In *Philosophical Subjects*, ed. Z. van Straaten. Oxford: Oxford University Press.

Everson, S. 1999. *Aristotle on Perception*. Oxford: Oxford University Press.

Fairchild, M. D. 1998. *Color Appearance Models*. North Reading, MA: Addison Wesley Longman.

Fairchild, M. D. 2013. *Color Appearance Models*, 3rd ed. Hoboken, NJ: Wiley.

Figdor, C. 2014. Verbs and minds. In *New Waves in Philosophy of Mind*, ed. M. Sprevak and J. Kallestrup, 38–53. London: Palgrave-Macmillan.

Findlay, J., and I. Gilchrist. 2003. *Active Vision: The Psychology of Looking and Seeing*. Oxford: Oxford University Press.

Fish, W. 2004. The Direct/Indirect Distinction in Contemporary Philosophy of Perception. *Essays in Philosophy* 5 (1):1-13.

Fish, W. 2009. *Perception, Hallucination, and Illusion*. Oxford: Oxford University Press.

Fish, W. 2010. *Philosophy of Perception: A Contemporary Introduction*. London: Routledge.

Flanagan, P., P. Cavanagh, and O. E. Favreau. 1990. Independent orientation-selective mechanisms for the cardinal directions of color space. *Vision Research* 30: 769–78.

Fodor, J. 1990. *A Theory of Content and Other Essays*. Cambridge: MIT Press.

Foster, D. H. 2003. Does colour constancy exist? *Trends in Cognitive Sciences* 7: 439–43.

Foster, D. H., and S. M. C. Nascimento. 1994. Relational colour constancy from invariant cone-excitation ratios. *Proceedings. Biological Sciences* 257 (1349): 115–21.

Frisch, K. v. 1914. Der Farbensinn und Formensinn der Biene. *Zoologische Jahrbucher. Abteilung fur Allgemeine Zoologie und Physiologie der Tiere* 35: 1–188.

Garber, D. 1992. *Descartes' Metaphysical Physics*. Chicago: University of Chicago Press.

Gaukroger, S. 1980. Descartes' project for a mathematical physics. In *Descartes: Philosophy, Mathematics and Physics. Hassocks*, ed. S. Gaukroger. Brighton, UK: Harvester Press.

Gaukroger, S. 1990. Introduction: The background to the problem of perceptual cognition. In *On True and False Ideas*, ed. S. Gaukroger. Manchester: Manchester University Press.

Gaukroger, S. 2006. *The Emergence of a Scientific Culture: Science and the Shaping of Modernity, 1210–1685*. Oxford: Oxford University Press.

Gegenfurtner, K., and D. Kiper. 2003. Color vision. *Annual Review of Neuroscience* 26: 181–206.

Gegenfurtner, K., and J. Rieger. 2000. Sensory and cognitive contributions of color to the recognition of natural scenes. *Current Biology* 10: 805–808.

Gegenfurtner, K. R., L. T. Sharpe, and B. B. Boycott. 2001. *Color Vision: From Genes to Perception*. Cambridge, UK: Cambridge University Press.

Gelb, A. 1938. Colour constancy. In *A source book of Gestalt psychology*, ed. W. D. Ellis, 196–209. London: Kegan Paul, Trench, Trubner.

Gert, J. 2008. What Colors Could Not Be: An Argument for Color Primitivism. *Journal of Philosophy* 105 (3):128-155.

Gert, J. 2012a. Color constancy and dispositionalism. *Philosophical Studies* 162 (2): 183–200.

Gert, J. 2012b. Crazy relations. *Croatian Journal of Philosophy* 12 (36): 315–30.

Gibbard, A. 2006. Moral feelings and moral concepts. In *In Oxford Studies in Metaethics*, vol. 1, ed. R. S. Landau, 195–215. Oxford: Clarendon Press.

Gibson, J. 1967. New reasons for realism. *Synthese* 17 (2): 162–72.

Gibson, J. [1979] 1986. *The Ecological Approach to Visual Perception*. Hillsdale, NJ: Lawrence Erlbaum.

Gibson, J. J. 1966. *The Senses Considered as Perceptual Systems*. Boston: Houghton Mifflin.

Giere, R. N. 2006. *Scientific Perspectivism*. Chicago: University of Chicago Press.

Gilchrist, A. 2006. *Seeing in Black and White*. Oxford: Oxford University Press.

Glanzberg, M. 2013. Truth. In *The Stanford Enyclopedia of Philosophy*, ed. E. N. Zalta. http://plato.stanford.edu/archives/spr2014/entries/truth/.

Goldstein, E. B. 1989. *Sensation and Perception*. Belmont, CA: Wadsworth.

Goldstein, E. B. 1999. *Sensation and Perception*, 5th ed. Pacific Grove, CA: Brooks/ Cole.

Gray, J. 2007. *Consciousness: Creeping up on the Hard Problem*. Oxford: Oxford University Press.

Gupta, A. 2006. *Empiricism and Experience*. New York: Oxford University Press.

Haddock, A., and F. Macpherson, eds. 2008. *Disjunctivism: Perception, Action, Knowledge*. Oxford: Oxford University Press.

Hanley, J. R., and D. Roberson. 2011. Categorical perception effects reflect differences in typicality on within category trials. *Psychonomic Bulletin and Review* 18: 355–63.

Hansen, T., S. Walter, and K. Gegenfurtner. 2007. Effects of spatial and temporal context on color categories and color constancy. *Journal of Vision (Charlottesville, VA)* 7: 1–15.

Harada, T., N. Goda, T. Ogawa, M. Ito, H. Toyoda, N. Sadato, and H. Komatsu. 2009. Distribution of colour-selective activity in the monkey inferior temporal cortex revealed by functional magnetic resonance imaging. *European Journal of Neuroscience* 30: 1960–70.

Hardin, C. L. 1988. *Color for Philosophers*. Indianapolis: Hackett.

Hardin, C. L. 1992. The virtues of illusion. *Philosophical Studies* 68 (3): 371–82.

Hardin, C. L. 1993. *Color for Philosophers*, 2nd ed. Indianapolis: Hackett.

Hardin, C. L. 2003a. A spectral reflectance doth not a color make. *Journal of Philosophy* 100: 191–202.

Hardin, C. L. 2004. A green thought in a green shade. *Harvard Review of Philosophy* 12: 29–39.

Hardin, C. L. 1983. Colors, normal observers and standard conditions. *Journal of Philosophy* 80: 806–13.

Hardin, C. L. 2003b. Byrne and hilbert's chromatic ether. *Behavioral and Brain Sciences* 26 (1): 32–33.

Harvey, J. 2000. Colour-dispositionalism and its recent critics. *Philosophy and Phenomenological Research* 61 (1): 137–56.

Hatfield, G. 1990. Metaphysics and the new science. In *Reappraisals of the Scientific Revolution*, ed. R. S. Westman and D. Lindberg. Cambridge, UK: Cambridge University Press.

Hatfield, G. 1998. The cognitive faculties. In *The Cambridge History of Seventeenth Century Philosophy*, vol. 2, ed. D. Garber and M. Ayers. Cambridge, UK: Cambridge University Press.

Hatfield, G. 2003. Objectivity and subjectivity revisited: Color as a psychobiological property. In *Colour Perception: Mind and the Physical World*, ed. R. Mausfeld and D. Heyer, 187–202. Oxford: Oxford University Press.

Hatfield, G. 2009. *Perception and Cognition: Essays in the Philosophy of Psychology*. Oxford: Oxford University Press.

Heft, H. 2001. *Ecological Psychology in Context*. Mahwah, NJ: Lawrence Erlbaum.

Heidegger, M. [1929] 1993. What is metaphysics? In *Basic Writings: From Being and Time (1927) to The Task of Thinking (1964)*, ed. D. F. Krell. London: Routledge.

Heidelberger, M. 2004. *Nature from Within: Gustav Theodor Fechner and His Psychophysical Worldview*. Pittsburgh: University of Pittsburgh Press.

Heil, J. 2012. *The Universe as We Find It*. Oxford: Oxford University Press.

Henry, J. 2002. *The Scientific Revolution and the Origins of Modern Science*, 2nd ed. Houndmills: Palgrave.

Hering, E. 1878. *Zur Lehre vom Lichtsinne*. Wien: Gerold.

Hilbert, D. R. 1987. *Color and Color Perception: A Study in Anthropocentric Realism*. Stanford: Stanford University CSLI.

Hilbert, D. R. 1992. Comparative color vision and the objectivity of color. *Behavioral and Brain Sciences* 15 (1): 38–39.

Hill, G. E., and K. J. McGraw. 2006. *Bird Coloration: Function and Evolution*. Cambridge: Harvard University Press.

Hiramatsu, C., A. Melin, F. Aureli, C. Schaffner, M. Vorobyev, Y. Matsumoto, and S. Kawamura. 2008. Importance of achromatic contrast in short-range fruit foraging of primates. *PLoS ONE* 3(10): e3356.

Hofer, H., B. Singer, and D. R. Williams. 2005. Different sensations from cones with the same photopigment. *Journal of Vision* 5: 444–54.

Holt, E. B. 1915. *The Freudian Wish and Its Place in Ethics*. New York: Henry Holt.

Horwitz, G., and C. Haas. 2012. Nonlinear analysis of macaque V1 color tuning reveals cardinal directions for cortical color processing. *Nature Neuroscience* 15: 913–19.

Hume, D. [1739] 1985. *A Treatise of Human Nature*, ed. E. C. Mossner. London: Penguin.

Hume, D. [1777] 1975. *Enquiries Concerning Human Understanding and Concerning Principles of Morals*, 3rd ed., ed. P. H. Nidditch. Oxford: Oxford University Press.

Hurlbert, A. 1998. Computational models of color constancy. In *Perceptual Constancies: Why Things Look the Way They Do*, ed. V. Walsh and J. Kulikowski. Cambridge, UK: Cambridge University Press.

Hurlbert, A. C. 2013. The perceptual quality of colour. In *A Handbook of Experimental Phenomenology: Visual Perception of Shape, Space and Appearance*, ed. L. Albertazzi. Hoboken, NJ: Wiley.

Hurley, S. L. 1998. *Consciousness in Action*. Cambridge: Harvard University Press.

Hurvich, L. 1981. *Color Vision*. Sunderland, MA: Sinauer Associates.

Hurvich, L., and D. Jameson. 1955. Some quantitative aspects of an opponent-colors theory. II. Brightness, saturation, and hue in normal and dichromatic vision. *Journal of the Optical Society of America* 45: 602–16.

Hurvich, L. M., and D. Jameson. 1956. Some quantitative aspects of an opponent-colors theory. iv. a psychological color specification system. *Journal of the Optical Society of America* 46: 416–21.

Ives, H. E. 1912. The relation between the color of the illuminant and the color of the illuminated object. *Transactions of the Illuminating Engineering Society* 7: 62–72.

Jackson, F. 1975. On the adverbial analysis of visual experience. *Metaphilosophy* 6 (2): 127–35.

Jackson, F. 1998. *From Metaphysics to Ethics*. Oxford: Clarendon Press.

Jackson, F., and R. Pargetter. 1987/1997. An objectivist's guide to subjectivism about colour. In *Readings on Color: The Philosophy of Color*, vol. 1, ed. A. Byrne and D. R. Hilbert. Cambridge: MIT Press.

Jacobs, G. 2004. Comparative color vision. In *The Visual Neurosciences*, ed. J. S. Werner and L. Chapula, 962–73. Cambridge: MIT Press.

Jacobs, G. H. 2009. Evolution of colour vision in mammals. *Philosophical Transactions of the Royal Society of London, Series B* 364: 2957–67.

James, W. 1904. Does 'consciousness' exist? *Journal of Philosophy, Psychology and Scientific Methods* 1 (18): 477–91.

James, W. [1907] 1981. *Pragmatism*. Indianapolis: Hackett.

James, W. [1892] 1985. *Psychology: The Briefer Course*. Notre Dame: University of Notre Dame Press.

Jameson, D., and L. M. Hurvich. 1955. Some quantitative aspects of an opponent-colors theory. i. chromatic responses and spectral saturation. *Journal of the Optical Society of America* 45 (7): 546–52.

Jameson, D., and L. M. Hurvich. 1956. Some quantitative aspects of an opponent-colors theory. III. Changes in brightness, saturation, and hue with chromatic adaptation. *Journal of the Optical Society of America* 46: 405–15.

Johansen, T. K. 1997. *Aristotle on the Sense-Organs*. Cambridge, UK: Cambridge University Press.

Johnston, M. 1989. Dispositional theories of value. *Proceedings of the Aristotelian Society* 63: 139–74.

Johnston, M. 1992. How to speak of the colors. *Philosophical Studies* 68 (3): 221–64.

Johnston, M. 1996. Is the external world invisible? *Philosophical Issues* 7: 185–89.

Jonas, H. 1954. The nobility of sight. *Philosophy and Phenomenological Research* 14 (4): 507–19.

Jones, L. A. 1943. The historical background and evolution of the colorimetry report. *Journal of the Optical Society of America* 33 (10): 534–43.

Jones, L. A. 1953. *The Science of Color*. New York: Crowell.

Jones, L. A., E. Q. Adams, B. R. Bellamy, C. Bittinger, E. C. Crittenden, C. Z. Davies, C. E. Foss, et al. 1943. The concept of color. *Journal of the Optical Society of America* 33 (10): 544–54.

Jraissati, Y., E. Wakui, L. Decock, and I. Douven. 2012. Constraints on colour category formation. *International Studies in the Philosophy of Science* 26 (2): 171–96.

Kail, P. J. E. 2007. *Projection and Realism in Hume's Philosophy*. Oxford: Oxford University Press.

Kaiser, P. K., and R. M. Boynton. 1996. *Human Color Vision*. Washington, DC: Optical Society of America.

Kalderon, M. E. 2007. Color pluralism. *Philosophical Review* 116 (4): 563–601.

Kalderon, M. E. 2011a. The multiply qualitative. *Mind* 120: 239–62.

Kalderon, M. E. 2011b. Color illusion. *Noûs* 45 (4): 751–75.

Kelber, A., M. Vorobyev, and D. Osorio. 2003. Animal colour vision—behavioural tests and physiological concepts. *Biological Reviews of the Cambridge Philosophical Society* 78: 81–118.

Kersten, D., P. Mamassian, and A. Yuille. 2004. Object perception as Bayesian inference. *Annual Review of Psychology* 55: 271–304.

Kim, J. 1999. Making sense of emergence. *Philosophical Studies* 95: 3–36.

Kingdom, F. 2003. Colour brings relief to human vision. *Nature Neuroscience* 6: 641–44.

Kingdom, F. 2008. Perceiving light versus material. *Vision Research* 48: 2090–2105.

Kingdom, F. 2011. Illusions of colour and shadow. In *New Directions in Colour Studies*, ed. C. P. Biggam, C. A. Hough, C. J. Kay, and D. Simmons. Amsterdam: John Benjamins.

Kingdom, F., C. Beauce, and L. Hunter. 2004. Colour vision brings clarity to shadows. *Perception* 33: 907–14.

Kneale, W. 1950. Sensation and the physical world. *Philosophical Quarterly* 1: 109–26.

Koenderink, J. J. 2013. Surface chape, the science and the looks. In *Handbook of Experimental Phenomenology: Visual Perception of Shape, Space and Appearance*, ed. L. Albertazzi, 165–80. Hoboken, NJ: Wiley.

Koffka, K. 1936. On problems of colour-perception. *Acta Psychologica* 1: 129–34.

Kriegel, U. 2011. The Veil of Abstracta. *Philosophical Issues* 21 (1):245-267.

Kuehni, R. G. 1997. *Color: An Introduction to Practice and Principles*. New York: Wiley.

Kuehni, R. G. 2003. *Color Space and Its Divisions*. Hoboken, NJ: Wiley.

Kuhl, P. K., B. T. Conboy, S. Coffey-Corina, D. Padden, M. Rivera-Gaxiola, and T. Nelson. 2008. Phonetic learning as a pathway to language: New data and native language magnet theory expanded (nlm-e). *Philosophical Transactions of the Royal Society of London, Series B, Biological Sciences* 363: 979–1000.

Ladyman, J., D. Ross, D. Spurrett, and J. Collier. 2007. *Every Thing Must Go: Metaphysics Naturalized*. Oxford: Oxford University Press.

Land, M. F., and D.-E. Nilsson. 2002. *Animal Eyes*. Oxford: Oxford University Press.

Langsam, H. 2000. Why colours *do* look like dispositions. *Philosophical Quarterly* 50: 68–75.

Levin, D. M., ed. 1997. *Sites of Vision*. Cambridge: MIT Press.

Levin, J. 2000. Dispositional theories of color and the claims of common sense. *Philosophical Studies* 100 (4): 151–17.

Lewis, D. 1989. Dispositional theories of value. *Proceedings of the Aristotelian Society* 63: 113–37.

Lewis, D. 1997. Naming the colours. *Australasian Journal of Philosophy* 75: 325–42.

Li, H.-C., and F. Kingdom. 2001. Motion-surface labeling by orientation, spatial frequency and luminance polarity in 3-D structure-from-motion. *Vision Research* 41: 3873–82.

Liebe, S., E. Fischer, N. K. Logothetis, and G. Rainer. 2009. Color and shape interactions in the recognition of natural scenes by human and monkey observers. *Journal of Vision (Charlottesville, Va.)* 9 (5): 14.

Lindberg, D. 1976. *Theories of vision from Al-kindi to Kepler*. Chicago: University of Chicago Press.

Lindberg, D. C., and R. S. Westman, eds. 1990. *Reappraisals of the Scientific Revolution*. Cambridge, UK: Cambridge University Press.

Ling, Y., and A. C. Hurlbert. 2008. Role of color memory in successive color constancy. *Journal of the Optical Society of America. A, Optics, Image Science, and Vision* 25 (6): 1215–26.

Livingstone, M., and D. Hubel. 1987. Psychophysical evidence for separate channels for the perception of form, color, movement and depth. *Journal of Neuroscience* 7 (11): 3416–68.

Livingstone, M., and D. Hubel. 1988. Segregation of form, color, movement and depth: Anatomy, physiology and perception. *Science* 240: 740–49.

Locke, J. [1690] 1993. *An Essay Concerning Human Understanding*, ed. J. W. Yolton. London: Everyman Library.

Logue, H. 2012. Why naive realism? *Proceedings of the Aristotelian Society* 112 (pt. 2): 211–37.

Longino, H. E. 2006. Theoretical pluralism and the scientific study of behavior. In *Minnesota Studies in the Philosophy of Science: Scientific Pluralism*, vol. 19, ed S. H. Kellert, H. E. Longino, and C. K. Waters. Minneapolis: University of Minnesota Press.

Lotto, R., and L. Chittka. 2005. Seeing the light: Illumination as a contextual cue to color choice behavior in bumblebees. *Proceedings of the National Academy of Sciences of the United States of America* 102: 3852–56.

Lovell, P., D. Tolhurst, C. Parraga, R. Baddeley, U. Leonards, J. Troscianko, and T. Troscianko. 2005. Stability of the color-opponent signals under changes of illuminant in natural scenes. *Journal of the Optical Society of America, Series A, Optics, Image Science, and Vision* 22: 2060–71.

Lythgoe, J. N. 1972. The adaptation of visual pigments to the photic environment. In *Photochemistry of Vision: Handbook of Sensory Physiology*, vol. VII/1, ed. H. J. A. Dartnall, 566–603. Berlin: Springer-Verlag.

MacAdam, D. 1997. The physical basis of color specification. In *Readings on Color: The Science of Color*, vol. 2, ed.A. Byrne and D. R. Hilbert. Cambridge: MIT Press.

Machamer, P., L. Darden, and C. Craver. 2000. Thinking about mechanisms. *Philosophy of Science* 67: 1–25.

Mackie, J. L. 1976. *Problems from Locke*. Oxford: Clarendon Press.

Maloney, L. T. 1986. Evaluation of linear models of surface spectral reflectance with small numbers of parameters. *Journal of the Optical Society of America, Series A, Optics and Image Science* 3:1673–83.

Maloney, L.T. 2003. Surface colour perception and environmental constraints. In *Color Perception: Mind and the Physical World*, ed. R. Mausfeld and D. Heyer, 285–86. Oxford: Oxford University Press.

Maloney, L. T., and B. Wandell. 1986. Color constancy: a method for recovering surface spectral reflectance. *Journal of the Optical Society of America, Series A, Optics and Image Science* 3: 29–33.

Maloney, L. T. 1999. Physics-based models of surface color perception. In *Color Vision: From Genes to Perception*, ed. K. Gegenfurtner and L. Sharpe. Cambridge, UK: Cambridge University Press.

Marr, D. 1982. *Vision: A Computational Investigation into the Human Representation and Processing of Visual Information*. San Francisco: Freeman.

Martin, P. R. 2009. Retinal color vision in primates. In *Encyclopedia of Neuroscience*, ed. M. D. Binder, N. Hirokawa and U. Windhorst. Berlin: Springer-Verlag.

Matthen, M. 1988. Biological functions and perceptual content. *Journal of Philosophy* 85: 5–27.

Matthen, M. 2005. *Seeing, Doing and Knowing: A Philosophical Theory of Sense Perception*. Oxford: Oxford University Press.

Matthen, M. 2009. Truly blue: an adverbial aspect of perceptual representation. *Analysis* 69 (1): 48–54.

Maull, N. 1978. Cartesian optics and the geometrization of nature. *Review of Metaphysics* 32 (2): 253–73.

Maund, J. B. 1981. Colour: A case for conceptual fission. *Australasian Journal of Philosophy* 59 (3): 308–22.

Maund, J. B. 2006. The illusory theory of colour: An anti-realist theory. *Dialectica* 60: 254–68.

Maund, J. B. 2012. Colour relationalism and colour irrealism/eliminativism/fictionalism. *Croatian Journal of Philosophy* 12 (36): 379–98.

Mausfeld, R. 1998. Color perception: From Grassmann codes to a dual code for object and illumination colors. In *Color Vision*, ed. W. Backhaus, R. Kliefl, and J. Werner. Berlin: De Gruyter.

Mausfeld, R. 2003. The dual coding of colour: 'Surface colour' and 'illumination colour' as constituents of the representational format of perceptual primitives. In *Colour—Mind and the Physical World*, ed. R. Mausfeld and D. Heyer. Oxford: Oxford University Press.

Mausfeld, R. 2010. Colour within an internalist framework: The role of 'colour' in the structure of the perceptual system. In *Color Ontology and Color Science*, ed. J. Cohen and M. Matthen. Cambridge: MIT Press.

Mausfeld, R., and J. Andres. 2002. Second order statistics of colour codes modulate transformations that effectuate varying degrees of scene invariance and illumination invariance. *Perception* 31: 209–24.

Mausfeld, R., R. Niederée, and D. Heyer. 1992. On possible perceptual worlds and how they shape their environments. *Behavioral and Brain Sciences* 15 (1): 47–48.

Maximov, V. V. 2000. Environmental factors which may have led to the appearance of colour vision. *Philosophical Transactions of the Royal Society of London, Series B* 355: 1239–42.

McDowell, J. 1985. Values and secondary qualities. In *Morality and Objectivity*, ed. T. Honderich. London: Routledge and Kegan Paul.

McDowell, J. 2011. *Perception as a Capacity for Knowledge*. Milwaukee: Marquette University Press.

McGilvray, J. 1994. Constant colors in the head. *Synthese* 100 (2): 197–239.

McGilvray, J. A. 1983. To color. *Synthese* 54: 37–70.

McGinn, C. 1996. Another look at color. *Journal of Philosophy* 93: 537–53.

McGinn, C. 1983. *The Subjective View: Secondary Qualities and Indexical Thoughts.* Oxford: Oxford University Press.

McGinn, C. 2000. *The Mysterious Flame: Conscious Minds in a Material World.* New York: Basic Books.

McIlhagga, W., and K. Mullen. 1996. Contour integration with color and luminance contrast. *Vision Research* 36: 1265–79.

McLaughlin, B. P. 2003. The place of color in nature. In *Colour Perception: Mind and the Physical World*, ed. R. Mausfeld and D. Heyer, 475–502. Oxford: Oxford University Press.

Menn, S. 1995. The greatest stumbling block: Descartes' denial of real qualities. In *Descartes and His Contemporaries: Meditations, Objections, and Replies*, ed. R. Ariew and M. G. Grene, 182–207. Chicago: University of Chicago Press.

Merleau-Ponty, M. 1969. *The Visible and the Invisible*, ed. A. Lingis. Chicago: Northwestern University Press.

Michna, M., and K. Mullen. 2008. The contribution of color to global motion processing. *Journal of Vision (Charlottesville, VA)* 8 (5).

Millikan, R. 1989. Biosemantics. *Journal of Philosophy* 86 (6): 281–97.

Misak, C. 2013. *The American Pragmatists*. Oxford: Oxford University Press.

Miscevic, N. 2007. Is color-dispositionalism nasty and unecological? *Erkenntnis* 66: 203–31.

Mitchell, S. D. 2012. Emergence: Logical, functional and dynamical. *Synthese* 185: 171–86.

Mollon, J. [1989] 1997. "'Tho' she kneel'd in that place where they grew....'": The uses and origins of primate color vision. In *Readings on Color: The Science of Color*, vol. 2, ed. A. Byrne and D. R. Hilbert, 379–96. Cambridge: MIT Press.

Mollon, J. 2006. Monge: The Verriest Lecture, Lyon, July 2005. *Visual Neuroscience* 23: 297–309.

Mollon, J. D. 2003. The origins of modern color science. In *The Science of Color*, ed. S. Shevell. Amsterdam: Elsevier.

Monasterio, F. M. D., and P. Gouras. 1975. Functional properties of ganglion cells of the rhesus monkey retina. *Journal of Physiology* 251:167–95.

Morgan, M., A. Adam, and J. Mollon. 1992. Dichromats detect colour-camouflaged objects that are not detected by trichromats. *Proceedings, Biological Sciences* 248: 291–95.

Mullen, K., W. Beaudot, and W. McIllhagga. 2000. Contour integration in color vision: A common process for the blue-yellow, red-green and luminance mechanisms. *Vision Research* 40: 639–55.

Nanay, B. 2014. Empirical problems with anti-representationalism. In *Does Perception have Content?* ed. B. Brogaard. Oxford: Oxford University Press.

Nascimento, S. M. C., and D. H. Foster. 2000. Relational color constancy in achromatic and isoluminant images. *Journal of the Optical Society of America, Series A, Optics, Image Science, and Vision* 17 (2): 225–31.

Nassau, K. 2001. *The physics and chemistry of color: the fifteen causes of color.* 2nd ed. New York: Wiley.

Newton, I. [1730] 1952. *Opticks, Or a Treatise of the Reflections, Refractions, Inflections and Colours of Light.* New York: Dover.

Nijboer, T., R. Kanai, E. Haan, and M. Smagt. 2008. Recognising the forest, but not the trees: An effect of colour on scene perception and recognition. *Consciousness and Cognition* 17 (3): 741–52.

Noë, A. 2004. *Action in Perception.* Cambridge: MIT Press.

Noë, A. 2009. *Out of Our Heads.* New Haven: Hill and Wang.

O'Callaghan, C. 2007. *Sounds: A Philosophical Theory.* Oxford: Oxford University Press.

O'Regan, J. 2011. *Why Red Doesn't Sound Like a Bell.* Oxford: Oxford University Press.

Osorio, D., and M. Vorobyev. 1996. Colour vision as an adaptation to frugivory in primates. *Proceedings. Biological Sciences* 263: 593–99.

Osorio, D., and M. Vorobyev. 2005. Photoreceptor spectral sensitivities in terrestrial animals: adaptations for luminance and colour vision. *Proceedings, Biological Sciences* 272: 1745–52.

Palmer, S. E. 1999. *Vision Science: Photons to Phenomenology.* Cambridge: MIT Press.

Parkes, L. M., J.-B. C. Marsman, D. C. Oxley, J. Y. Goulermas, and S. M. Wuerger. 2009. Multivoxel fMRI analysis of color tuning in human primary visual cortex. *Journal of Vision (Charlottesville, VA)* 9 (1): 1–13.

Pasnau, R. 2009. The event of color. *Philosophical Studies* 142: 353–69.

Pautz, A. 2010. Review of Jonathan Cohen, the red and the real: An essay on color ontology. *Notre Dame Philosophical Reviews.* https://ndpr.nd.edu/news/24305-the-red-and-the-real-an-essay-on-color-ontology/.

Pautz, A. 2011. Can disjunctivists explain our access to the external world? *Philosophical Issues* 21 (1): 384–433.

Pautz, A. 2013. The real trouble for phenomenal externalists: New evidence for a brain-based theory of consciousness. In *Consciousness Inside and Out: Phenomenology, Neuroscience, and the Nature of Experience,* ed. R. Brown. Berlin: Springer-Verlag.

Peacocke, C. 1984. Colour concepts and colour experiences. *Synthese* 58 (3): 365–81.

Perry, R. B. 1935. *The Thought and Character of William James*. Boston: Little Brown.

Pettit, P. 1999. A theory of normal and ideal conditions. *Philosophical Studies* 96: 21–44.

Philipona, D. L., and J. K. O'Regan. 2006. Color naming, unique hues, and hue cancellation predicted from singularities in reflection properties. *Visual Neuroscience* 23: 331–39.

Prete, F. R. 2004. *Complex Worlds from Simpler Nervous Systems*. Cambridge: MIT Press.

Prindle, S. S., C. Carello, and M. T. Turvey. 1980. Animal-environment mutuality and direct perception. *Behavioral and Brain Sciences* 3: 395–97.

Rao, R., B. Olshausen, and M. Lewicki, eds. 2002. *Probabilistic Models of the Brain: Perception and Neural Function*. Cambridge: MIT Press.

Regan, B. C., C. Julliot, B. Simmen, F. Vie not, P. Charles-Dominique, and J. D. Mollon. 2001. Fruits, foliage and the evolution of primate colour vision. *Philosophical Transactions of the Royal Society of London, Series B* 356: 229–83.

Rescher, N. 2000. *Process Philosophy: A Survey of Basic Issues*. Pittsburgh: University of Pittsburgh Press.

Rickless, S. C. 1997. Locke on primary and secondary qualities. *Pacific Philosophical Quarterly* 78 (3): 297–319.

Roberts, P., J. Andow, and K. Schmidtke. 2014. Colour relationalism and the real deliverances of introspection. *Erkenntnis* 79 (5): 1173–89.

Rorty, R. 1970. In defense of eliminative materialism. *Review of Metaphysics* 24:112–21.

Rorty, R. 1979. *Philosophy and the Mirror of Nature*. Princeton: Princeton University Press.

Rorty, R. 1999. *Philosophy and Social Hope*. New York: Penguin.

Rubin, J. M., and W. A. Richards. 1982. Color vision and image intensities: When are changes material? *Biological Cybernetics* 45: 215–26.

Rushton, W. A. H. 1965. Chemical basis of colour vision and colour blindness. *Nature* 206: 1087–91.

Russell, B. [1912] 1980. *The Problems of Philosophy*. Oxford: Oxford University Press Opus.

Sacks, O. 1995. *An Anthropologist on Mars*. London: Picador.

Schellenberg, S. 2008. The situation-dependency of perception. *Journal of Philosophy* 105 (2): 55–84.

Schellenberg, S. 2011. Perceptual content defended. *Noûs* 45 (4): 714–50.

Schiller, P. 1996. On the specificity of neurons and visual areas. *Behavioural Brain Research* 76 (1–2): 21–35.

Schütz, A., D. Braun, and K. Gegenfurtner. 2009. Object recognition during foveating eye movements. *Vision Research* 49 (18): 2241–53.

Schwartz, R. 2006. *Visual Versions*. Cambridge: MIT press.

Schwitzgebel, E. 2011. *Perplexities of Consciousness*. Cambridge: MIT Press.

Seibt, J. 2012. Process philosophy. In *The Stanford Encyclopedia of Philosophy*, ed. E. N. Zalta. http://plato.stanford.edu/archives/fall2013/entries/perception-contents/.

Sekuler, R., and R. Blake. 1985. *Perception*. New York: Knopf.

Sellars, W. 1956. Empiricism and the philosophy of mind. In *The Foundations of Science and the Concepts of Psychoanalysis, Minnesota Studies in the Philosophy of Science*, vol. 1, ed. H. Feigl and M. Scriven. Minneapolis: University of Minnesota Press.

Sellars, W. 1963. Philosophy and the scientific image of man. In *Science, Perception and Reality*, ed. W. Sellars. London: Routledge Kegan Paul.

Sellars, W. 1971. Science, sense impressions, and sensa: A reply to Cornman. *Review of Metaphysics* 23: 391–447.

Sellars, W. 1981. Foundations for a metaphysics of pure process. *Monist* 64 (1): 3–90.

Shevell, S. 2012. The Verriest Lecture: Color lessons from space, time and motion. *Journal of the Optical Society of America, Series A, Optics, Image Science, and Vision* 29 (2): A337–45.

Shevell, S., and F. Kingdom. 2008. Color in complex scenes. *Annual Review of Psychology* 59: 143–66.

Shoemaker, S. 2003. Content, character, and color. *Philosophical Issues* 13: 253–78.

Shoemaker, S. 2006. On the way things appear. In *Perceptual Experience*, ed. T. Gendler and J. Hawthorne, 461–80. Oxford: Oxford University Press.

Siegel, S. 2013. The contents of perception. In *The Stanford Encyclopedia of Philosophy*, ed. E. N. Zalta. http://plato.stanford.edu/archives/fall2013/entries/perception-contents/.

Simons, P. J. 2000. Continuants and occurrents I. *Aristotelian Society Supplementary* 74 (1): 59–75.

Skorupski, P., and L. Chittka. 2011. Is colour cognitive? *Optics and Laser Technology* 43: 251–60.

Smart, J. 1959. Sensations and brain processes. *Philosophical Review* 68: 141–56.

Smart, J. 1975/1997. On some criticisms of a physicalist theory of colors. In *Readings on Color: The Philosophy of Color*, vol. 1, ed. A. Byrne and D. R. Hilbert. Cambridge: MIT Press.

Smith, A. D. 1990. Of primary and secondary qualities. *Philosophical Review* 100: 221–54.

Smith, A. D. 2002. *The Problem of Perception*. Cambridge: Harvard University Press.

Smith, M. 1989. Dispositional theories of value. *Proceedings of the Aristotelian Society* 63: 89–111.

Smithson, H. 2005. Sensory, computational and cognitive components of human colour constancy. *Philosophical Transactions of the Royal Society of London, Series B, Biological Sciences* 360: 1329–46.

Smithson, H., and Q. Zaidi. 2004. Colour constancy in context: roles for local adaptation and levels of reference. *Journal of Vision* 4: 693–710.

Smythies, J. 1999. Consciousness: Some basic issues—A neurophilosophical perspective. *Consciousness and Cognition* 8: 164–72.

Solomon, S., and P. Lennie. 2007. The machinery of colour vision. *Nature Reviews. Neuroscience* 8: 276–86.

Sorabji, R. 1974. Body and soul in Aristotle. *Philosophy (London)* 49: 63–89.

Stebbing, L. S. 1958. *Philosophy and the Physicists*. New York: Dover.

Stevens, M. 2013. *Sensory Ecology, Behaviour, and Evolution*. Oxford: Oxford University Press.

Stoughton, C. M., and B. Conway. 2008. Neural basis for unique hues. *Current Biology* 18: R698–99.

Stroud, B. 2000. *The Quest for Reality: Subjectivism and the Metaphysics of Color*. Oxford: Oxford University Press.

Sumner, P., and J. D. Mollon. 2000a. Catarrhine photopigments are optimized for detecting targets against a foliage background. *Journal of Experimental Biology* 203: 1963–86.

Sumner, P., and J. D. Mollon. 2000b. Chromaticity as a signal of ripeness in fruits taken by primates. *Journal of Experimental Biology* 203: 1987–2000.

Switkes, E., A. Bradley and K. K. DeValois. 1988. Contrast dependence and mechanisms of masking interactions among chromatic and luminance gratings. *Journal of the Optical Society of America, Series A, Optics and Image Science* 5: 1149–62.

Taylor, C. 2007. *A Secular Age*. Cambridge, MA: Belknap Press.

Thompson, B. 2009. Senses for senses. *Australasian Journal of Philosophy* 87 (1): 99–117.

Thompson, B. 2010. The spatial content of experience. *Philosophy and Phenomenological Research* 81 (1): 146–84.

Thompson, E. 1995. *Colour Vision*. London: Routledge.

Thompson, E., A. Palacios, and F. Varela. 1992. Ways of coloring: Comparative color vision as a case study for cognitive science. *Behavioral and Brain Sciences* 15: 1–74.

Tolliver, J. 1994. Interior colors. *Philosophical Topics* 22: 411–41.

Travis, C. S. 2004. The silence of the senses. *Mind* 113: 57–94.

Tresiman, A., and G. Gelade. 1980. A feature-integration theory of attention. *Cognitive Psychology* 12: 97–136.

Troland, L. T. 1929. *Psychophysiology* II. New York: Van Nostrand.

Troscianko, T., R. Montagnon, J. Le Clerc, E. Malbert, and P.-L. Chanteau. 1991. The role of colour as a monocular depth cue. *Vision Research* 31 (11): 1923–30.

Tye, M. 1984. The adverbial approach to visual experience. *Philosophical Review* 93 (2): 195–225.

Tye, M. 2000. *Consciousness, Color, and Content*. Cambridge: MIT Press.

Tye, M. 2003. Blurry images, double vision, and other oddities: New problems for representationalism? In *Consciousness: New Philosophical Perspectives*, ed. Q. Smith and A. Jokic. Oxford: Oxford University Press.

Tye, M. 2006a. The puzzle of true blue. *Analysis* 66: 173–78.

Tye, M. 2006b. The truth about true blue. *Analysis* 66: 340–44.

Tye, M. 2007. True blue redux. *Analysis* 67 (1): 92–93.

Tye, M. 2012. Cohen on color relationism. *Analytic Philosophy* 53 (3): 297–305.

Valberg, A. 2001. Unique hues: An old problem for a new generation. *Vision Research* 41: 1645–57.

van Fraassen, B. C. 1980. *The Scientific Image*. Oxford: Oxford University Press.

von Uexküll, J. 1934/1957. A stroll through the worlds of animals and men: A picture book of invisible worlds. In *Instinctive Behavior: The Development of a Modern Concept*, ed. C. H. Schiller, 5–80. New York: International Universities Press.

Wade, N., and J. Brožek. 2001. *Purkinje's Vision*. Mahwah, NJ: Lawrence Erlbaum.

Watkins, M. 2002. *Rediscovering Colors: A Study in Pollyanna Realism*. Dordrecht: Kluwer.

Watkins, M. 2005. Seeing red: The metaphysics of color without the physics. *Australasian Journal of Philosophy* 83: 33–52.

Watkins, M. 2010. A posteriori primitivism. *Philosophical Studies* 150: 123–37.

Weber, M., and A. Weekes. 2009. *Process Approaches to Consciousness in Psychology, Neuroscience, and Philosophy of Mind*. Albany: SUNY Press.

Westphal, J. 1987. *Colour: Some Philosophical Problems from Wittgenstein*. Oxford: Blackwell.

Whitehead, A. N. [1929] 1979. *Process and Reality: An Essay in Cosmology*. New York: Macmillan.

Wichmann, F., L. Sharpe, and K. Gegenfurtner. 2002. The contributions of color to recognition memory for natural scenes. *Journal of Experimental Psychology: Learning, Memory, and Cognition* 28 (3): 509–20.

Wilson, M. 1999. History of philosophy in philosophy today; and the case of the sensible qualities. In *Ideas and Mechanism: Essays on Early Modern Philosophy*, ed. M. Wilson. Princeton: Princeton University Press.

Wilson, M. 2006. *Wandering Significance: An Essay on Conceptual Behaviour*. Oxford: Oxford University Press.

Wittgenstein, L. 1953. *Philosophical Investigations*. Oxford: Blackwell.

Witzel, C., and K. R. Gegenfurtner. 2013. Categorical sensitivity to color differences. *Journal of Vision (Charlottesville, VA)* 13 (7): 1–33.

Wolfe, J. M., K. R. Kluender, D. M. Levi, L. M. Bartoshuk, R. S. Herz, R. L. Klatzky, and S. J. Lederman. 2006. *Sensation and Perception*. Sunderland, MA: Sinauer Associates.

Wuerger, S., and L. Parkes. 2011. Unique hues. In *New Directions in Colour Studies*, ed. C. Biggam, C. A. Hough, C. J. Kay, and D. Simmons. Amsterdam: John Benjamins.

Wyszecki, G., and W. S. Stiles. 2000. *Color Science: Concepts and Methods, Quantitative Data and Formulae*, 2nd ed. Hoboken, NJ: Wiley Interscience.

Yablo, S. 1995. Singling out properties. *Philosophical Perspectives* 9: 477–502.

Yang, J., and S. Shevell. 2002. Stereo disparity improves color constancy. *Vision Research* 42: 1979–89.

Yarbus, A. L. 1967. Eye movements during perception of complex objects. In *Eye Movements and Vision*, ed. L. A. Riggs, 171–96. New York: Plenum Press.

Yolton, J. 1984. *Perceptual Acquaintance from Descartes to Reid*. Minneapolis: University of Minnesota Press.

Zaidi, Q. 1998. Identification of illuminant and object colors: Heuristic-based algorithms. *Journal of the Optical Society of America, Series A, Optics, Image Science, and Vision* 15: 1767–76.

Zaidi, Q., and A. Li. 2006. Three-dimensional shape perception from chromatic orientation flows. *Visual Neuroscience* 23: 323–30.

Zeki, S. 1978. Functional specialisation in the visual cortex of the rhesus monkey. *Nature* 274: 423–28.

Zeki, S. 1983. Colour coding in the cerebral cortex: The reaction of cells in monkey visual cortex to wavelengths and colours. *Neuroscience* 9: 741–65.

Zeki, S. 1993. *A Vision of the Brain*. Oxford: Blackwell.

Index

Achromatopsia, 71, 85–86, 93–94. *See also* Color blindness

Adaptationism, 108

Adverbialism
  in philosophy of color, 18, 99, 132, 139, 142–46, 148–55, 157–62, 167–75, 177–78, 181, 183, 185–88, 203, 208–13
  in philosophy of perception, 140n, 152–53, 177–78

Akins, Kathleen, 69, 76, 112–13, 126

Alhazen, 21, 34

Allen, Keith, 193, 211

Antirealism, in philosophy of color, 12, 14, 16–17, 22, 26, 29, 38, 40, 42, 44, 48–50, 53–54, 58, 62, 65, 70–71, 99, 102–104, 118–19, 124–26, 130, 144, 154, 162. *See also* Eliminativism

Aquinas, Thomas, 15, 19, 22–23, 35

Aristotle, 20n, 21–23, 27, 29–30, 34–35, 142n, 175

Armstrong, David, 13, 29, 31n, 45, 188n

Attention. *See* Saliency

Audition, 125. *See also* Hearing

Averill, Edward Wilson, 44n, 62–63, 162

Benham disc, 84

Binary hues, 59–63. *See also* Unique hues

Berkeley, George, 26, 31n

Block, Ned, 195, 200n

Boghossian, Paul, 144, 160–62, 167–68, 171, 178, 192n

Boyle, Robert, 10, 24, 41n

Broackes, Justin, 146n, 180n

Brogaard, Berit, 48n, 149

Brown, Derek, 42, 81, 133

Burnyeat, Myles, 6, 20n, 21n

Byrne, Alex, 45, 56, 126–27, 157

Campbell, John, 47, 172, 174–75

Campbell, Keith, 8

Chalmers, David, 36, 53n, 189, 198–204, 205n

Churchland, Patricia, 112n

Churchland, Paul, 14, 46n, 60, 112n

Cohen, Jonathan, 6, 14, 42, 47–48, 52, 67–68, 103, 116, 117n, 132n, 139, 143n, 149–50, 163, 170n, 179–80, 183–85, 188, 190, 192–95, 198n, 211

Color
  blindness, 4, 85, 90, 93 (*see also* Achromatopsia; Dichromacy)
  categorization, 46, 63, 65, 89, 114n, 121–30, 185–86
  cognition, 87–89, 137n
  constancy, 45–46, 54–58, 71, 86, 89, 97–98, 102–103, *117*, 140, 179–80, 183–84, 209–11, 213
  contrast effect, 74–76, 163, 182–83
  language, 44–45, 51, 122–23, 165, 179, 185–86, 213

Color (cont.)
opponency, 58, 60–63, 125, 140
shading effect, 95–96
Common sense, in theory of color, 14–
16, 26, 31–33, 44–45, 49–54, 188n,
191, 212
Common sensible, 27
Cones, 4, 59–60, 64, 85, 93, 122–23. See
also Photoreceptors
contrast, 141n
Consciousness
problem of, 13, 18, 60, 134n, 136,
157–58
representationalist theory of, 202–203

Democritus, 6, 9–10, 12, 19n, 154
Depth perception, 79–82
Descartes, René, 10, 13, 19, 23–24, 27–
28, 30, 33, 37–39, 41
Dichromacy, 92–93, 120, 180n
Direct realism, 170
Disjunctivism, 156, 170, 171n, 175–77
Dispositionalism, 14, 39–42, 48–49, 52,
66–68, 139, 146n, 154, 169, 172,
188, 192, 198n, 199
Dual reference theory, 42, 133
Dummett, Michael, 52, 118
Dupré, John, 148n, 152, 212

Ecological psychology, 14–15, 49, 63,
68, 109n, 134–36, 157–58
Eddington, Arthur, 7–12, 51,
Eliminativism, in philosophy of color,
13, 44, 65, 68, 138, 187. See also
Antirealism
Enactivism, 114, 145–46
Error theory, 25–26, 44, 187, 198
Evolution, of color vision, 4, 80, 85–86,
92–93, 99, 129, 180n
Exteroception, 199–200, 202–203

Folk color theory, 14, 32n, 33–34, 49–
50, 52, 184. See also Common sense,
in theory of color

Functionalism, in philosophy of color
realizer functionalism, 67–68
role functionalism, 48n, 67–68, 198n
Fregean, theory of content, 163,
167–70
Frugivory hypothesis, 92–93, 98, 180n

Galileo, 9–10, 19, 22–26, 30, 35, 39
Gegenfurtner, Karl, 70, 88, 137
Gert, Joshua, 47n, 146n, 167n, 169
Gestalt psychology, 16, 56, 74, 76n
Gibson, James, 49, 107, 109n, 134–36,
160
Giere, Ronald, 43, 103, 121n, 139, 143,
212
Gilchrist, Alan, 76n
Gupta, Anil, 106n, 161

Hallucination, argument from, 153,
155–56
Hardin, C. Larry, 9, 13, 14n, 17, 38, 44,
48, 58–61, 63–65, 102, 124–25, 133,
138
Hearing, 23, 108, 129. See also Audition;
Sound
Heraclitean flux, 149–50
Helmholtz, Hermann von, 59–60
Hering, Edwald, 59–63
Hilbert, David R., 29, 32, 42, 45, 56,
64–65, 126–27
Holt, Edwin, 109n, 136, 157–58
Hubel, David, 71–73, 80, 82, 84, 89–90
Hume, David, 37, 54
Hurlbert, Anya, 77n, 82, 88n, 98, 103n,
132
Hurvich, Leo, 58, 60, 132–33

Illusion, 44–45, 48, 75, 83–84, 116–18,
125–26, 179–84
argument from, 153
Intentional species, 15, 19–22, 26–28,
30, 35, 39, 53
Interception, 199–200, 202–203
Introspection, 196, 202, 204, 209

Jackson, Frank, 23, 38, 46, 49, 64n, 67, 136, 162, 166, 178
James, William, 109n, 135–36, 154, 157–58
Jameson, Dorothea, 58, 60
Johnston, Mark, 48, 50, 66–67, 172–73, 187, 192–94

Kalderon, Mark Eli, 5n, 6, 8n, 31n, 47n, 157
Kingdom, Frederick, 73, 75, 77, 93–95, 128

Lewis, David, 14, 212
Lightness constancy, 57, 84–86
Livingstone, Margaret, 71–73, 80, 82, 84, 89–90
Locke, John, 9–10, 19, 24, 26, 37, 39–41, 52, 199, 206

Mackie, J. L., 40, 44, 50
Maloney, Laurence, 103
Manifest image, 7, 9, 11, 12–13, 31, 143
Marr, David, 107, 111n, 160
Matthen, Mohan, 49n, 108–109, 167n, 180n
Maund, Barry, 31n, 42, 44n, 50, 133, 186
Mausfeld, Rainer, 42, 53, 76n, 132–33
McDowell, John, 13, 52, 106n, 188n
McGilvray, James, 143, 152–53, 160n
McGinn, Colin, 134n, 189–90, 197, 206
McLaughlin, Brian, 64n, 67
Metamerism, 64–65, 98, 126
Mind-independence, 5, 33–36, 118–20
Mitchell, Sandra, 151–52
Mode of presentation (MOP), 167, 169–70
Monochromacy, 84–85
Monism, 132–36, 154–55
Mollon, John, 62–63, 72, 87, 90–91, 129

Motion perception, 83–84
Mullen, Kathy, 70, 72, 82

Naïve realism, 46, 159, 161, 170–77. See also Direct realism; Disjunctivism; Relationism, in the philosopy of perception
Neo-Platonism, 21, 34
Newton, Isaac, 1, 10, 19, 23, 40–41, 45, 121, 134, 186
Noë, Alva, 115, 145–46, 157

Objectivity, 5, 11, 22, 119–20
Olfaction. See Smell
Ontological commitment, 20, 32–33, 35, 49–52, 97, 101, 105, 201, 208, 210, 212
Ontology, 9, 13, 22–25, 32–34, 44, 47, 60–61, 65, 101–106, 118–20, 133, 136, 145–52, 158
Orange, 59, 61, 129, 162

Pain, 13, 51, 125, 189, 198–201, 203
Palmer, Stephen, 103, 110, 139
Pautz, Adam, 112n, 125, 170n
Perceptual variation, 3, 5–7, 9, 31n, 47–48, 132n
Phenomenology, of color, 22, 32, 95, 129, 144, 157, 164, 187–212
Photoreceptors, 4, 29, 59–60, 85, 89, 112, 115, 122, 141
Physicalism
   in general metaphysics, 11, 13, 50, 51
   nonreductive, 8n, 13, 151 (see also Primitivism)
   in philosophy of color, 17, 29, 45–47, 55, 64–65, 68, 74, 83, 103, 113n, 126–27, 138, 141n, 151, 162. See also Reflectance realism
Plato, 12n, 175
Platonism, 118, 137n. See also Neo-Platonism
Pragmatism, 109, 120n, 121n, 136

Primary quality, 24–26, 41n, 67, 177

Primitivism, 8n, 47, 50, 55, 102, 150–52, 157, 171. *See also* Physicalism, nonreductive

Process ontology, 146–48, 152, 158

Proper sensible, 21, 23–24, 27, 29

Properties, 5–6, 8, 11, 16, 21, 23–29, 32–33, 50–52, 67, 143, 146, 148, 150, 185

Psychophysics, 76, 192

Qualia, 60, 158

Rainbow, 42, 84, 121, 142

Realism
   in philosophy of color, 9, 14, 16–17, 22–23, 25, 27, 29 31–33, 35–38, 40, 42, 45, 46–50, 53–54, 56, 58, 64n, 65, 67, 86, 98–99, 102–103, 105, 118–20, 126–28, 130–31, 144–45, 148–49, 154, 180n, 187, 210
   in philosophy of science, 11n, 31, 121n,

Realizer functionalism. *See* Functionalism

Reflectance realism, 46, 84, 103. *See also* Physicalism, in philosophy of color

Relationism
   in philosophy of color, 6, 14–15, 18, 43, 47–49, 53, 66, 68, 99, 101–104, 116, 118, 128, 130–33, 138–39, 142–46, 148–50, 152, 154, 162, 170, 172–73, 183–84, 185n, 187–96, 199–200, 203–205, 208
   in philosophy of perception, 152, 170, 172, 175, 178 (*see also* Disjunctivism; Direct realism; Naïve realism)

Relativism, in philosophy of color, 48n, 149

Representationalism, in philosophy of perception, 159–70, 175, 177, 202–203

Role functionalism. *See* Functionalism

Russell, Bertrand, 3–4, 6–7, 9, 171–72

Russellian theory of content, 161–63, 165, 168, 170n, 203

Sacks, Oliver, 85–86, 93–94

Saliency, 91–93

Scientific revolution, 10, 23, 30, 35, 133

Secondary quality, 12–13, 20, 24, 26, 37, 40–41, 48, 52, 66–67, 134, 177

Segmentation, of scenes and colors, 77, 83, 89–93, 99, 164–66, 180

Selectionism, 5n

Sellars, Wilfrid, 9, 12, 143, 158, 191n, 209, 212

Sense data, 3, 153, 172

Sensory-classification theory, 49n

Shape perception, 82–83, 89–91

Siegel, Susanna, 167–68n

Smart, J. J. C., 13, 19n

Smell, 8, 10, 12, 20, 22, 41, 108, 113n, 124–25

Smith, A. D., 24–25, 153n

Sound, 8, 10, 12, 20, 22–24, 41, 108, 113n, 141n. *See also* Hearing

Species. *See* Intentional species

Spectral surface reflectance (SSR), 13, 29, 42, 46–47, 55–57, 63–65, 74, 83–84, 86, 88, 91, 97–99, 103, 126–27, 169, 182–83

Standard observers, 4, 67, 105, 179n

Standard conditions, 67, 105, 179n

Taste, 6, 8, 10, 12, 20, 22, 24, 41, 108, 113n, 124–25, 142n

Taxonomy, of color theories, 43

Thompson, Brad, 162n, 167–69

Thompson, Evan, 14–15, 39–40, 48–49, 68, 133, 145, 162–63

Touch, 23, 115–16, 176n

Transparency, of perceptual experience, 200–203

Travis, Charles, 161

Trichromacy, 4, 59–60, 63, 65, 87, 92–
    93, 98–99, 126, 129
Tye, Michael, 55–56, 75, 116, 178, 184,
    190n

Unique hues, 47, 61–63, 127n, 167n. *See
    also* Binary hues
Unsteady colors, 192–93

V4 cortical area, 71–72
Velleman, J. David, 144, 160–62, 167–
    68, 171, 178, 192n

Watkins, Michael, 8n, 13, 47, 150, 179
Wavelength, of light, 13, 29, 45–47, 55,
    59–60, 69–70, 72, 80, 85–86, 88, 92–
    93, 103, 108, 121–22, 128, 140, 184
Wavelength specific behavior, 88,
    140–41
Wittgenstein, Ludwig, 51

Yellow, color experience, 4–6, 38, 44,
    46–47, 50, 56, 59–61, 63–64, 67, 74,
    88–89, 97, 127, 150, 153, 183–85

Zeki, Semir, 71

Figure 4.3 [Plate 1]
Blue Mountains panorama. The colors of very distant objects appear less saturated because of atmospheric scattering. They will often appear blue because short wavelengths of light are scattered least. In the Blue Mountains near Sydney, vaporized eucalyptus oil from the forest increases scattering. Loss of color saturation and bluing phenomena are known to cue depth to human observers.

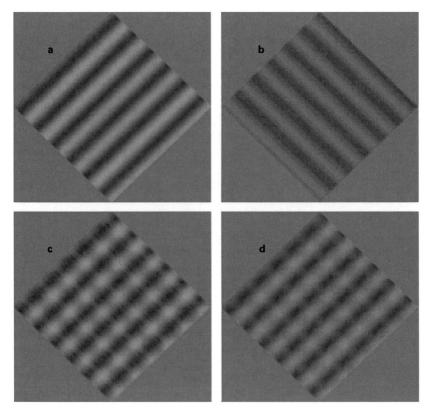

Figure 4.4 [Plate 2]
Color-shading effect. A sinusoidal luminance grating (a) and red-green equiluminant grating (b) are not found to elicit an impression of depth or corrugation. However, when these two images are superimposed (c), there is a strong depth effect. This effect is abolished if a colored grating is then superimposed onto the luminance grating (d). Image reprinted with permission from Shevell, S. and F. Kingdom (2008). Color in complex scenes. *Annual Review of Psychology 59*, 143–66. Copyright © 2008 by Annual Reviews.

Figure 7.1 [Plate 3]
Tree Fungus. Photographs of tree fungus among the undergrowth of a north Australian rainforest.

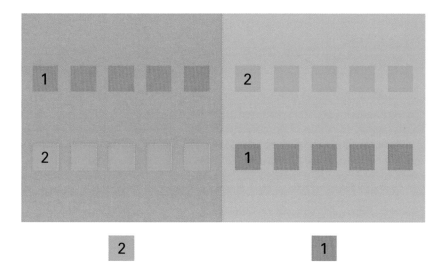

Figure 7.2 [Plate 4]
Color contrast effect. Squares in the top row all appear as roughly the same gray color. However, squares on the top left have the same physical spectral values as the other squares labeled 1, which appear mushroom pink in other contexts, and squares on the top right have the same physical spectral values as the other squares labeled 2, which appear sage green in other contexts. Image adapted from website of Akiyoshi Kitaoka, reproduced with permission.

Figure 7.3 [Plate 5]
Color contrast effect and color constancy. The top tiles of Rubik's cube, which appear blue on the left-hand side and yellow on the right-hand side, actually have the same reflectance, which appears gray if seen against a white background. The equivalence can be demonstrated by viewing these tiles through a paper cutout that masks the surrounding area. Image created by Beau Lotto, reproduced with permission.

20513844R10148